GUIDEPOSTS FOR EFFECTIVE SALESMANSHIP*

ROBERT R. BLAKE & JANE SRYGLEY MOUTON

*Original title: The Grid® for Sales Excellence

A JOVE BOOK

GUIDEPOSTS FOR EFFECTIVE SALESMANSHIP

A Jove Book / published by arrangement with
McGraw-Hill, Inc.

PRINTING HISTORY
McGraw-Hill edition published 1970
Playboy Press Paperbacks edition / August 1981
Jove edition / June 1984

All rights reserved.
Copyright © 1980, 1970 by Robert R. Blake and Jane Srygley Mouton
This book may not be reproduced in whole or in part,
by mimeograph or any other means, without permission.
For information address: McGraw-Hill, Inc., 1221 Avenue of the Americas,
New York, N.Y. 10020.

ISBN: 0-515-08088-8

Jove books are published by The Berkley Publishing Group,
200 Madison Avenue, New York, N.Y. 10016.
The words "A JOVE BOOK" and the "J" with sunburst
are trademarks belonging to Jove Publications, Inc.

PRINTED IN THE UNITED STATES OF AMERICA

DO YOU SELL YOUR PRODUCT OR YOURSELF?

HAVE YOU EVER TRIED TO SELL SOLUTIONS?

Authors Blake and Mouton, with their Sales Grid®, have helped thousands develop secure, financially rewarding selling careers. And now, in this completely updated and improved edition of their classic sales book, you can gain even more practical, immediately useful ideas for turning the toughest prospects into confirmed customers.

ABOUT THE AUTHORS:
Dr. Robert R. Blake is president of Scientific Methods, Inc., a behavioral science firm headquartered in Austin, Texas, which lists among its customers: Westinghouse, Reynolds Metals, Alcoa, United Airlines, DuPont, IBM, Monsanto, Union Carbide, and many others.

Dr. Jane Srygley Mouton is vice-president of Scientific Methods, Inc. She is an associate of the American Psychological Association and a member of the American Association for the Advancement of Science and the International Association of Applied Social Scientists.

Most Jove Books are available at special quantity discounts for bulk purchases for sales promotions, premiums, fund raising, or educational use. Special books or book excerpts can also be created to fit specific needs.

For details, write or telephone Special Sales Markets, The Berkley Publishing Group, 200 Madison Avenue, New York, New York 10016; (212) 686-9820.

CONTENTS

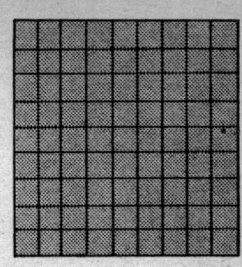

PREFACE vii

CHAPTER 1
The Sales Grid: The Human Side of Selling   1

CHAPTER 2
Grid Elements: The Grid as Your Mirror
19

CHAPTER 3
9,1: Domineering   25

CHAPTER 4
1,9: Eager to Please   51

CHAPTER 5
1,1: Indifferent   71

CHAPTER 6
5,5: Status Conscious   91

CHAPTER 7
9,9: Solution Seeking   119

CHAPTER 8
Mixed Theories   155

CHAPTER 9
On Being Deceptive   163

CHAPTER 10
Self-Development   175

CHAPTER 11
Effective Selling: Summary and Implications
193

APPENDIX
Grid Study of Behavioral Approaches   217

REFERENCES   227
INDEX   229

PREFACE

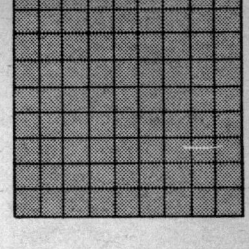

This book is for people who sell. The treatment is a behavioral science analysis of the fundamentals of selling, concentrating on the human relationship between sales representative and customer. The approach is comparative. Sales behavior that is likely to be weak and ineffective is examined and the underlying reasons for this identified. This behavior is compared with approaches to selling that tend to be stronger and more effective.

Tremendous benefits are available to salespeople who really know how to use their skills in a sales presentation. To achieve successful sales where others with comparable products have failed is the contribution that this book can make to you. Readers worldwide who have independently studied the first edition of this book or who have read it as part of their preparation for Sales Grid Seminar attendance have found it of significant value.

This second edition of *The Grid ® for Sales Excellence* was written to add more strength and clarity to the original work. It is more tightly organized. The sales relationship is examined in sequence, beginning with new customers from opening, through all aspects of the sales interview, to closing. A separate treatment is also provided for dealing with established business.

Dialogue has been added to this edition to more clearly illustrate the concepts, adding a "real life" character to aid comprehension and application. Additionally, we have endeavored to provide updated examples which have more relevance to today's salesperson and purchaser.

Although this is not its direct purpose, the Grid framework depicted in this book has been found to be equally interesting to those on the buying or purchasing side—purchasing agents, wholesalers, retail store proprietors, merchandise buyers, and others for whom purchasing is an occupation. From the customer's point of view, a greater understanding of the features of selling—of what is sound and what is unsound in a salesperson's approach—can lead to more effective decisions on what to buy, from whom, when, how many, and for how much.

The many individuals who brought a rich and varied background of sales and purchasing experience to the study and critique of this book are acknowledged with appreciation. Reginald C. Tillam, R. Anthony Pearson, and many other members of Scientific Methods, Inc., have offered valued suggestions. The same is true of Dr. Frederick D. Sturdivant, Associate Professor of Marketing, The University of Texas at Austin. Walter Barclay of Scientific Methods, Inc., made a significant contribution to this second edition, which incorporates many new features while strengthening the positive features of the first edition.

ROBERT R. BLAKE

AUSTIN, TEXAS

JANE SRYGLEY MOUTON

THE SALES GRID

The Human Side of Selling

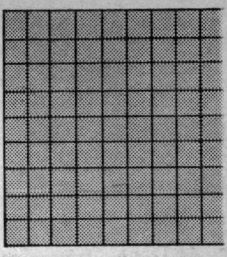

The objective of this book is to help you strengthen your selling through better relationships with your prospects or customers. How you relate to customers makes all the difference between failure and success. By "relate" we mean all the things you do, or fail to do, that have the effect of turning people off or on. Once you are aware of these things and the effects they have on your prospects, you are then in a position to strengthen the relationships you create with them. In this way you mobilize your effectiveness as a salesperson.

The book focuses on face-to-face sales situations, whether of products or services, and an approach involving the application of behavioral science principles to improve everyday selling is described. We encourage you to adopt an attitude of self-analysis while you read it. Look inside yourself. You will find facts, opinions, attitudes, and emotions that either get in your way or add strength to your sales effectiveness. Because selling involves two or more people, you are only one-half of the sales relationship. By looking inside your customers, and seeking their points of view, you will find facts, opinions, attitudes, and emotions that relate to their readiness to purchase. If you ignore these feelings, you are more than likely building barriers to a successful closing, almost from the moment of initial contact. However, if you become aware of the attitudes and emotions of your prospect, and deal with them as realities, you will find yourself able to turn indifference into enthusiasm and resistance into respect for you as a salesperson.

Relationships between sales representatives and customers are evaluated here from a behavioral science point of view. "You-and-each-customer," interacting together, is what is emphasized. A salesperson's thinking and action, as well as a customer's, can be analyzed separately. In real life, however, they often occur together as a rapid-fire interchange.

The Sales Grid is a set of theories that help you understand your own sales style, your personal reactions to the customer, and the customer's reactions to you. These theories are invaluable because they aid you in planning constructive ways of dealing with situations that may have baffled you in the past. Nothing is more practical in selling than sound theory to guide action. It enables you to see the assumptions on which your behavior is based, and it provides a framework for predicting the consequences of your actions. It opens up alternatives and options for dealing with customers in ways that otherwise might not occur to you. Only with good theory is it possible to gain the powerful insights so essential for effective selling.

How the theories apply is demonstrated by examining the fundamentals of selling. These include making initial contact, identifying the real customer, carrying out a needs analysis to ensure an understanding of what the customer really wants, establishing sound expectations, dealing with objectives, setting up the closing, maintaining and strengthening established accounts, and handling complaints and rush business. The importance of communication between you and the customer is also investigated. Communication encompasses the skills of listening, of getting the customer's involvement and active participation in the purchasing decision, and of dealing with feelings and emotions—both yours and the customer's—that enter a sales interaction.

This book contains no gimmicks; nor does it offer any pat formulas for success. It is not a magic pill or a shot in the arm. There is no rah, rah, rah; no siss, boom, bah. Rather, the book presents a scientific foundation for building fundamental sales skills. When the techniques are understood and applied, it is no longer necessary to rely on gimmicks to get the order. Once sound understanding has been established, you will see that every sales contact is a challenging experience in human interaction that demands imagination, innovation, and creativity. Additionally, it will become apparent that the selling relationship is one of the most rewarding relationships in business today.

WHAT IS THE SALES GRID?

Now to get started. When you are selling, at least two thoughts come into your mind. One is *concern for making the sale*. The other is *concern for the customer as a person*. These are represented graphically in a diagram composed of two scales. The way in which the two concerns mesh determines your selling strategy.

What does "concern for" mean when a salesperson is dealing with a customer? It does not indicate "how much," such as the quantity of sales volume. The emphasis is on the degree of concern that is present in the mind of the salesperson, because actions are based on personal assumptions and thus emerge from them. What is significant is how sales representatives are concerned with making a sale, their concern for their customers, and the manner in which these two concerns are intertwined.

Concern for Making a Sale

The idea of concern for making a sale covers a wide range of considerations. Locating new prospects reflects one facet of this concern. This is often expressed in the number of calls made, the number of hours worked, the number of deliveries expedited, the character of service given, and so on. Furthermore, the term "sales results" is not restricted to the sale of a targeted number of specific articles or services. It includes much more: whatever people are trying to accomplish by way of selling activities. Much of sales work is a profit-seeking, private-enterprise activity, but this is not always the case. Voluntary associations, educational institutions, and other nonprofit organizations have ideas and programs to offer to the citizen, to the community, to legislatures, and to government agencies. Agency officials and field workers, in turn, are often trying to interest, inform, persuade, or respond to citizen complaints, which places them in a selling orientation too.

Thus, "concern for" indicates not the *actual* sales results in orders, invoices, or purchased items, but the character of the thoughts and feelings about how to achieve results. If your concern for sales results is low, you are less likely to exert the kind of effort that leads to high sales volume than you would exert if your concern were high. One salesperson may have a high degree of concern for achieving a sale based on the desire to make the company more profitable. Another may have a high degree of concern solely because of the desire to achieve a high commission, and a third may possess a low degree of concern due to "burnout." Whatever the underlying rationale, the degree of concern for sales production greatly influences behavior and actual sales volume.

Concern for making the sale is only one part of the story. Let us now turn to the human factor in sales relationships.

Concern for Customers

Concern for customers is another component and is also revealed in various ways. One salesperson expresses concern by providing special services or a "deal" in favor of the customer. Another does so by calling frequently and chatting in a friendly fashion about trade matters or social events. A third may show concern for the customer by seeking to comprehend the customer's actual requirements and by presenting product facts that ensure a sound understanding. There are a host of other ways, but what is significant is how the salesperson, in words and behavior, expresses concern for the customer and the influence this has on personal selling effectiveness.

Each salesperson's degrees of concern on these two scales—for making the sale and for the customer—relate back to the assumptions; that is, the salesperson's personal *strategy* for conducting a sales transaction. The concern for making a sale and the way in which it is linked with the concern for the customer are at the foundation of this selling strategy. These two concerns are expressed in vastly different ways, depending upon the specific manner in which they mesh. A high concern for making a sale joined with a *low* concern for the customer results in a significantly different sales approach than that encountered when a high concern for the sale is joined with a *high* concern for the customer, or when a high concern for the customer is coupled with a low concern for the sale.

Grid Sales Strategies

The "Grid strategy" diagram of Box 1 shows these two concerns and the many ways they may interact.[1]* The horizontal axis indicates concern for making a sale. The vertical axis indicates concern for the customer. Each is a nine-point scale. The number *1* represents minimum concern, while *9* represents maximum concern, and *5* represents an intermediate degree. The other numbers, *2* through *4* and *6* through *8*, indicate an uninterrupted sequence of degrees of concern. They do not represent anything so measurable as the speed of your car as shown on the speedometer or the amount of fuel in the tank. Nevertheless, they do signify recognizable amounts, more like "Empty" and "Full" on your gas gauge and the successive degrees in between.

In the lower right corner is the 9,1 orientation to selling. This is where a high concern for getting the sale is coupled with little or no concern for the customer. Prospects or customers are seen as things to be processed in a juice-extracting way. Squeeze the oranges one by one for as much juice as you can get, then throw away the pulp. Such 9,1 assumptions can result in behavior that alienates the customer because it is hard-driving, insensitive, and hard-sell. At one time or another almost every buyer has had an experience with a salesperson so bent on "making the pitch," on pushing a product or service, as to be blind

---

*Numbered references are collected in an annotated list at the end of this book.

6 GUIDEPOSTS FOR EFFECTIVE SALESMANSHIP

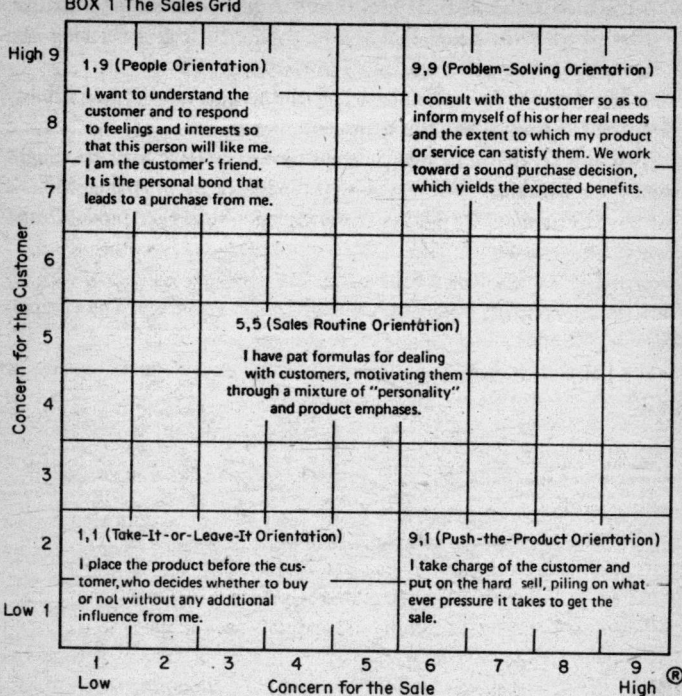

BOX 1 The Sales Grid

to what was on the prospect's mind; to how the customer felt; to the reservations or doubts that resulted in hesitation and eventually caused the customer to walk away—with no purchase but with considerable resentment.

The 1,9 strategy is in the upper left corner. Here a minimum degree of concern for the sale is joined with a maximum concern for the customer. Little direct persuasive influence is brought to bear on the customer to make a purchase under this selling style. The salesperson is so concerned with the feelings of the customer that most of the time is spent being nice. The salesperson strives for a friendly relationship, initiating pleasant small talk in an attempt to be more socially acceptable to the prospect. The desired sale is viewed as a by-product of friendliness rather than as a direct consequence of selling initiative. This parallels the belief that you only have to feed a clucking hen enough mash and she will lay a fertile egg.

The desire to be likable may win friends, but it can also be a liability to a salesperson. When this desire becomes an overriding concern and there is a *dependency* on friendships for success, one may get caught in the unproductive trap so masterfully portrayed in Arthur Miller's *Death of a Salesman*.[2] Willie Loman could no longer produce sales because his customer "friends" had retired or turned to other suppliers who better met their needs.

At the lower left corner of the Grid is the 1,1 strategy. The salesperson's concern for making a sale and concern for the customer are both at a low ebb. This lack of concern for each of the basic ingredients in the selling situation results in passive behavior. Minimal influence is exerted during the sales interview, with no attempt to establish an improved relationship with the prospect or to build acceptance for the product or service. The basic pattern of sales behavior is best summed up as "going through the motions." The salesperson contributes very little to the development of the transaction. It is hard to say that this individual is a *salesperson* at all. However, given the benefit of the doubt, such a person might be called an "order taker" or "package wrapper," even though the "package" that never gets wrapped might be a million-dollar contract.

In the center is the 5,5 strategy, which is "middle of the road," containing half of each kind of concern. There is no hard push; the selling pressure is better described as sustained nudging. Concern for the customer is shown by trying to create a cordial atmosphere for the proceedings. This resembles the hail-fellow-well-met approach—telling a joke, talking about sports, or chatting about the weather as a way of breaking the ice. Underneath all this is a reliance on set routines with pat presentations and rehearsed "sophistication," all of which come through as mechanical because that is exactly what they are.

The 9,9 strategy is in the upper right corner, where high concern for making a sale and high concern for the customer are combined in an integrated way. The 9,9 high concern for the sale is evident from the salesperson's thorough product knowledge, which is related convincingly to the customer's requirements as these are discussed during the sales interview. High concern for the customer becomes evident through such considerations as the usefulness of the product in this situation, meeting the customer's expectations, and the benefits the customer is likely to gain from the purchase. Thus, the 9,9 orientation reflects a deep concern for the customer's interests and for the satisfaction the customer receives when the product or service is purchased.

Eighty-one different combinations of these two concerns are represented in a nine-by-nine point system. The focus here, however, is on analyzing the theories and strategies of selling behavior that are represented by the corner and midpoint Grid positions, as these five positions are most easily understood. Sales fundamentals such as prospecting, opening, presenting the product or service, closing, following up, and so on will be analyzed for how a salesperson, operating according to each of these basic Sales Grid orientations, attempts to make a sale. Later, more complex aspects will be examined, such as the sales approach of a paternalist, or of a facadist, i.e., the manipulative salesperson.

How Assumptions Guide Behavior

Each of the five Grid theories is based on a unique set of *assumptions* that lead to a fundamentally different way of orienting oneself to selling. By "assumptions" we mean those things you take for granted as being true or reliable in producing an effect. They are at the center of your customary selling strategy, whether you recognize them or not. Without assumptions, you would have no sales strategy at all when interacting with a customer. Your behavior would be random, aimless, purposeless.

Assumptions, then, are what give your style of selling its special character, and the assumptions you act on to get the sale are what make you a star or limit your effectiveness in various ways and in varying degrees. Even so, it is not enough just to have any old style or strategy with its corresponding sales tactics. Faulty assumptions can lead to poor sales results. Salespeople, however, do not often question their own basic assumptions. It is a good practice to do so as a way of checking on your selling "health."

The important point is this: *People can change their behavior by learning to use different assumptions.* In Chapter 2 you will be invited to identify the most natural set of assumptions you rely upon to get sales results. Then you will be ready to compare these with others that may boost your sales effectiveness.

CUSTOMER GRID

Now let us take an x-ray of the situation from another angle. Enter the customer, who also has two concerns. One is the concern for making a purchase. This is indicated along the horizontal axis of the Customer Grid (Box 2). The vertical axis represents concern for you, the salesperson, the individual from whom the customer may or may not buy. Each of these also ranges from low to high. Depending on how they combine, they reveal five basic Customer Grid styles, each with its own unique strategies and tactics for interacting with salespeople.

The 9,1-Oriented Customer

In the lower right corner is the 9,1-oriented customer, whose maximum concern is for making a purchase and whose minimum concern is for you, the salesperson. The attitude is "This character is determined to sell me, no matter what. I've got to take control. Otherwise I'll be taken advantage of against my will."

What are the assumptions of a 9,1-oriented customer during a sales presentation? There is a strong desire to make a purchase but little concern for the salesperson. Thus, this individual wants to be satisfied that the product is what is wanted, and it will be immediately rejected if there exists any doubt. Desires, data, and thought processes are shielded from the salesperson to avoid being tricked into making a purchase. Thus, the customer plays down personal desires, indicating no particular interest in what the salesperson has to sell. The customer may assert or imply that competitors are quoting lower prices or may give the impression of being better informed than is actually the case. Expectations are likely to be pessimistic, distrusting the product and doubting that it can meet concealed desires.

This customer has the tendency to turn the sales interview into

10 GUIDEPOSTS FOR EFFECTIVE SALESMANSHIP

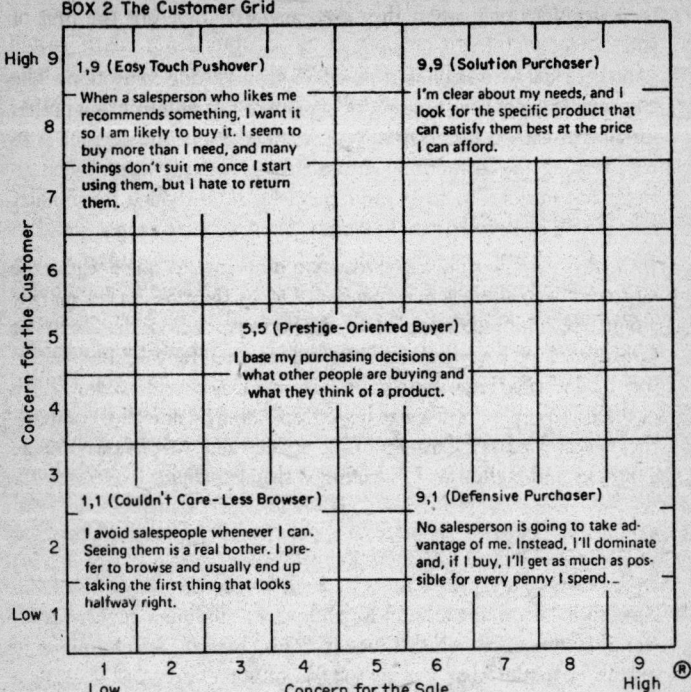

BOX 2 The Customer Grid

1,9 (Easy Touch Pushover) — When a salesperson who likes me recommends something, I want it so I am likely to buy it. I seem to buy more than I need, and many things don't suit me once I start using them, but I hate to return them.

9,9 (Solution Purchaser) — I'm clear about my needs, and I look for the specific product that can satisfy them best at the price I can afford.

5,5 (Prestige-Oriented Buyer) — I base my purchasing decisions on what other people are buying and what they think of a product.

1,1 (Couldn't Care-Less Browser) — I avoid salespeople whenever I can. Seeing them is a real bother. I prefer to browse and usually end up taking the first thing that looks halfway right.

9,1 (Defensive Purchaser) — No salesperson is going to take advantage of me. Instead, I'll dominate and, if I buy, I'll get as much as possible for every penny I spend.

a win-lose contest. Though a purchase may ultimately result, it is only after the sales representative has been forced on the mat, with the 9,1-oriented customer making every attempt to get the product cheaper or faster than it can be delivered, or of better quality yet at the same price, or on better terms. Typically, such customers provoke you to "prove" yourself and your product. They may even accuse the product of any number of weaknesses and limitations, remarking that you do not seem to know enough about the particular product or service. The burden is placed on you to disprove these charges. As you complete your presentation and move toward the closing, the customer vigorously resists, wrangling over the price and pushing for extra services. Such customers feel "good" about their decisions only when they are convinced they got the best of you.

So here you are up against a closed mind and strong convictions. The customer may not have a clear idea of personal requirements but pushes for all that can be gotten from you, whether or not the decision is to buy, turning the relationship into a battle. This tendency, when allowed to run riot, can result in no purchase, even though the product may satisfy real needs, simply because the customer cannot stand to capitulate. It may produce other "wild" results. The customer may "win" and take away something that is believed to be a "good buy," even though it actually is not. You are blamed for this later, of course. The customer's high concern for making a purchase (if a purchase is made at all) is evident in the strength of these personal convictions.

An opposite attitude toward purchasing that may appear still reflects the 9,1-oriented customer's way of going about buying. Here, the customer is all in favor of your product and wishes to buy it, not because you have been convincing, but because there is a reluctance to reveal weakness or lack of knowledge by having to ask questions. There are no in-betweens for 9,1-oriented customers.

The 1,9-Oriented Customer

The 1,9-oriented customer, with a low concern for making a purchase coupled with a high human concern for the salesperson, leaves no doubt about experiencing pleasure in receiving a visit from the salesperson. Interest in the product is often exaggerated so as not to offend the sales representative. By revealing a lack of product knowledge, the customer gives the salesperson something to talk about and readily accepts the propositions made without requesting proof or substantiation. A presentation is responded to with affirmative shakes of the head. The 1,9-oriented customer is easily persuaded that the product will satisfy personal desires even though, when the product is reconsidered at a later time, it often does not. In the salesperson's presence, however, the customer is suggestible and easily influenced.

This customer prefers to buy from a salesperson he or she likes and by whom the customer feels accepted. This desire to be accepted makes the customer susceptible to flattery and compliments, for this indicates approval. The 1,9-oriented customer is the original pushover, a real sucker for the salesperson who shows personal interest by remembering birthdays, children's names, golf scores, and hobby interests. Whatever makes this person feel appreciated is likely to result in a sale. The 1,9-oriented customer cannot afford to decline. To do so would be to reject the salesperson, and the warmth and approval would be withdrawn.

The 1,9-oriented customer's concern for making a purchase differs according to whether there is an initial purchasing intention or not. If you are called upon by a 1,9-oriented customer, you can assume that competitors' products will not even be considered. The customer likes you and is practically sold before arriving. Unless you are conscientiously set on describing the product and demonstrating it, there will be little more than a cursory look or feel. Quality, service, appropriateness, and so on are all accepted on faith. "I'll take your word for it." The customer may have no real need for what is being purchased or may be purchasing more than is financially wise, but those realizations are likely to come later.

The 1,1-Oriented Customer

A 1,1-oriented customer, with low concern for making a sound purchase and low concern for the salesperson, quickly communicates disinterest to the salesperson. The resulting inertia places full weight on the salesperson to carry the discussion and to provide the momentum if the sale is to be made. A typical attitude is "Salespeople try to influence you, so I avoid them if I can." When it is necessary to deal with a salesperson, purchases are made in a perfunctory, disinterested way, and often not because the product is wanted or needed, but as a way of escaping a pressure situation. It is easier than resisting.

When a 1,1-oriented customer does respond to a sales presentation, the major motivation is to find the path of least resistance while at the same time keeping out of hot water with whoever would reprimand sloppy or thoughtless purchasing. In order to avoid purchasing something that could be criticized for either volume, price, quality, or need, the 1,1-oriented customer is likely to stall or to serve as a message passer, presenting the salesperson's specifications verbatim to a superior with a minimum of evaluative comment. The customer thus avoids attack or being drawn into controversy because the buy/no-buy decision has been shifted to the shoulders of others.

The 5,5-Oriented Customer

The 5,5-oriented customer expects to be treated in a polite, give-and-take way. This customer does not want to be challenged to think deeply, but wants a solution that can be accepted with confidence, one that is consistent with what others have judged best to do in similar situations. The salesperson's confidence moves the 5,5-oriented customer from tentativeness toward a decision as long as what is being presented does not go against conventional thinking. This customer can be expected to raise objections to aspects of the presentation that might cause uneasiness. Because desires are rooted in conformity to the norms and values of social groups to which the customer belongs—in terms of "what other people think"—the salesperson may sometimes have difficulty in understanding how this prospect views the situation and in pinpointing the prospect's desires.

The 5,5-oriented customer is tentative and uncertain in any kind of purchasing situation except those that are standard or routine. To avoid overcompliance or being overly solicitous, this customer is likely to make a decision to purchase based upon the status of *others* who have bought the item in the past. Thus the customer avoids the risk of trying a new product and possibly making a mistake that would result in the loss or reduction of personal status in the eyes of others.

This customer is fearful of being taken and seeks to avoid criticism and derision by the salesperson and others. Unless the product has a recognizable degree of prestige, the customer may worry that there might be something better. While trying to remain pleasant, this person avoids complying blindly with the sales representative's suggestions and, for this reason, is responsive to "bait" such as name-dropping, suggestions on how to keep up with the Joneses, or interesting tidbits about past satisfied customers.

The 9,9-Oriented Customer

A customer with a high concern for making a sound purchase and high concern for the salesperson is accustomed to thinking in a logical, straightforward way. When a salesperson is not on the same wavelength, the 9,9-oriented customer is prepared to exercise leadership and bring the discussion up to a problem-solving level. The customer recognizes the personal limitations that some salespersons have but is unwilling to purchase in terms of those limitations—on the basis of either partial knowledge or unsound relationships.

The customer has assessed real needs in general terms if not in specifics before the sales interview and is prepared to buy or not buy on the basis of facts, data, logic, and reason. This customer responds favorably when the sales representative discusses or consults in an open, problem-solving way on how well the product fits requirements. By knowing the product's strengths and limitations relative to real needs, the customer is in a position to make a purchase, fully convinced that the decision to buy is sound.

As is true for the Sales Grid, the Customer Grid possesses five basic positions that picture the "pure" buying strategies. There are more combinations and mixtures of these five, but these are the fundamental ones.

ANOTHER DEGREE OF COMPLEXITY

Do sales representatives and customers have just one strategy, or do they skip over the surface of the Grid, shifting and adapting according to how the situation looks?

All but a few salespeople (and customers) do have dominant styles. That means that each person's basic approach resembles either 9,1; 1,9; 1,1; 5,5; or 9,9 assumptions. This, however, suggests that salespeople and customers are rigid and unchanging, which, of course, is not so. How the dominant strategy affecting a person's behavior can shift and change from time to time can be understood in the following way. Besides having a dominant style, everyone possesses a backup strategy, and sometimes another strategy as well. A backup Grid strategy is the one a person falls back on, particularly when feeling the strain of tension, frustration, or conflict. For you, as a salesperson, this can happen when your best efforts meet nothing but resistance or when, at the point of closing, the customer's enthusiasm turns to stubborn reluctance.

Any Grid style can back up any other. For example, even a 1,9-oriented person, when sharply challenged, might turn stubborn and go into a 9,1 orientation. Additionally, a person who normally sells in a 9,9 way may meet continued resistance from a customer. Unable to get onto a problem-solving level, this salesperson may shift to a 5,5 approach, negotiating for a compromise purchase under which both the salesperson and customer will be at least partially satisfied.

There are no natural links between one Grid style and another in terms of dominant-to-backup. Much depends on the individual and the situation. You sometimes see a salesperson who habitually comes on in a 9,1 way, pressing hard for a time, suddenly break off, crestfallen. This individual has switched away from a 9,1 orientation to a different set of assumptions and has moved back to a 1,1 state of resignation, feeling a sense of powerlessness, a victim to hostile fate. In such a case, had a different set of backup assumptions been used to continue the interview, a sale might have resulted. It is this great variety of optional dominant-backup behavioral combinations applied by both salespeople and customers in daily transactions that makes selling such a fascinating profession.

There are only ten major Sales Grid styles: five that relate to the salesperson and five that apply to the customer. But the number of possible dominant-backup combinations in a salesperson-customer interaction is quite large. Fortunately the dynamics between the salesperson and customer are not too difficult to understand and use when interpreting and responding to the customer—in any sales situation. As soon as the underlying motivations become clear, you are well on the way toward mastering the selling environment.

Effectiveness in selling can be enhanced through the application of sound behavioral science principles of behavior. Of course, selling will still depend to some degree on the artistic skill in being able to sense nuances, biases, and emotional colors in their innumerable combinations and dealing with them creatively, moving toward a good sale-and-purchase result.

GUIDEPOSTS FOR EFFECTIVE SALESMANSHIP

BOX 3 Effectiveness of Salesperson Grid Styles

Salesperson Grid Style	Customer Grid Styles				
	1,1	1,9	5,5	9,1	9,9
9,9	+	+	+	+	+
9,1	0	+	+	0	0
5,5	0	+	+	−	+
1,9	−	+	0	−	+
1,1	−	−	−	−	−

Various combinations of sales strategies and customer styles can bring a sale about, while others result in headaches and lost sales. The question dealt with here is: Which Sales Grid styles are most likely to be effective when the salesperson is facing each of the Customer Grid styles? This is depicted in Box 3, where the plus (+) represents "likely to be effective," a zero (0) indicates "intermediate between effective and ineffective," and a minus (−) stands for "generally ineffective in producing sales results."

Because of the many other variable factors that influence a sale—the product itself, its price, competing products, and prevailing economic conditions—these judgments can never be absolute. Other influences in the situation include the prospect's financial circumstances as well as the frame of mind of both parties prior to a presentation. The general trends apparent in Box 3 are the best predictions that can be made in the light of current knowledge. The more significant complexities of relationships between salespeople and their customers will be examined in detail in later chapters.

One more point should be made before we launch into a study of each of the Grid orientations. There is good reason to believe that the salesperson's Grid strategy is more important than the customer's with respect to a successful sales outcome. Salespeople, by reason of what they do or do not do, are in a position to set the climate in the selling relationship. The climate they initiate often causes customers to respond in kind, possibly slipping quite early from a dominant style into the 9,9-oriented backup set of assumptions, which is more favorable to a successful closing. Just as certainly other salesperson initiatives—such as 1,9; 5,5; 1,1; 9,1—may create a climate that starts the sales interview moving in a downward spiral. How the salesperson gets going with the customer is an important consideration. It means that in any sales contact the salesperson *can* be a leader if he or she knows how, leading the customer to become a *sound* purchaser. This is what creates a lasting relationship, repeated sales, and mutual respect.

GRID ELEMENTS

The Grid as Your Mirror

Given two more or less equal products, the salesperson who more fully satisfies the customer is more likely to get the sale. The salesperson either tips the balance, turning the prospect into a customer, or loses the sale altogether. Successful salespeople have proved this a thousand times over.

How a salesperson *thinks* about selling is all-important in determining the way customers are dealt with. Thinking is something everyone does, but we are not often aware of exactly *how* we do it. Yet it is critically important for us to understand how we think, because only in this way do we stand a chance of strengthening our thinking and thereby improving our sales effectiveness.

How we think about selling can be examined by discussing six elements of thought that influence the manner in which we deal with customers.[3] These elements are Thoroughness, Involvement, Convictions, Conflict, Energetic Enthusiasm, and Resilience.

Before getting into the minute-by-minute activities involved in selling, take a quick look at yourself as a salesperson. This can enable you to cut beneath the surface and see yourself as a salesperson dealing with customers.

The five alternatives under each element portray various attitudes toward selling, and one of them is probably an accurate description of you. Read the sentences beneath the element. Consider each as a possible description of yourself. Put a 5 beside the sentence you think is *most* like yourself. Place a 4 beside the sentence you think is next most like yourself. Continue ranking the other sentences with 3 for the third, 2 for the fourth, and 1 for the fifth choice. Thus, you will be putting the 1 beside that sentence that is *least* characteristic of you. There can be no ties.

These six elements describe qualities of personal behavior through which you can see your own assumptions about selling.[4] Preceding the sentence descriptions for each element is a statement describing the significance of the element to selling.

ELEMENT 1: THOROUGHNESS

A salesperson is an *expert* when he or she is thorough—really on top of product facts and the benefits buyers can expect from a purchase. Such a salesperson knows the product inside and out—its construction and features and how well it fits the customer's needs—and can describe the range and applicability of various financing options. Being an expert, the salesperson has the confidence that goes with it. This is what people mean when they say, "Knowledge is power." With such extensive product knowledge, the professional salesperson is in the best possible position to sell on the basis of facts, data, logic, and reasoning. This means designing a presentation that is powerful because it is valid. The validity of it is what transfers to the customer the confidence of the salesperson's convictions. It also places the salesperson in the position of maximum flexibility for responding in a constructive and problem-solving way to customer queries regarding the product.

This description of *thoroughness* pictures its importance as a factor in how a salesperson thinks about selling. Yet we know that not all salespersons think in this way.

The alternatives below portray various attitudes toward thoroughness. Record your 5, 4, etc., in the space provided.

_____ A1. I am reasonably well-informed of facts but not in sufficient depth to respond to challenges.

_____ B1. I collect and validate both negative and positive facts, continuously updating them, so that I can give the customer an objective basis for a sound decision.

_____ C1. I take facts given to me at face value. When asked for them I pass them on without embellishment.

_____ D1. I investigate facts in depth and personally satisfy myself as to their accuracy; no one is going to catch me short when it comes to facts.

_____ E1. I concentrate on learning the positive facts and tend to rationalize negative facts to diminish their importance.

ELEMENT 2: INVOLVEMENT

We know human beings get involved. It is as natural as breathing. Involvement entails feeling something in a personal way. When the emotions of positive involvement are aroused, they produce commitment to buy; if negative, not to buy.

Participation is the key to bringing involvement about. This means give-and-take between salesperson and customer. It means aiding a customer to "try on," "get a feel," "test out," or experience a trial run. There are any number of ways to activate direct experience. When these are out of the question, participation can be achieved by helping a prospect to "feel" by imagining what cannot be directly experienced or encouraging a prospect to visit a customer who is now using the product being considered.

Although we know the importance of involvement in decision making, salespersons often make far less use of it than would be desirable, and some seem to completely disregard its importance.

There are a variety of ways of thinking about involvement, and we need to understand each of them. In the sentences below we find various attitudes toward involvement. One of them is likely to be a quite accurate match for you.

_____ A2. It is a coincidence when the customer wants what I offer.

_____ B2. Being actively interested in customers as people allows them to feel secure in evaluating the products I offer.

_____ C2. Showmanship, plus a little participation, sells customers.

_____ D2. I am involved in selling the customer, whom I expect to listen and take my advice.

_____ E2. Customers sell themselves whenever I am able to get them to be active in thinking about, trying out, or experiencing a demonstration.

ELEMENT 3: CONVICTIONS

People are expected to think for themselves, and the most highly respected are those who have sound convictions and hold on to them. When a person has clear convictions, there is a certainty about that person—life has a sense of purpose, character, and direction. When a person has no convictions, or when personal convictions are easily given up, the individual appears weak, insecure, uncertain or anxious, or just plain indifferent to the real issues.

_____ A3. I listen for and seek out ideas, opinions, and attitudes different from my own. I have clear convictions but respond to sound ideas by changing my mind.

_____ B3. I stand up for my ideas, opinions, and attitudes, even though it sometimes results in stepping on toes.

_____ C3. I prefer to accept opinions, attitudes, and ideas of customers and others rather than push my own.

_____ D3. I go along with opinions, attitudes, and ideas of customers and others or avoid taking sides.

_____ E3. When ideas, opinions, or attitudes different from my own appear, I initiate middle-ground positions.

ELEMENT 4: CONFLICT

Disagreement and conflict are likely to result when people have different points of view, such as reservations and doubts about buying, and readily express them. The effects of conflict can be either disruptive and destructive or creative and constructive, depending upon how conflict is met and handled. An individual who can face conflict with another person and resolve it to their mutual understanding evokes respect and admiration. Inability to cope with conflict constructively and creatively leads to disrespect and oftentimes to increased hostility and antagonism. One makes a relationship; the other breaks it.

_____ A4. When conflict arises, I try to remain neutral or stay out of it.

_____ B4. When conflict arises, I try to identify reasons for it and to resolve underlying causes.

_____ C4. When conflict arises, I try to cut it off or to win my position.

_____ D4. When conflict arises, I try to be fair but firm and to get an equitable solution.

_____ E4. I try to avoid generating conflict, but when it does appear, I try to soothe feelings and to keep people together.

ELEMENT 5: ENERGETIC ENTHUSIASM

Healthy people have the capacity for using their unbounded energy in positive and constructive ways. When they do, enthusiasm is contagious; others catch it. It produces a "Can do!" spirit of optimism and progress. When enthusiasm is absent, life is drab and conversation is dull and boring. Then pessimism creeps in, hopelessness appears, and a sense of "Why try?" results.

_____ A5. I offer positive suggestions to keep things moving along.

_____ B5. I support, encourage, and compliment others on what they want to do.

_____ C5. I put out enough to get by.

_____ D5. I know what I want and pressure others into acceptance.

_____ E5. I direct my full energies into what I am doing and others respond enthusiastically.

ELEMENT 6: RESILIENCE

Not even the best salesperson will make every sale. A salesperson is often subject to low morale and despair when a sale is lost.

Resilience is the ability to bounce back, to keep performance in perspective. By doing so, a salesperson can avoid discouragement, and a "no sale" experience in dealing with one customer does not rub off and contaminate the next contact.

_____ A6. Whether I fail or succeed doesn't make too much difference; another customer will come along.

_____ B6. Failure doesn't affect my enthusiasm. There is always another prospect around the corner.

_____ C6. When I appear to be unsuccessful with a customer, I come back with alternative approaches. I don't let one failure diminish the prospect of success with another customer.

_____ D6. When I am turned down by a prospect, I approach the next one with the fear that I might be rejected again.

_____ E6. Failure to make the sale with one customer makes me cautious with the next.

Remember, this is a self-description and it may not represent the "true" you. Most of us are prone to self-deception when picturing ourselves. But it is a point of departure to keep in mind as you read through the book. In the last chapter, you will be able to summarize these rankings to depict your Grid style. It is important to rerank yourself after completing the book and to compare this latter ranking with the one just completed. To a certain extent this aids you to strip away self-deception and to improve the objectivity of your self-evaluation. This is an important first step in changing toward a more effective selling strategy.

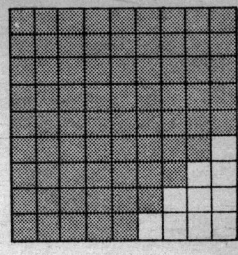

9,1

Domineering

The behavior of salespeople who act on 9,1 assumptions is motivated by a drive toward mastery. These people are *volume-oriented,* wanting to prove themselves through high performance, which satisfies the personal urge for control and domination. Consequently, there is a strong inner sense of direction. This is the positive motivation. Other people's opinions, which might require a shift from the present course of action, are disregarded. Furthermore, 9,1-oriented salespeople tend to be impervious to criticism. If anyone disagrees or stands in the way, there are no second thoughts about arguing down the objections—the need to prevail takes priority.

A negative motivation—failure—also influences the behavior of 9,1-oriented salespersons. Defeat may mean not getting a sale. It could be an unfavorable decision from a repeat customer regarding a refill order. Salespersons with a 9,1 orientation seek to avoid failure in either case by applying greater and greater persistence. When defeat must be acknowledged, their first reaction is to blame others. The 9,1-oriented response is "That guy wouldn't know a good deal if it looked him in the face." The resolution is "I won't let that happen again."

Having this orientation, the salesperson is highly committed to making a sale and getting a closing. The underlying assumption is "I have the right answer." Convictions are strong. Such a person stands up for personal ideas, opinions, and attitudes and presses forcefully for their acceptance, even when others have conflicting points of view. These strong convictions move a person to initiate action, to grab the ball and run with enough impetus to overcome the opposing forces. Though not always right, this salesperson is seldom in doubt. Categorical thinking of the right-or-wrong sort becomes the characteristic mode of analysis. Everything is black or white, and there are few if any grays. Once a position is taken or a course of action set, the 9,1-oriented salesperson is likely to hold tenaciously to it. As this becomes a customary way of relating to life, the person is more inclined to interpret facts to uphold personal points of view rather than make conclusions consistent with the objective situation.

Additionally, this self-sealing tendency keeps the 9,1-oriented salesperson detached from the true needs and feelings of other people. However, when the general desire to "win" is brought into the sales-interview situation, the friendly approach to the customer is often conditional. A pleasant demeanor is maintained so long as the salesperson is the driving power moving the customer along toward a positive decision. If the customer bows to the salesperson's will and is influenced, all is well. The warning light comes on, however, if the customer questions what is being said. To the salesperson, this means that the interview is in danger of veering out of control. Usually the first reaction is to try to override or discount the customer's disagreement. If the customer persists in objecting, though, the time has come to demonstrate the error of the customer's position. A salesperson acting under 9,1 assumptions finds little reason to shy away from conflict. Upholding the validity of one's stance is more important than maintaining friendly relations with the customer. "It is weak to let yourself be challenged." Momentum builds up as conflict with the customer grows, and this salesperson is quite unaware of the impact of the words that are expressed. Temper can easily be aroused when things are not going well. Humor, as well as anger, can be hard-hitting—it is likely to carry a sting. The total effect, of which the salesperson may be quite unaware until it is too late, is that this personal behavior goes beyond the customer's tolerance limit. Suddenly the interview is broken off, and another sale is lost.

KNOWLEDGE: PRODUCT, COMPETITOR, AND CUSTOMER

Assumptions of the 9,1 character can strongly influence a salesperson to get to know the product forward and backward. The salesperson gains expertise and becomes a genuine specialist, the rationale being never to be caught short by anyone. There is no excuse for ignorance; product knowledge is a strength. The attitude is that the salesperson's product is good—and good for the customer—despite what the customer thinks.

The same basic attitude impels the 9,1-oriented salesperson to get to know competitors and the products *they* are pushing. Competition becomes a win-lose fight. If the competitor wins, the sales representative loses, and vice versa. To be done in by a competitor is a bitter pill to swallow. As a result of this attitude, the salesperson is likely to be quite familiar with the competitor's strategies, pricing, and product characteristics, especially with regard to any weakness or defect, real or reputed. This too can add force, if the facts are used to demonstrate the relative merits of one's own product compared with the competitor's. When dealing with a customer, the salesperson uses this knowledge as ammunition for shooting down the competitor, frequently by name. The impact of this depends partly on how well grounded the criticisms are and partly on whether the customer is already favorably impressed with a competitor's product. The salesperson's strong "It's absolutely no good!" attitude can sometimes influence a customer against what a competitor is offering. Thus, the now-shared antagonism against the third party can promote a feeling of solidarity between customer and salesperson. However, when the customer already has respect for a competitor's product, having heard of it or having used it before, there will not be much regard for the person who degrades it. To the customer, such an individual appears unfair, arbitrary, and unworthy of trust. This is so particularly if the salesperson's criticism has been loaded with caustic remarks. In essence what the salesperson has actually done is unwittingly sell the competitor's product.

In contrast to a well-developed product and competitor knowledge, the 9,1-oriented salesperson's customer knowledge is likely very superficial. Being so unconcerned for customers as individuals, the salesperson feels little need to prepare in advance or understand a customer's own situation with its accompanying needs. The question, "What are the unique circumstances facing this customer?" is not in the salesperson's mind. Rather, a customer is a customer is a customer—all exist for the purpose of buying. If a prospect volunteers information, the salesperson is listening only for an entry point into which the product can be singled out as the standard solution to any problems the prospect has.

PARTICIPATION AND INVOLVEMENT

A person oriented with 9,1 attitudes feels obligated to take over and dominate the interview. An attempt is made to mold and shape most of the customer's responses and to suppress others. Objections to the product are out of line. The salesperson has no interest in the customer as a person with unique thoughts and emotions and special needs. The object is to *tell* it and then *sell* it. Listening is all-important, but it is the *customer* who is expected to listen. No time is wasted so long as the customer remains silent. The sales speech is delivered forcefully, sometimes continuing longer than would be necessary if there were any way of knowing when the customer was feeling ready to purchase. It does not occur to the salesperson that a customer's spontaneous participation in the interview could accelerate the progress toward a favorable buying decision. Customer participation is desired only if it is in the form of an agreement to buy—a nod, a brief word, or a signature—and preferably as soon as the sales talk is over.

Inviting customer participation is to invite trouble. Therefore questions are likely to be of only two types: a rhetorical question that the salesperson answers, emphasizing a selling point, or one calculated to get only a "yes" response from the customer, which enhances momentum toward the decision to purchase. Customers are thought of as crafty, always looking for excuses to get out of buying something. Given half a chance, they would probably bring up all sorts of objections to be overcome. The salesperson is, of course, willing to do this should it become necessary but considers it a waste of time. It is far better to rush the customer into a quick buying decision and then to move on to another prospect.

There are many customers, of course, who are not as passive as the salesperson wants them to be. They become involved, but in not buying. They may even rebel by interrupting, talking about what *they* want. The salesperson jumps to counterargue as soon as an opening is detected. This allows the customer to be silenced and the sales presentation continued.

9,1-oriented salespeople may search for and seize opportunities to give help, but they do this only to create an obligation and rarely do anything to increase credibility. The whole 9,1 approach communicates a pushing, sometimes blatantly exploitative attitude toward the customer. The salesperson's sudden switch to apparent helpfulness carries overtones of deception that perceptive customers quite often notice. The less perceptive recipient may become obligated as a result of accepting help, later recognizing, however, that an obligation has been created rather than assistance provided. This can easily convert a positive attitude toward the salesperson into resentment and long-lasting antagonism.

Thus in these and other ways the salesperson who behaves in a 9,1 manner cuts off possibilities of sound involvement with the customer. Little real back-and-forth discussion of the sort leading to a logical purchase decision takes place. Previous misunderstandings about the product are likely to be retained. Present prejudices against the product, if any, are reinforced, and new ones may be created as a result of the salesperson's powerfully exploitative approach.

COMMUNICATION

There are many sources from which people get information: books, TV, newspapers, and other communications media. Many of these are not very useful to a salesperson because they do not contain the kind of facts and data that are needed in order to sell customers. The essential kind of information the salesperson needs is what each customer possesses as a unique individual. The key to gaining this information is to ask questions to elicit needs and desires, to test the level of knowledge, and to determine what the customer's expectations are. Questions allow a sales representative to become acquainted with what a customer is thinking and why. But posing questions can be a tricky business. If they are good questions, you get the kind of information you need and can make a contribution to the customer. However, if the questions are weak and unsound, they may do a great disservice to you and your efforts to make a sale.

The typical 9,1 orientation to asking questions is simply to put forth the query but neglect explaining to the customer why the information is sought. A 9,1-oriented salesperson does this because it is a speedy and direct way to get to the point and avoid wasting valuable time. If a question is deemed necessary, that is sufficient reason for asking it, period.

However, if the customer is unaware of why you want certain information, a free and open exchange is hampered. Rather, the customer is more likely to become closed, hidden, secluded, and distrustful. Without knowing why the information is needed, the customer may become defensive at being coerced into a contractual arrangement.

Questions can also be asked in a way that makes customers feel they are being pumped. This kind of questioning is very suspect; it only reinforces a customer's fear that other forms of exploitation will follow.

9,1 listening is defensive listening to what the customer is saying, viewing any hesitation as a threat to an effective closing. If the salesperson perceives something in what the customer is saying that may prevent a sale, an attack is immediately launched to dispose of such comments quickly. Defensive listening does have its advantages, though. It keeps the salesperson alert to the opinions, thoughts, and attitudes being revealed which, if not understood, could lead to difficulty. However, the disadvantage is that this kind of listening is not all that perceptive. What the sales representative hears stimulates an internal sensitivity that often triggers an aggressive attitude. Faulty and filtered listening can lead to a customer's emotionally neutral question being translated into a strong objection—as the salesperson hears it. An attempt is then made to shoot down the objection, and the customer, feeling rebuked, begins to feel emotions of resistance. Once aroused, these emotions may in fact turn the initial query into an outright criticism, and a win-lose battle begins. The ensuing fight may be stimulating, but it is only stimulating to the glands, respiration, and pulse rate—not to sales volume.

Let us now look at the pattern of a 9,1-oriented salesperson responding to a customer's interruptions. This sales representative views interruptions as slowing down a presentation. They are considered irrelevant and unworthy of being dealt with. In either event, they are likely to be ignored or, with a figurative swing of the arm, simply brushed aside.

A customer trying to express a point of view responds to such treatment with resentment and resistance. What appears to be irrelevant to the salesperson may be highly relevant to the customer. Its significance may be related not to the sale itself but rather to the customer's desire for the salesperson to understand what is being said. For example, it may be that the customer has recently had personal problems and simply wants to use a part of the sales interview to blow off a little steam. If the salesperson does not allow this release of pressure, the customer may remain preoccupied with the problem and not listen to the presentation. Or the customer may want to tell the sales representative about something that has caused pride and excitement—for example, a recent promotion or a child's graduation from college. This interruption may have no relevance to the subject of the sales interview. However, the fact that such information is being given indicates that the salesperson is seen as someone who, until proved otherwise, does not consider the customer a nonentity. Thus, being ignored or brushed aside may raise barriers in the customer's mind against the salesperson and, by extension, the product being represented.

When a salesperson's emotions are out of tune with the situation, they undoubtedly get in the way of establishing a sound relationship with a customer. That is why it is important to look deeply into the whole matter of emotions and feelings.

A 9,1-oriented salesperson views emotions as a source of weakness. An individual should keep a stiff upper lip and not let emotions get in the way of action. A person acting from 9,1-oriented assumptions has learned to deny and disregard personal feelings—or, at least, the sentimental kind. These emotions may have been suppressed and internalized so deeply that the person no longer recognizes that they are there. Disregard for people may slip through in the use of humor—it is hard-hitting and carries a sting for those who are its targets. Sometimes emotions are discharged through intense prejudices and hates, such as against minority groups or certain ideologies in politics or religion. Negative emotions may be experienced not for what they really are but as righteous indignation against various features of society. Only when a situation gets out of control are emotions likely to become apparent. Then the salesperson's temper flares and may even result in a fit of rage.

To a 9,1-oriented person who controls emotions in these ways, all is business: no play, no interruptions, no irrelevancies; get to the point, drive hard, move in, close the deal, get out. What gets lost is the richness of understanding, human sympathy, and the ability to sense how the other person feels. Furthermore, controlling negative emotions in this way often results in an inability to enjoy the positive ones. Success is not gratifying, achievement not rewarding. Life affords few pleasures.

NEW CUSTOMERS

Opening

The key to the 9,1-oriented salesperson's attitude to gaining rapport lies in getting right down to brass tacks. The feeling is that time wasted is money lost; therefore, gaining rapport as such is merely excess baggage. Instead, credibility is established through product knowledge, with no time spent on wasteful chit-chat or preliminary discussions that are not to the point of making the sale.

The salesperson jumps right in and demands attention. Taking "no" for an answer is avoided, even in the initial few moments. This sales representative does not like to be put off. The goal is to keep talking, to keep the conversation alive on a never-say-die basis. For example, the sales representative might say, "This will take no more than 5 minutes of your time. I'll explain it briefly and I'm sure you'll immediately see its advantages."

Two examples of this approach to opening are briefly described below. The first is concerned with a customer who comes into the salesperson's (SP) establishment.

SP: Come right in. What can I do for you? (No smiles, all business, and a firm, strong handshake.)

Here's how a 9,1-oriented salesperson sounds when answering the phone.

SP: Harvey & Company; Smith here, what can I do for you?

Just the minimum is offered by way of contact with the customer. The objective is to get to business right away.

Identifying the Customer

The salesperson either makes the automatic assumption that the person being dealt with is the customer, or bluntly poses the question "Are you looking at this for yourself or for someone else?" If the answer is "someone else," the salesperson evaluates how to do a needs analysis through this intermediary, or, depending upon the circumstances, seeks to make direct contact with the customer. The attitude is "Take me to your leader" in an effort to get to the real decision-making source. In this way the person representing the customer becomes little more than a conduit or message passer.

The following conversation between a typical 9,1-oriented salesperson (SP) and a prospective customer (PC) describes the automatic assumption that this is the real customer.

SP: No time to breathe. Seven more calls today. So let's get to it, shall we?

PC: I'm sorry, I didn't get the name.

SP. Jones.

PC: Thank you, Mr. Jones.

SP: There is no question but that our company produces the highest quality in the industry.

PC: Sorry, what was your organization again?

SP: XYZ.

PC: Oh, yes. We've done business with you before.

SP: Now, as I was saying, our quality is unmatched, our delivery 100 percent, and our service top-notch.

PC: But I heard recently . . .

SP: Same old stuff. Our competitors can't compete, so they spread wild stories. Untrue, of course. But let me be more specific. There are seven steps in our product line. The third step is what you really need. It has all the essentials while using the same frame.

PC: But, wait a minute, I just want to collect information before making a decision. That's really my boss's job.

SP: Well, then I should be speaking directly to your boss.

PC: I'm afraid she's too busy for that.

SP: Aren't we all? I think it would be best if I went to her office and met with her. Can you set it up?

PC: I really don't know about that . . .

The salesperson is determined to get on with the interview regardless of who is listening.

Needs Analysis

The salesperson realizes the importance of establishing exactly what the prospect is after. However, it is anticipated that the customer will be wary, and thus the sales representative proceeds very carefully to explore the prospect's needs through subtle and sometimes not so subtle interrogation. The salesperson wants to know what kind of purchase the customer has in mind, the price that the customer expects to pay for it, the kind of service contract the customer is willing to sign, etc. In other words, it becomes necessary to know the maximum ability of the customer to buy so the salesperson can get top benefit from the purchase. The salesperson, however, is not always satisfied with the customer's answers and continues to test their validity and limitations. The sales representative might say, "Have you considered these options?" thereafter presenting additional possibilities, which might lead to a more expensive purchase, a longer service contract, and so on. If the need that the prospect formulates fails to square with the salesperson's product knowledge or the availability of the product, the prospect is pressured to accept alternatives, with the sales representative insisting on their importance, even though this may violate previously established expectations. The goal is to get the customer to buy a substitute if the particular product being sought is not available.

The following dialogue between a salesperson and a prospective customer illustrates this approach to needs analysis.

SP: What are you looking for?

PC: This is a once-in-a-lifetime purchase, but I'm afraid the product will be out of date within a year or two. Innovations are coming so fast that a better piece of equipment will probably appear, so perhaps I should wait.

SP: No way. The basic features are set. They won't change. There's no need for you to worry about that. By buying now you avoid the next price rise, which is going to be substantial.

PC: I love this one, but in the long run wouldn't I be better off to wait?

SP: I understand that you are concerned about when to buy, but my conclusion is just the opposite. You're much better off buying now. Get your basic equipment and then add to it if something important comes along.

PC: But I worry . . .

SP: Hey, forget it. Your anxiety is uncalled for. The problem is in your imagination, not in our equipment.

The salesperson, eager to push the sale in view of a positive customer attitude, fails to probe in depth regarding the specifics of the customer's requirements.

Establishing Expectations

The salesperson builds high expectations that the product can satisfy customer needs, and this is maintained throughout the interview. "What you asked for is available and perfect for your situation. It is exactly what you need." Thus, when a need can be satisfied, the solution is pushed to get a quick sale.

The following dialogue illustrates how 9,1 convictions are used to establish expectations.

SP: This product is the best there is; that about sums it up.

PC: I don't doubt your word. But can you elaborate on that?

SP: First, I've been in this business 30 years, and I know what I'm talking about. Second, we have a good number of customers who have come to us in disgust after not being satisfied by our competitors. Third, the craftsmanship we put into it is second to none. Next, the warranty offers "absolute" protection. Finally, we can offer an excellent service contract at a small additional charge. All that has got to tell you it's the best on the market. Believe me, there is no doubt in my mind.

PC: Those are quite impressive reasons. But I heard the testing laboratory ratings for your product were below those of your primary competitor.

SP: Poor test work is the only possible explanation. Don't pay attention to faulty data.

Here we see an illustration of what was described earlier as a 9,1 characteristic: self-sealed convictions. There is not even a hairline crack in the salesperson's projection of confidence.

If specific requirements cannot be met, some way is sought to get around them in order not to lose the sale. This might mean promising a 30-day delivery when, in fact, it is known that delivery takes 45 days. It might mean promising one model but substituting another, or claiming a capability for performance at a given level above that which is possible. Establishing expectations that satisfy the customer gets the sale. If a little slippage creeps in, an apology can reduce tensions and keep the contract in force until delivery can be made.

Presentation

A 9,1-oriented salesperson launches into the presentation with:

> I've solved this problem many times. Here is exactly what you need. Let me describe it for you in detail and I think you'll have few if any questions about its value when I finish. First of all, these are the positive features, many of which are new and available only on our products. This product is engineered to be foolproof. There is nothing to match it. It will give you continuous service year after year. It is possible for us to offer this at an unusually low price because of the efficiency of our R&D, the productivity of our manufacturing system, and the quality of service that we rigorously maintain. You may think that these add to our expense, but because of no returns, we are able to beat the field.

In this way the 9,1-oriented salesperson promises exceptional performance and quick service, and all positive features are emphasized, if not exaggerated.

The 9,1-oriented salesperson might start by listing the array of benefits to be gained through purchase of the product and then proceed through the major selling points, all calculated and marshaled to prove that the benefits are for everyone. The points of emphasis are selected mainly for their dramatic possibilities. On first glance this might appear as a customer-oriented presentation, since the emphasis is on benefits and satisfactions. However, in truth, it is not. This is because there is no genuine exploration of this customer's particular situation. Consequently, there can be little deliberate matching of needs to possibilities. Without this kind of exploration, the presentation is pitched to "Here is what the *product* can do" instead of "This is what you can expect from our product when *you* use it."

This sales presentation is not only a one-way street; it is also one-sided propaganda. The product's positive features are emphasized to the limit, but any performance limitations are ignored. Along the way, the weaknesses of competitors' products may be discussed in detail. The general notion is that the customer, whose attention is focused on the benefits and favorable aspects of the salesperson's product against the dark background of other products' defects, will have no option but to be persuaded of the wisdom of making a purchase.

The entire presentation is calculated to be a pitch that gives little opportunity for doubts or reservations to arise in the customer's mind. More than any other type of sales representative, the 9,1-oriented hard-seller cultivates and uses an impressive appearance, voice, and manner to give weight to the content of what is being said. The presentation is also engineered to be highly persuasive. The evidence is carefully selected to anticipate and prevent customer objections or to divert them if they arise. A customer is never allowed to say "no." The salesperson has few scruples about causing the customer to become overly committed financially. In these ways, a 9,1 sales presentation boxes in the customer and makes it difficult to escape. Carried to an extreme, the 9,1 orientation is characterized by the "snake oil" sales representative so often seen in motion pictures. Salespeople such as these have given the entire profession a bad name.[5]

The thoroughness with which a 9,1-oriented sales representative presents a product is illustrated in the following example.

SP: Let me tell you about this product. It is really fantastic, the result of years and years of research and field testing. There is no equal.

PC: Doesn't look that different, and it seems to have the same operational properties as all the others.

SP: Not so. Let me start at the beginning. The materials that go into it are of the highest quality and are quite expensive. We have to go farther west to get them, but it means we start ahead of all the rest.

PC: What about West Coast suppliers?

SP: Well, except for them. But they lose out in the expense of shipping the finished product east, you see?

PC: Well, you've got a point there.

SP: To go on, we maintain a rigid, I mean rigid, inspection program during manufacture. Twenty-seven different checkpoints. Can you imagine that? Checkers are held accountable. They don't spot-check like everyone else does. They check every single item. Defects are taken out of the line and sent to a special department for correction or disassembly.

PC: What is the warranted product life?

PS: We accept returns up to 90 days for any defects not caused by misuse. With the number of moving parts in it, you'd think 30 days might be maximum, but not with us. We know that when it goes for 90 days, it'll go for 900, or 9000, or right on up into eternity.

PC: What percent of returns do you get?

SP: Good question. Practically none. At any rate, too few to count.

PC: But how many?

SP: In the last 4 years, using the same equipment as now, we've had an annual average of 3.5 percent. Often it looks like customer misuse, but we can't prove it, so we accept returns, no questions asked, except when it's an open-and-shut case.

PC: Anything else?

SP: Yes. I started telling you about the product from the beginning, and believe me, I've just begun. Maybe it would be better if I tell you the *whole* story before you ask questions, okay? Then I'll deal with any remaining questions you might have at the end.

In this example, the salesperson knows the product in terms of raw materials, manufacturing process, inspection system, elimination of rejects, the warranty, and whatever else there is to know. The 9,1 character is seen in the sheer accumulation of facts, and the impact on the customer tends to be overwhelming.

9,1-oriented salespeople may be so impressed with the information they possess that customers are drowned in a sea of facts and data. This is self-reinforcing for such salespeople in the sense that they are impressed with product-knowledge prowess, but what is presented is far beyond a customer's need to know.

Results are what count to the 9,1-oriented salesperson. The end justifies the means. One's product is the best ever, and the intent is to go for broke to move it. Things are either good or bad, up or down, but never sideways, in the selling situation. When a customer raises a question, the answer given is whatever will sell. If the customer resists, the salesperson increases the pressure and, often without realizing it, allows some factual distortion to creep in.

A common reaction on the part of the customer to the big 9,1 presentation buildup is to convert the interaction into a test ground with an "I'm from Missouri" attitude. The customer looks for the salesperson's clay feet by asking questions to which the answers are already known. If given an incorrect reply under these circumstances, the customer loses confidence in the salesperson. The customer has shown the sales representative to be wrong. There is little opportunity to get back into the customer's good graces—once a liar, always a liar. On the other hand, the customer might not have sufficient background information to be able to detect a flaw in the salesperson's presentation. Nevertheless, customers can usually recognize exaggerated claims. Some customers are highly capable, once stimulated, of conducting an inquisition that can become a win-lose battle, and the blood that gets spilled is not the customer's.

To a customer, integrity is a matter of an individual's being consistent in what is said and done. It is seen when there is an unbroken connection between spoken and actual behavior and the degree to which these both adhere to a code of high moral values. The issue of integrity comes through clearly in connection with those promises which create firm expectations in the customer's mind. The matter of delivery promises already mentioned is an example of how some basic 9,1 attitudes show through. Having made a delivery commitment, and thereby having obtained the order, the salesperson's conscience usually is satisfied by a brisk "Now see here, you guys . . ." message or pep talk to the Production people concerning the urgency of this order. If they cannot produce, the customer can be told afterwards, when it is too late to back out, that it will be necessary to wait a little while. The salesperson is confident, if this happens, that the customer can be retained and any damage done repaired.

These kinds of factual distortions stretch the truth; they make it elastic. But this is not "lying" in the malicious sense of falsehood. The salesperson may very well be convinced at the time the promise is made that what is being said is truth itself. The attitude is that the key element in each statement is basically true. In one sense it might be said that truth begins when the elements in a selling presentation, taken as a whole, are 51 percent or more valid. In other words, if the majority of a statement is true, the whole is true, because the valid elements outweigh the invalid ones. This is what permits the 9,1-oriented salesperson to polarize a presentation in categorical terms of "all good" or "all bad." It allows an oversimplification of issues, and relevant facts may be left out because, in the salesperson's view, they are trivial and unimportant. As a result, the sheer strength of one's convictions can be highly persuasive, both personally and to others, because as far as the 9,1-oriented sales representative is concerned, the exceptions or contradictions do not count.

Objections

If the customer manages to get a word into the conversation, to put forward an objection or to lodge a criticism, the 9,1-oriented salesperson jumps to the challenge. Objections are a sign that a contest is on. They bring a win-lose orientation into play and intensify black-white thinking rather than stimulate an effort to understand the customer's feelings as the basis for working through the disagreement. There has been a threat to the sales representative's need for control, mastery, and domination, and therefore it is difficult for this salesperson to refrain from polarizing the issues. When a customer's attitude does not square with personal thinking, it is neither examined nor evaluated; it is rejected. The salesperson triumphantly stamps "Wrong" on it.

The most typical response is to overwhelm the objection. This can be done in a number of ways—for example, by piling up the "evidence" as a rational approach, or by suppression tactics that repudiate the emotional overtones of the customer's negative remark. An objection can be dealt with by giving the customer several reasons for the misconception and then getting a statement of admission for this error. The salesperson can also subject the customer to ridicule. Alternatively, some previously unrevealed information may be produced to nullify the objection. Another tactic, by no means unusual, is to ignore the objection as though it had never been spoken and to press on with the sales presentation. The salesperson seems deaf to the word "no." This is a straightforward brush-off. The salesperson might simply cut off the customer's statement and suppress objections with an attitude that implies, "Yours is not to question why. . . ."

The consequence of these attitudes toward winning the sale by suppressing objections is usually reinforcement of customer resentment and resistance. The 9,1-oriented salesperson who suppresses an objection by overwhelming the prospect is basically saying, "Don't ask questions. I will shoot you down if you do." From the prospect's point of view, silence is sometimes preferable.

The following illustrates how an objection creates a win-lose conflict situation for the 9,1-oriented salesperson.

SP: This guarantee is foolproof. No exceptions.

PC: What makes it so binding?

SP: Our word, of course.

PC: I'm afraid I must take exception to that. I know a person whose warranty you refused to honor.

SP: You must be mistaken. I give you my word it is a foolproof guarantee and my company has never welched on our warranty. That's pure and simple fact. Do you have other questions you would like to discuss?

The salesperson has won agreement on this point, but the sale may be lost because of the customer's feelings of antagonism toward what might be described as an "impossible" salesperson.

Closing

When the customer truly desires a product, the decision to buy will be positive regardless of the salesperson. This is true for any Grid style. Otherwise, closing is a potential mine field for the 9,1-oriented sales representative. New objections start to arise and old ones suddenly reappear. The salesperson mounts each in turn, presuming that when all skirmishes have been won, the customer will have no alternative but to sign on the dotted line. An objection, however, is like the cat with nine lives who refuses to die. Under these circumstances, the customer may be stimulated to counterattack with high-pressure tactics. Although desiring the product, the customer may refuse to take it simply to establish domination over the salesperson. Quite often the customer who has been frustrated by a 9,1-oriented sales presentation focuses on price, not because of the amount per se, but because price is one of the strongest tools for fighting back. If the salesperson wants the sale in a very intense way, as most 9,1-oriented salespeople do, then reaching agreement on the price can become a bitter battle. When events such as these come to pass, 9,1-oriented salespeople come face to face with what they most fear—failure to close the deal, which communicates an inability to control the situation.

Another customer may capitulate and buy against better judgment, simply because buying is seen as the only means of escape. However, the salesperson can rest assured that this is the last time business will occur with this customer. A short-term victory may hide an actual longer-term loss. These varied reactions tell us that 9,1-oriented selling is filled with land mines that can go off at the most unanticipated times.

The 9,1 orientation of persistence in closing is revealed in the following telephone conversation.

- SP: Well, I'm sorry you are uncertain, but it does take time to make up your mind.
- PC: Thank you for your help, anyway.
- SP: You're welcome. Please be in touch when you decide. I'm sure you'll want to buy.

Later,

- SP: Hello. I thought I'd give you another call. Can I wrap it up?
- PC: No. I've decided on another solution.
- SP: Perhaps I can help you avoid a big mistake by changing your mind.
- PC: No, I don't think so.
- SP: I think I might be able to sweeten up the deal for you.

PC: No, thanks. I've already made a firm decision.

SP: But I can promise faster delivery!

PC: Sorry. Goodbye.

SP: I want you to know you're making a real mistake!

PC: (Hangs up.)

Putting the phone back on the hook symbolizes defeat to the salesperson and victory to the prospect, who has terminated any future relationship with this salesperson.

ESTABLISHED BUSINESS

A salesperson who acts on 9,1-oriented assumptions is inclined to treasure an established account much as a dog guards its favorite bone. The salesperson is on the customer's side now and extends the protection and benefits at his or her command. The customer becomes very much like the salesperson's own property.

Maintaining Accounts

Because of an intense ambition to raise sales volume, the 9,1-oriented sales representative may unwittingly concentrate emphasis on the larger accounts and make little additional effort to cultivate marginal or low-volume accounts. But whenever an account is lost, however small, this salesperson becomes a tiger in trying to get it back. The feeling is that the customer has acted unfairly. What the sales representative fails to recognize is that the true problem lies in neglecting those actions that would have helped to nurture many of the small, uncertain accounts into steady ones. With regard to more lucrative accounts or those that have potential for increased volume, no amount of effort is too much if this is what it takes to retain them. The result is that the 9,1-oriented salesperson may spend a great amount of time maintaining contact with some established customers at the cost of losing others or failing to develop new accounts for the future.

Complaints

Complaints from customers quickly activate this salesperson. A complaint may foreshadow failure, so the 9,1-oriented sales representative speedily gets alongside the complainer and does whatever can be done to bring that customer around. The objective is to keep the problem in bounds and prevent it from looking too serious. Just as during the sales presentation, the salesperson tries to dominate the discussion, but this time the goal is to avoid creating an irate customer. If the customer becomes angry, the 9,1-oriented salesperson is willing to move to the customer's side against the company, saying perhaps, "Those bums—I'll really give them a hard time when I get back to the factory and get quick action to have this matter put right. In the meantime, don't you worry about a thing." Salesperson and customer have found a common purpose by uniting against a third party. When the salesperson can deliver by correcting the problem back in the organization, the bond may even be reinforced.

Rush Business

The 9,1-minded salesperson tends to be a "rush-business generator." Enticing a customer by promising earlier deliveries than could normally be expected, even when the salesperson realizes the factory cannot handle it, is better than losing the order. The factory becomes committed by virtue of the salesperson's unilateral initiative. Manufacturing is pressured to meet the promised delivery date. The salesperson may have influence back in the company to get priority on rush orders, even though the orders booked by the rest of the sales force must suffer delays. This is just another indication of a low concern for people in general. The self-justification is "If you don't look out for Number One, who will?" Enemies among one's sales colleagues are less to be feared than are disappointed customers who take their business elsewhere.

SELF-MANAGEMENT

A 9,1-oriented salesperson is inner-directed and keeps a tight rein on personal actions. A sense of purpose is maintained in all situations. This can result, however, in inflexible and rigid self-prescription, which, in the extreme, can program the salesperson like a computer. Once the course is set, it becomes difficult to veer to either one side or the other. The positive aspect is that behavior is well organized and guided by purpose, and trivial or extraneous factors do not enter the picture. The negative side, however, is that this salesperson is blinded to the unforeseen opportunities that may surface during an interview. When new information becomes available that should be interpreted as the basis for redirection, it is likely to be brushed aside. The original path is maintained.

SCHEDULING AND TIME MANAGEMENT. I plan a fixed schedule of activities several days in advance and do my best to avoid deviating from it. By having my activities well organized, I can use my time with customers to the maximum advantage. I don't tolerate much disturbance in my schedule.

PROSPECTING. I track down every prospect brought to my attention. No stone is left unturned. I push myself to make a specific number of new contacts, on a cold-canvassing basis if necessary, every week.

SERVICING. Since I intend to sell more, the customer is the boss. I keep constant pressure on my company to ensure that service requirements are satisfied.

EXPENSES. I am ready to answer for every penny I spend. The expenses I incur while with customers are a means to an end: getting increased sales. The expenses I incur for myself are in line with the effort I put out.

SELF-STEERING. I analyze the record of my ongoing sales results to make sure I'm keeping ahead. Some self-appraisal may be useful if failures occur, but for me it's diligent effort that makes for better performance.[6]

CUSTOMER REACTIONS

There is no doubt that a 9,1 orientation can be a very successful selling strategy. One reason for this is that the 9,1-oriented sales representative is a take-charge type. This salesperson is likely to move fast, to exercise positive persuasion on the customer, to communicate enthusiasm for the product, and to brush aside objections as trivial and unimportant. In this way, a customer can be swept into an impetuous decision to buy.

What are the probable consequences of this kind of selling approach? First of all, the customer is likely to feel hemmed in, impressed by the benefits and unable to muster a statement of reservations or doubts that exist. Second, the customer may sense that the sales presentation, persuasive as it is, does not deal directly with the problem—but the customer may be unsure of which way to turn. Third, resentment and hostility are likely to build up if anything in the presentation is contradictory to what the customer *does* know about the product or if it fails to satisfy real needs.

Thus a hard-driving approach is likely to have one of two results. On the one hand, it may bring about submission, even though disguised resentment may be present. The salesperson, meeting no open resistance, proceeds swiftly through the presentation and then presses the customer to buy. The customer may do so, and possibly the product will prove satisfactory. But if the customer *is* subsequently disappointed with the purchase, there will be a recollection of the hard-sell tactics and a mental note will be made to stay clear of this salesperson in the future.

Another result is that the 9,1-oriented approach may promote active hostility on the part of the prospect. When this happens, the salesperson is in a no-win or a lose-win situation. Objection after objection is given, no one of which is the real reason for reluctance, but the unexpressed attitude is "There is just no way I'll buy from this clown." The 9,1-oriented way of pressuring to close a sale often heightens a customer's feeling that the salesperson's objective is to make a sale rather than to provide what the customer needs.

More specific consequences of the 9,1 approach can be anticipated, depending on the *customer's* Grid style.

9,1

The 9,1 exploitative kind of purchaser immediately recognizes the salesperson as one who will take advantage of the situation. While 9,1-oriented salespeople can suppress participation simply by preventing questions from being asked, they cannot control customers' involvement. The more customers are prevented from participating, the more involved they become in pushing their own control, domination, and mastery. A discussion quickly evolves into a win-lose fight, a battle of wits, with intense involvement on both sides. The karate match is on, with each contestant looking for an opening. The salesperson tries to create enthusiasm; the customer remains unimpressed, or at least tries to give that impression so as not to be seen as "knuckling under." It is a situation where someone is going to emerge the winner and someone else the loser. Unless the 9,1-oriented customer has some basis for winning, satisfaction will be derived solely from beating the salesperson down on some minor point. The salesperson is unlikely to capture the sale through proving the 9,1-oriented customer wrong in a debating match. There can be no consensus; the sale is made only if each of the two is convinced, for reasons unknown to the other, that an argument has been won. Sometimes the salesperson may win a sale if, during the argument, the customer wins a few points and thereby becomes convinced that a good bargain has been derived from the salesperson. But equally as often there is a standoff, and no sale is made.

1,9

If the customer's style is 1,9, the response may be submission and acquiescence in order to avoid the 9,1-oriented salesperson's rejection. The salesperson sees this customer as a pushover, recognizing that here is someone who can be induced to buy readily and quickly. The tactic then is to short-circuit the sales presentation on the knowledge side and to hammer on the benefits by showing how the product will satisfy the customer's desires. The salesperson, who is unlikely to probe the customer for a realistic assessment of the situation and what the actual needs are, usually raises the 1,9-oriented customer's expectations to an exaggeratedly high level regarding what the product will do. The chances are that a purchase will be made, even though the customer will probably be disappointed with the result at a later time. But there are no complaints; rather, the customer will avoid having an unpleasant follow-up discussion with the salesperson and will look for others to satisfy future desires. So this customer is unlikely to become an established long-term account.

1,1

With a 1,1-oriented customer, the 9,1-oriented salesperson has a great opportunity to continue the sales presentation monologue uninterrupted. Product knowledge and selling points are rattled off nonstop. The customer's lack of response is unlikely to cause uneasiness; the salesperson simply continues without testing whether the customer has a good understanding. Because of the force of the presentation, a 1,1-oriented customer is inclined to withdraw even further and find ways to retreat from the situation. The customer may go along, however, if there is an obvious fit between the product, as the salesperson describes it, and a customer need. If the customer is a company purchasing agent, the 9,1 presentation can be persuasive, but only if the product meets the criteria set by the company the agent represents. If the product does not fit buying specifications, the customer is likely to defer making a decision and procrastinate indefinitely. If this path of retreat is cut off by the salesperson's tight closing maneuvers, the customer might evoke an unexpectedly strong backup and even fight with the ferocity of a "natural" 9,1. Alternatively, the customer may just take the easy way out and avoid further tension by establishing a direct contact between the salesperson and the ultimate purchaser.

5,5

The force and drive of a 9,1-oriented salesperson's presentation may put some reinforcement into the tentativeness with which the 5,5-oriented customer enters the selling situation. However, there are two ways in which a 9,1-oriented salesperson's approach makes a negative impact on a 5,5-oriented customer. One is that the customer's questions, interruptions, and objections may be brushed aside in an abrupt and unfeeling way. The customer may recoil from this kind of treatment and become resistant to the salesperson's efforts. Even though the product is desired, the customer might become so piqued as to refuse to buy.

The second pitfall a 9,1-oriented salesperson encounters is that the presentation of the product's benefits might not square with the customer's expectations of what this kind of product should be able to do. This is due to the salesperson's being unlikely to probe in depth to understand the source of the 5,5-oriented customer's desires.

The 5,5-oriented customer is susceptible to a 9,1 approach so long as the salesperson's presentation strikes the right chord in appealing to what is held in high esteem—the product's prestige as demonstrated by the fact that a number of illustrious people or companies are using or at least endorsing it, or even the reputation of the organization that the salesperson represents. If not immediately convinced on the basis of product reputation, the customer may become very choosy. Whether the product will eventually be purchased depends, to a great extent, on the salesperson's treatment of inquiries.

9,9

The 9,1-oriented salesperson's emphasis on product knowledge stimulates the 9,9 customer's interest in a sound purchase. The customer can be expected to question the salesperson at points where the presentation does not square with the customer's own factual knowledge or assessment of the situation. The 9,1-oriented salesperson's attempt to brush aside or diminish the importance of these checking points is met with customer persistence in having them answered. When challenged, the 9,1 salesperson is inclined to convert the previously objective interview into a win-lose argument. The sales representative is likely to be disappointed in this effort to provoke a more heated discussion, since this customer maintains composure and continues probing for facts and data. If unable to make progress under these conditions, the 9,1 salesperson may throttle down and become more factual in providing explanations when requested to do so, or may acknowledge an inability to provide the needed information at the present time. The salesperson's attempts to display product benefits and to arouse desire only meet with success when it can be shown that the product really fits. As the 9,1-oriented salesperson follows the usual selling approach, it is unlikely that the customer's current understanding of the situation will be enhanced or that the customer will be aided to see the situation in a different light. Thus, if the salesperson's product explanations meet with the customer's self-formulated requirements, a sale will result. If not, the salesperson is unlikely to possess the flexibility of alternative ways of viewing the customer's situation so as to make it possible to come to a successful closing.

SUMMARY

This salesperson's attitude might be summed up in the following way: "By working hard and driving myself, I operate in the best interest of the company. Getting more and more business is the most important aspect of my job, and that means increasing sales volume. Profit is the direct result. This is not easy, and prospects have a million reasons for not becoming customers, and every reason has to be overcome one at a time. It is easy to lose your sense of proportions when you are trying to help customers and all you meet with is resistance."

Given the limitations and barriers to effective selling that are created by a 9,1 orientation, the question still remains: What is the probable impact of a 9,1 orientation on the profitability of selling? A "push the tons and profit dollars will result" mentality is the hallmark of 9,1-oriented thinking. It is correct in that dollars will not result unless the product moves. However, it may be very erroneous, too, because the 9,1 way of selling, which undercuts competitors and makes customers feel small, can also undercut profits. It may get the sale but have such costly servicing consequences that no sale at all would have been less damaging. Or it may move the product this time but alienate the customer forever.

1,9
Eager to Please

The 1,9-oriented salesperson is primarily concerned with being responsive to other people, being liked by them, and gaining their acceptance. The positive motivation behind a 1,9 orientation is to gain approval, sometimes almost without regard for personal effort or the degree of acquiescence involved. High value is placed on good relationships, on being a "nice guy." A customer's frown is a bad sign, whereas a smile means all is well. When an interview is over, the 1,9-oriented sales representative is more likely to reflect on the emotions in the situation or the nuances of emotions felt rather than on logic of the presentation itself or even the outcome.

The negative motivation of a 1,9-oriented salesperson is fear of rejection, which mesmerizes this type of person into a submissive attitude. Instead of confronting customers with sound logic and debate, the 1,9-oriented salesperson is involved in placating, mollifying, and other efforts to pacify customers when tensions arise and disapproval and rejection are felt. It is said that "out of dissent comes the most elegant solution." However, the 1,9-oriented salesperson adopts the attitude of "out of dissent comes the loss of friends," which is personally devastating because this person has built-in uncertainties about being liked.

To avoid rejection, the sales representative tries to keep from giving the impression of being negative or critical in any respect. One way to do this is to embrace the opinions, attitudes, and ideas of others in preference to forwarding one's own. This permits agreement with others and also reduces the possibility that disagreements will occur. Even when an opinion is expressed, it is more likely to reflect what the sales supervisor or the customer has said rather than to be an attitude founded on personal convictions. The salesperson is inclined to be an oversensitive listener and encourages others to act on their feelings, regardless of the validity or soundness of them.

As far as exercising initiative goes, the 1,9-oriented sales representative is no leader; he or she is a follower. However, there is an active effort to initiate contacts and to establish bonds of friendship, thus creating an atmosphere of congeniality. The salesperson rarely generates conflict, but when it does appear, whether the salesperson is personally involved or not, an attempt is made to soothe the bad feelings. This attribute of looking on the bright side has a quality of "Wanting will make it so," in contrast with the optimistic "Can do!" attitude of a person who sets a course and then works to bring it about. When there are tensions between people, humor is aimed at reducing the tensions, lightening the atmosphere, and in this way smoothing over the differences. To allay tensions the salesperson keeps an inventory of amusing anecdotes relating to the product and its users, which can divert criticism and invite interest and more favorable reactions. Temper is not easily triggered in the sense of lashing out in anger, but similar emotions in others increase the level of anxiety in a 1,9-oriented salesperson.

The 1,9 orientation is a friendly, likable approach to selling. This sales representative is *other-directed*, with cues for behavior taken from *outside*, not from inside, the person.

KNOWLEDGE: CUSTOMER, COMPETITOR, AND PRODUCT

With these characteristics of a low concern for outcomes and a high concern for people, the 1,9-oriented salesperson has an active interest in developing an understanding of the customer as a person. Where possible, some inquiry about the prospect is undertaken in advance to discover what sort of person the customer is and to look for conversational leads to promote friendly discussion. When meeting with a customer, the salesperson is genuinely interested in hearing the other person's thoughts, attitudes, and opinions, and this interest is not limited to business matters. Finding out about hobbies, family, the progress of children in school, as well as career aspirations, is a pleasure in itself. Through acquaintances this salesperson is attuned to a widely ranging network of hearsay, rumor, and gossip. It is enjoyable to pass on this news and to hear the latest from prospects, customers, and others with whom amicable relationships have been established. A salesperson with 1,9 attitudes often significantly increases sales costs by insisting on picking up the check for meals, drinks, and entertainment. The rationale seems sound to this person because it builds friendships.

A 1,9-oriented salesperson is unlikely to develop a deep knowledge and understanding of competitors. There are more agreeable things to think about. The attitude of businesslike vigilance, so essential for becoming aware of and informed about competition, is in itself a potential form of conflict; something so unpleasant is not deemed worthy of attention. With this self-destructive blind spot, the salesperson is frequently unable to cope with customer-supplied information with regard to competitors.

The desire to be liked by one and all leads the salesperson with 1,9 attitudes to be complimentary about competitors in a way that can be disquieting to the customer. This is not to say, of course, that the salesperson bursts forth with spontaneous praise, but the basic attitude is "Don't say anything unless you can say something nice." When invited to comment on a competitor's product, the salesperson's response is to avoid saying anything that might be interpreted as critical.

There is, of course, a likelihood that the salesperson's compliments and warm attitudes may enhance the competitor's product in the eyes of the prospect and thereby make what the 1,9-oriented salesperson is presenting seem less attractive. When the customer probes beneath these compliments, it is evident that the salesperson is actually deficient in an understanding of the competitor—unaware of the sales strategies, products, pricing, and so on—and the salesperson's credibility is reduced.

Product knowledge also tends to be superficial. The sales representative is more likely to be able to recount features that appeal to the senses than to give a technical explanation of "how it works." Knowledge is a means to an end rather than an end in itself. To be helpful, this salesperson learns what it is that customers *want* to know rather than what it is they *need* to know as a basis for making sound purchase decisions.

PARTICIPATION AND INVOLVEMENT

A salesperson with a 1,9 orientation seeks to establish a congenial relationship with the customer while touching lightheartedly on agreeable aspects of the product. This is the salesperson's idea of participation and involvement. When people like one another, it is easy to do business together. This is the ideal vocation in this person's eyes—being paid to make friends.

Listening is all-important. The salesperson would never think of preventing the customer from expressing personal feelings and desires and is always ready to listen receptively to whatever the customer wishes to discuss. Whenever the conversation lags, a new way is found to keep the topic going. The effect of this is relaxing, and the customer may be influenced to see the salesperson as someone with whom it is pleasant to do business.

But this friendly discussion has a pseudo quality. Although congenial, unhurried, and sociable, it does little to create a suitable atmosphere for completing a business transaction. It is more in the nature of a coffee-break visit and is not the kind of involvement that heightens a customer's interest in the product. The characteristic approach and the very assumptions that dictate personal conduct cause the salesperson to hold back from any kind of guiding initiative toward "getting down to basics" concerning the product.

Some customers are pleased to see their 1,9-oriented friend during a visit. After an enjoyable chat about social events, the salesperson may mention something of interest to show the customer—for example, a brochure on a high-priced piece of equipment. In this case, the customer is likely to remark, "That's really interesting, Tom. Leave it with me and I'll look through it and discuss it with our technical people." Both parties lapse back into an irrelevant conversation, and eventually the salesperson leaves with a smile and a handshake. The customer thinks, "Nice guy, that Tom. Good to have him stop by, but, gee, it's really getting late." The customer writes a colleague's name on the brochure and shoves it into the "out" box. That is the end of that.

On the other hand, a 1,9-oriented salesperson may come in with a fairly low priced, novel item, and the customer, in a good mood, says, "They're great little gadgets, Anne. I'll take a couple right away." The salesperson is delighted, for her theory has been borne out—a sale is made. Maybe, though, if she had probed to find out from her friend the objective needs of the company that the product could satisfy, she could have sold a couple of gross.

Some customers, however, are not so chummy. "Oh, you're here again. You've caught me between two appointments. We've got just 3 minutes at the outside, so what is it today?" Busy people prefer to participate and involve themselves in profitable and productive transactions.

1,9-oriented helpfulness is of a still different character and quality. Many times a 1,9-oriented salesperson's assistance caters to weakness in the customer who receives it; something is done for the customer that is superfluous, as the customer is perfectly capable of doing it. It is much like having an oversolicitous parent who, by cloying attentions, deadens the child's initiative to act under his or her own steam. It makes the salesperson feel good, but it does little in the way of constructively aiding the customer to become more effective. Although it reflects a high concern for the individual to whom it is given, the salesperson unwittingly makes the receiver more dependent, though not obligated. The customer simply gets accustomed to "letting George do it," accepting the assistance as a matter of course with very little sense of appreciation.

COMMUNICATION

The 1,9-oriented sales representative is inclined to ask questions that the customer might see as irrelevant. The salesperson asks such questions in a loose and indirect way, proceeding in this manner in order to avoid saying anything that could be challenged. These open-ended questions allow plenty of room for the customer to talk and to express needs and desires.

But the results are that the customer is very likely to feel that time is not being used constructively by a salesperson acting in this manner. The conversation is perceived as too soft and lacking the "brass-tacks reality" quality that the customer has come to expect. Rather than moving the customer toward a purchase, these questions often have the opposite impact.

The 1,9-oriented sales representative is sensitive to the emotions in the situation and interprets the message differently, depending on whether what is perceived is hostility or friendliness, acceptance or rejection. This is particularly so in the case of objections, which are unpleasant and disconcerting. The salesperson does not like to hear them and thinks, "Surely you don't mean that!" Rather than listening for the sake of gaining a better understanding of the customer's situation, the salesperson dwells solely upon the emotions present in a statement. Therefore, answers are likely to be off base, responding to feelings rather than focusing on a sound resolution of an objection. Listening for what one wants to hear, though, does have certain advantages. A salesperson can sometimes supplement an approving remark made about the product with a series of additional points of information, all of which further a positive attitude on the part of the customer. Despite this, however, the customer is unlikely to find much gratification in the sales discussion. When a question is posed or objections raised, the answers the customer receives have a bland and insipid quality. Whereas the customer seeks food for thought, the salesperson merely provides tranquilizers.

The 1,9 way of dealing with interruptions is to treat them with utmost interest and respect. The salesperson sincerely wishes to avoid giving customers any indication that they are not valued as persons. At the same time, a negative tone in the interruptions produces personal anxiety, based on the fear of being rejected. So the salesperson responds warmly. The subjective aspects of the interruption are put in the forefront, to be fully discussed, while the content of the sales interview is set aside indefinitely.

The result is that the interview stretches out to an indeterminable length, wandering and meandering all over the place, having little crispness and even less direction. One topic of the free-flowing conversation stimulates another, and so on. The closing recedes farther into the horizon. The sales interview finally is closed, but the sale is not. The customer has run out of time and has not gathered enough information to see how the product could meaningfully solve the problem. Unless the customer is also 1,9-oriented, it is unlikely that this kind of meandering and wandering will be seen as very beneficial. Rather, the customer concentrates on what could have been done without this distraction. So although the 1,9-oriented salesperson's intention is to create fondness and respect—an atmosphere in which a purchase may be made—the methods employed tend to be self-defeating.

1,9 ways of adjusting to emotions accent the positive, and enjoyment comes not during the action or from achievement, but in togetherness. This means veering away from situations that could lead to personal rejection. Warmth and affection are emotions with which a 1,9-oriented salesperson feels quite secure. Situations that produce harmony and good feelings are sought, while those likely to produce tension or conflict are strictly avoided. This latter reaction makes it difficult for a 1,9-oriented salesperson to deal with objections and to respond validly to complaints. Yet it is by dealing with objections, interruptions, complaints, and questions that a sales representative can aid a customer to establish firm convictions about a particular product.

NEW CUSTOMERS

Opening

The initial step for a 1,9-oriented salesperson is to become acquainted with the customer by establishing a comfortable atmosphere in order to develop a secure feeling of acceptance. The 1,9-oriented assumption is that people usually do business with those they like. The salesperson approaches the customer and smiles, saying, "Hello, how are you today? Nice day, isn't it?" The salesperson may inquire about the customer's background, hobbies, family, and so on, all open-ended and aimed at establishing rapport and enabling the prospect to talk about things of personal interest, keeping the prospect self-focused. The sales representative may talk and joke with the customer to create a relaxed and receptive mood. Flattery is used as a means of singling out favorable aspects with regard to the customer and the organization the customer works for.

The following example reflects the warmhearted, congenial atmosphere that the sales representative seeks to establish with the potential customer during an opening in the customer's house.

SP: I know you're busy . . .

PC: That's okay. Come right in, I've been waiting for you.

SP: Oh, well, thank you. We are so pleased that you invited our company to make a bid on this project.

PC: Well, let's get down to business then. We'd like you to enter a bid on these specifications. Have you already seen them?

SP: Yes, I did glance at them. They told me the purpose of this call was to bid on finishing this room . . . Does that mean wallpaper, painting the woodwork, valances for the windows, and so on . . . ?

PC: That's part of it, yes. Do you think you would be interested?

SP: Oh, yes, yes, very much. I just love this room. Such a beautiful view, just magnificent . . . I am really going to enjoy this . . .

The salesperson immediately launches a display of gratitude at having been invited. This provides the opportunity to make friends and creates a climate where unpleasant issues are unlikely to arise. The salesperson possesses an endless reservoir of small talk and often leaves

1,9: EAGER TO PLEASE

it to the customer to initiate the shift from social chat to the sales interview.

Identifying the Buyer

The salesperson is genuinely interested in the present contact regardless of whether this is the ultimate customer or an intermediary. Because of the salesperson's high personal concern for the immediate contact, little or no initiative is exercised in finding out if the prospect is the ultimate buyer; the sales representative only gives consideration to the latter possibility if and when the prospect brings it up. At that point the salesperson offers help and assistance to this intermediary in satisfying the ultimate customer.

Needs Analysis

The 1,9-oriented sales representative believes the prospect's needs will unfold and be revealed in the context of a friendly, social relationship. The basic assumptions underlying this approach are essentially customer-centered. The salesperson believes in responding solely to the customer's definition of need. Questioning or challenging this stated need must be indirect, if at all, in order to avoid being offensive or invading the customer's privacy.

The following example illustrates these assumptions.

SP: Interior decoration makes people happy when it expresses the personalities of those who live in it.

PC: What do you mean? How does a house express a personality?

SP: Oh, in so many, many ways. For example, what is your favorite color?

PC: Brown.

SP: Well, that's a little dark for the walls, perhaps, but we could make the woodwork brown. It would be absolutely beautiful.

PC: But what about the walls?

SP: Would you like a lighter brown or beige perhaps? We have so many different gorgeous shades for you to choose from.

Prospects are encouraged to participate and talk about themselves. Reflection, open-ended remarks, and comments about the obvious are ways in which this is done. The hope is that the invitation to express preferences, e.g., "What colors do you most enjoy?" and so on, will lead to requests for samples or for descriptions and brochures. If not, the salesperson pieces together probable needs and invites reactions of interest in a way that communicates a desire to be helpful.

Establishing Expectations

The 1,9-oriented salesperson avoids establishing anything about the product beyond minimum expectations. When asked a direct question that implies a higher expectation than can be delivered, this salesperson does not want to disappoint the prospect and avoids doing so by saying, "I'll see what we can do." The salesperson is also easily influenced by a 9,1-oriented customer to urge the company to give quantity discounts or other price concessions that might be unwarranted when related to manufacturing costs and the current market situation.

The following example is typical of the 1,9-oriented sales representative's evasiveness when dealing with a customer's inquiries.

PC: I suspect my requirements are quite unique and you may be unable to be of assistance.

SP: Well, we would truly like to help. What exactly do you have in mind?

PC: The unit I need is 9 by 5 feet and 2 feet deep. Ideally the color should be black with a chrome trim.

SP: Oh, I am sorry, but our demonstration models are a little larger than that. However, they do come in all shapes, sizes, and colors. Perhaps you would like to look in our catalog.

PC: Well, that depends. If you order, how long is delivery?

SP: Oh, usually not too long. If we don't have what you want, we might even be able to get it from another store. We could arrange for you to use a demonstration model that is fairly close to your specifications in the meantime.

PC: I don't know. Could you give me a definite date on the delivery time?

SP: I'm just not sure . . . You know, so much depends on things not under our control, I'm afraid to make a commitment when I may have to disappoint you later.

Since the salesperson does not correct falsely high expectations, the possibility exists that they will subsequently be violated. When this occurs, the salesperson is profuse with apologies regarding the mistake.

Presentation

In discussing the product, the 1,9-oriented salesperson mentions the attractive features and identifies other aspects the customer might like. The approach involves waiting to express personal opinions until "reading the signs" from the customer.

The presentation usually starts off very low key, with the sales representative describing a number of interesting and perhaps novel features. These are conversational appetizers to induce the client to express favorable opinions or to mention what feature of the product seems most appealing. As soon as an opinion is expressed, the salesperson reinforces it if it is favorable, complimenting the customer's good taste and agreeing that the feature is indeed a most desirable benefit to be accrued from purchase. On the other hand, if the customer's expressed opinion is negative, the salesperson cushions its impact by implicitly yielding the point and even apologizing, then quickly moving on to a positive feature. Product features that are not so attractive from the customer's point of view are ignored or glossed over in order to maintain a pleasant atmosphere.

In the following example the 1,9-oriented salesperson uses the presentation for the purpose of establishing a friendly relationship with the customer. The salesperson's lack of in-depth product knowledge becomes quite evident as the customer seeks more detailed information.

SP: Well, here it is. How do you like it?

PC: It seems to be more or less what I had in mind.

SP: That's wonderful. I know you'll be satisfied . . .

PC: I've never operated one of these. May I see how it works?

SP: Oh, well, let me see. Hmmm. . . . Let me get Bill over. He's a real expert on the operation of this equipment, and he can answer all your questions. I love to listen to his presentation—it's so clear, and he has so many facts and details right on the tip of his tongue. It's really a pleasure to hear him. Hey, Bill, can you help us for a minute, please?

As we see, the 1,9 salesperson breaks down when called on to deliver based on thoroughness of product knowledge. Leaning on others rather than developing the needed skill to deal with tough spots is certainly typical of the 1,9 sales orientation.

Objections

How a salesperson with 1,9 assumptions deals with disagreement and conflict can be very revealing of the basic approach. The conversation is steered away from topics that might provoke controversy and ill feelings, but when objections do arise, they are quickly smoothed over. An objection is seen as a breach in the harmony that the salesperson is seeking to establish. The objection may be played down by saying, "It's not important," or "Let's set this aside for a moment; we can discuss it later on." Yielding to the customer's point or shifting the conversation with a joke eases tension and aids in bypassing objections.

Since it is thought that everything will turn out all right, there is no need to paint anything but the brightest picture for a potential customer. Misrepresentation may be the result at times, but this is by no means due to any conscious deception on the part of the salesperson. The 1,9 attitude toward truth can be understood when it is recognized that personal wishes and desires tend to be confused with data and facts. The sales representative wants above all to keep the customer happy. The possibility that the customer may become irate with the purchase at a later point in time is, at present, only a small cloud on the horizon. Truth is found only in what the salesperson wishes or hopes for at the moment. If a customer states a number of requirements and asks whether the product can meet them, the sales representative remains more interested in retaining personal acceptance than in satisfying the literal requirements that have been specified.

If the salesperson does not possess enough detailed product knowledge to give specific answers to critical remarks, generalizations are given, which envelop the query but fail to answer it. Another technique of this salesperson is to take a negative point and abstract it to the point where it becomes meaningless or insignificant. In this way the 1,9-oriented sales representative is a master of the tactics of depolarization. All these responses serve to blur objections and make what the customer wished to discuss appear less critical than it truly is. It is almost impossible to get an argument going!

The following illustrates the 1,9-oriented salesperson's approach to dealing with reservations and objections.

SP: Are there any other matters we might discuss?

PC: Yes, there is one. Don't you think this product will be out of date within a year or so? Innovations are coming so fast that a better piece of equipment may appear before I get my money's worth.

SP: They're coming out with things so fast these days that it's hard for even us to keep up with them.

PC: Then maybe I'd be better off waiting. This is a once-in-a-lifetime decision for me, you know.

SP: It's rather difficult for me to counsel you on that, unfortunately. I'd really hate for you to be disappointed.

PC: I'm glad you understand. Perhaps I'd better think on this a while.

Objections that have been deflected work against the possibility of a sale, particularly when the customer becomes suspicious that unanswered objections have pinpointed true limitations in the product. These may become magnified out of proportion. The salesperson, sensing that some specifications cannot be met, emphasizes the positive. If the negatives cannot be eliminated, a profuse apology is in order. Worse yet, the sales representative may hastily reply to a customer, "Yes, I'm sure it will meet all your requirements," without running a mental check on the possibilities that it may not. This, of course, is *not* dishonesty; it is only an overenthusiastic desire to please. Unfortunately, the end result may be an extremely dissatisfied customer.

Thus, the desire to please always tips the balance beyond the salesperson's ability to maintain a realistically objective awareness of what can be provided. The effect on the customer of a 1,9 optimistic, head-in-the-clouds statement is likely to be an initial acceptance. Sometimes reservations and doubts are withheld so as to avoid making the 1,9-oriented salesperson feel personally uncomfortable. The customer may keep silent about these objections rather than cause the salesperson embarrassment, but the end result is ultimately the same—no sale.

Closing

The sales representative with 1,9 assumptions worries about throwing the customer off balance if too much selling pressure is exerted, and to this salesperson, any amount seems to be too much. There is a great fear that the customer will say "no," and the salesperson is delicately tuned to this possibility. Thus, it seems preferable to refrain from pushing the customer for a declaration so as not to risk a turndown. The salesperson hangs back, waiting for the customer to make a spontaneous buying decision. If this does not come, the salesperson is quite willing to acquiesce in the face of procrastination or indecisiveness. Suggesting that the customer think about it and keep in touch, the salesperson at the same time indicates pleasure and appreciation for the opportunity to visit.

In the following example, the customer is leaning toward a favorable decision, but the indecisiveness of the sales representative may jeopardize the potential sale.

SP: Oh, I am so pleased you have asked me to give you a bid on this. I hope you will be very pleased with our work.

PC: Well, I hope so, too. When can you let me know your approximate cost figures?

SP: Oh, real soon. Shall I bring my wallpaper samples tomorrow? Or would you like to come by our . . . ?

PC: Well, can you be a little more definite on when you can get those costs to me? Perhaps you could give me an approximation now?

SP: Oh, I really wish I could, but I had better not. I am just not sure yet, and I'd hate to give you an estimate that would have to be changed later.

PC: I really need to know right away. My boss is pressuring me for a decision.

SP: Oh, well, yes, of course. I'm sure I can get those cost figures for you in a day or two.

PC: Okay, if that's the best you can do. I've got another appointment right now. Goodbye, and be sure to get back to me on that.

SP: Goodbye. Thanks again for calling on us. We have so much regard for our customers, and we really love our work. I know you will be pleased with our . . .

PC: I've got to go. Goodbye!

If the customer has any initial doubts about the wisdom of making a purchase, the salesperson's lack of confidence only serves to reinforce this hesitation. The reason is that a customer expects the salesperson to provide a sound rationale for buying. If this is not communicated, its absence provokes doubt about the wisdom of completing the purchase. If and when a customer asks about prices or terms, the 1,9-oriented salesperson avoids speaking about the matter directly, preferring to hand the customer a price list.

If a sales interview gets as far in the sequence as the closing, the chances are that the outcome will be successful. The reason is that the customer has taken on the role of salesperson and has chosen to close the deal. Reflective commentary and supportive helpfulness by the salesperson may have contributed to this, but these kinds of comments are unlikely to be conclusive factors in a successful outcome. Nonetheless, the salesperson's behavior may be appreciated by the customer who feels some contribution has been made. Closings are happy affairs —the salesperson feels wanted and approved of, and the customer's convictions that a sound decision has been made are reinforced. We know from experimental research that after the decision to buy has been reached, customers continue to sell themselves. This process of self-reinforcing behavior is greater when the salesperson has a 1,9 orientation and resonates with the customer's enthusiasm for having made the purchasing decision.

ESTABLISHED BUSINESS

The 1,9-oriented salesperson spends a lot of time with established customers, enjoying their company and the easygoing relationship that has been formed with them.

Maintaining Accounts

The sales representative with a 1,9 approach believes that social contacts are necessary for success in selling. If one cultivates social contacts and manages to be in the right place at the right time, business will naturally fall one's way. An excessive expenditure of time is rationalized in this way.

The 1,9-oriented salesperson is less keen about visiting those established accounts who tend to be abrupt and abrasive. Because their harsh attitudes make this salesperson put off meeting with them, these accounts become open targets for competitors. Fractures in these relationships widen, leading to a loss of accounts, which the salesperson interprets as lack of interest in buying or possibly the result of an unfair advantage taken by a "ruthless" competitor.

Complaints

The 1,9-oriented sales representative dreads facing a customer who is angry or frustrated. Complaints tend to raise the salesperson's anxieties. This causes the salesperson to delay meeting with an irate customer, but when such a meeting occurs, the salesperson shows solicitude by being very apologetic. The customer is made aware of the fact that the salesperson, too, suffers deeply for this inconvenience. Through this joint commiseration, they may return to a friendly basis. Sometimes the salesperson's regret for the inconvenience caused the customer leads to promises of greater restitution than can realistically be accomplished. Meanwhile, as a personal gesture of apology, the salesperson goes overboard to do a special favor for the customer as soon as possible.

Rush Business

To avoid having to say "no" and risking a customer's displeasure, the 1,9-oriented salesperson reluctantly enters into commitments that have little prospect of being fulfilled. The 1,9 statement is likely to be "I'll do everything I can to meet your request. I hope it can be delivered on Thursday." The salesperson will ask the factory production manager—as a personal favor—to try to speed the order through, knowing the factory workers are all good people and will do their best. Only later, when the facts loom so large, is it realized how disappointed the customer will be when the delivery is not made on schedule. The salesperson tries to persuade the customer to be patient—even in advance of the event. Contrite and apologetic, the salesperson explains,

1,9: EAGER TO PLEASE

"So many unexpected difficulties have cropped up, but we are doing everything possible. Really, I feel so badly about disappointing you . . . What can I do to make up for your disappointment?"

To keep out of trouble with the company's Operations people, however, the salesperson lets them know that an attempt is being made to keep these unnecessary demands to a minimum. This kind of shuttle between customer and company is painful for the 1,9-oriented salesperson, because it is next to impossible to please everyone.

SELF-MANAGEMENT

A salesperson oriented in a 1,9 way tends to be managed by others. Since this sales representative is a responder, there is not likely to be much self-regulation in the areas of planning, scheduling, and organizing at the detail level. In this sense, the 1,9-oriented salesperson is directed from outside by whoever exercises influence—the customer, the sales manager, family, and friends. Not every influence from the outside has the same magnetic effect, however. Rather, the salesperson is drawn to those influences that are positive, and repelled by those that are not.

SCHEDULING AND TIME MANAGEMENT. I am at the disposal of my "good" customers. My work schedule has flexibility so that I can help my customers when they need me.

PROSPECTING. I follow up when an indication of positive interest has been shown. I ask the customers with whom I have a good relationship for suggestions concerning new people to contact.

SERVICING. I visit with the customer and am happy when I can provide a requested service, even one that is beyond the customer's expectations of what I should contribute. Nothing is too good for my customers.

EXPENSES. I need a reasonable expense account. If I spend beyond the policy limit, it's because I feel I am serving the company through promoting customer goodwill. To a large extent, business is built on my ability to present myself in a pleasing manner.

SELF-STEERING. I am wide awake to how others react to me and to what I do that increases my acceptance by them. A good personality is what sells products and services.[7]

CUSTOMER REACTIONS

9,1

The 9,1-oriented customer's attitudes of strength, determination, and suspicion convey hostility and rejection to the 1,9-oriented salesperson. The sales representative may initially try to respond with friendliness but quickly retreats and seeks ways to withdraw. This can be an extremely brief encounter in which the salesperson is likely to buckle under the pressure of direct or implied criticism, quickly closing the briefcase and thanking the customer for the interview, even though it nets nothing.

1,9

The 1,9-oriented sales presentation is most successful when made to a sociable 1,9-oriented customer, because the needs of each to be liked by the other are consummated in a purchase. It is a situation in which there is mutual admiration; the customer's friendliness strikes a responsive chord with the salesperson. Thus the presentation becomes essentially a social visit, much of which is unrelated to the issue at hand. The customer is inclined toward a positive decision even though it may be unsound when tested against needs or expectations.

1,1

The 1,1-oriented customer, feeling little impact from a 1,9 presentation, finds it relatively easy to give a noncommittal answer and so to escape by indicating a lack of interest. This lack of customer responsiveness can be disturbing to the 1,9-oriented salesperson. A typical reaction is to continue the effort to develop a mutual social interest with the customer. If this fails, there remains little to be done except to offer alternatives and to thank the customer for the time spent thus far. With this low-pressure, apologetic approach, a successful closing is most unlikely.

5,5

A 5,5-oriented customer might buy if there is a clearly recognized need for the product and assurance that everyone who has bought it has also been satisfied. The 1,9-oriented salesperson inspires little confidence in a 5,5-oriented customer, however, because this salesperson is likely to become discouraged and uncertain under questioning. If the presentation fails to convey a sense of product prestige and reputation, the customer may lose confidence in the salesperson. The end result of this presentation may be the loss of a sale but the development of a good social relationship.

9,9

A 9,9-oriented customer is likely to feel impatient with the irrelevancy and "soft touch" qualities—the slow movement and lack of solid facts—that characterize the 1,9 sales presentation. This approach simply does not meet the solution-seeking requirements of the 9,9-oriented customer. Sometimes, however, 9,9-oriented customers may in effect take over the 1,9-oriented sales presentation in such a way as to insist that the salesperson move away from the soft behavior toward a style more compatible with that of a professional salesperson. Usually, however, the salesperson does not find the situation attractive and is unlikely to understand why the 9,9-oriented customer does not reciprocate friendliness and congeniality by making a decision to do business.

SUMMARY

The sales representative operating under the 1,9 orientation is likely to follow the customer, adjusting to the latter's tempo. This salesperson is unlikely to take one of the customer's proposals and shift into an alternative way of thinking the customer might not like it and this might provoke a backlash. Rather, the 1,9-oriented salesperson listens keenly for positive customer attitudes toward features of the product and then adds constructive support to what has been said. In this way, objections are avoided while support and encouragement can be continuously added to the customer's "buy attitude," whatever that may be. The customer becomes the salesperson. Thus if a closing is reached, it may be the occasion for mutual appreciation.

What is the impact of a 1,9 orientation on profitable selling? The attitude is "Profit is desirable but should not be the key factor when good customer relationships are at stake. I prefer a customer whose business is easy to handle and good for the company." The salesperson clearly puts people ahead of profit. By pursuing personal inclinations, the 1,9-oriented sales representative may get some established accounts, but sales are not often high volume or for any extended period of time. The closings that do result are, in the long term, sometimes more costly to the company than they are profitable.

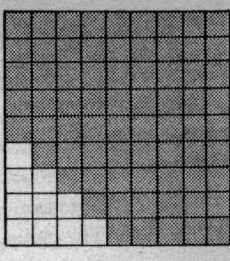

1,1
Indifferent

The salesperson who has adopted a 1,1 orientation is committed neither to mastering the sales environment nor to being admired by the people in it. This sales representative has turned inward, and survival within the business system represents the dominant concern. The level of personal satisfaction is simply that of "feeling no pain." The salesperson moves along the path of least resistance, going through the expected motions without any convictions or personal warmth. Rather, the behavior is more like that of a jellyfish, which floats, responding to the motion of the waves, without moving in any direction of its own. Enthusiasm for selling has disappeared, but selling is still necessary to keep the job, undoubtedly for financial or retirement benefit reasons. So the salesperson trudges around, meeting minimum sales quotas, calls, or hours behind a counter, as passively as an automaton.

The positive motivation in a 1,1-oriented approach is a minimum of effort to "hang on," to "keep in the system." Appearing occupied and seeming to be concentrating on some activity directs the attention of others from oneself. The degree to which a 1,1-oriented person can remain passive, nonresponsive, and undisturbed is governed by the minimum others are prepared to tolerate. This combination of being inconspicuous and yet physically present is the key to avoiding resentment from others. By staying aloof and not becoming emotionally entangled with things or people, a 1,1-oriented salesperson avoids facing up to personal inadequacies or inabilities. The motto is "See no evil, speak no evil, and hear no evil, and you are protected by not being noticed." The "silent" expectation that security is guaranteed places few demands on 1,1-oriented people beyond providing their own food, clothing, and shelter.

The negative motivation of salespeople with a 1,1 orientation is to avoid ostracism, dismissal, or separation. This means taking whatever steps are necessary to conceal, frequently even from themselves, the bored and tired attitudes that might lead to such disassociation. A semblance of commitment is maintained in order to avoid accusations of not following through. Thus 1,1-oriented salespeople will answer whatever questions are posed, though probably in vague terminology. In this manner they seek to remain within the boundaries of what others are likely to accept or tolerate.

Withdrawal, with the consequent lack of conviction about sales, shows through to customers and others. There is a generalized indifference about the product or service and the prospect as well. The justification is "The decision is up to the customer." The salesperson is governed by the principle of least effort and does not tamper with the customer's thinking about the purchase decision, giving little more than token support to the product and rarely expressing any point of view. Mental energy is low. This is a colorless character, devoid of feeling. This has a deadening effect, even on hostile customers, for there is minimum response even if a customer tries to pick a fight. The salesperson just crouches in a mental foxhole, with the verbal bullets flying overhead. Emotions are disengaged, so the sales representative rarely gets stirred up. Humor is seldom exhibited, or if it is, it is likely to be seen by others as rather pointless.

1,1: INDIFFERENT

The notion of a person, in the selling context, having both a low concern for customers and a low concern for making a sale may at first glance seem improbable. Yet on deeper reflection you may recall individuals who have adopted this orientation. Because they make no dramatic splash and do not stir up trouble, they seem almost invisible, particularly in a situation of low competition and high demand. Many sales representatives, not normally apathetic or unconcerned, can have 1,1 as a backup style or as a temporary response to failure or defeat. This 1,1-oriented retreat occurs when there does not seem to be any available action to take to overcome an obstacle or barrier to a sale. Then the salesperson is likely to take an "I don't care" attitude and mentally or physically retire from the situation. The salesperson has become depressed by what is seen as customers' indifference and the rejection implied when customers refuse to purchase. The response becomes "It doesn't really matter anyway. There are more important things to do," or "Since it's the customer's decision, it makes no difference whether I agree or not." Thus, the 1,1 orientation is common as a backup or temporary style, and many salespersons can readily identify particular kinds of conditions under which they too are likely to "go 1,1."

Also, as people go through life, a backup 1,1 orientation may become prominent and crowd out some other Grid style that previously dominated their behavior. When this happens, salespersons who come to 1,1 orientations via the routes to be described below may not appear to be 1,1 at all. They often retain the manner of another Grid style, such as continuing to dress in a way characteristic of their past, being easy to talk with, maintaining a subdued interest in daily events, or smiling and nodding acceptance. However, something has happened deep inside, and the real motivation now is simply to go through the paces. There are several explanations for how this originates.

It has been observed that energy resources may diminish as a person advances in years. The old "pep" is no longer there to be called on and the person slips into a 1,1 orientation. This notion is difficult to substantiate, but the main evidence to support it lies in the fact that many middle-aged people say that they really "feel" this way.

Discouragement takes its toll along the way in one's abortive attempts to be successful. Failures and discouragements accumulate, and though they may be relatively few in absolute numbers, they begin to tip the balance, indicating that the next experience will also be unsuccessful. This shift into pessimism and hopelessness becomes a self-fulfilling prophecy. Now one unwittingly postures oneself in the next sales situation in such a way as to foreordain failure. Once this vicious cycle is confirmed, each new failure adds to further discouragement and increases the attitude of "why try?" A 1,1 orientation blossoms. Resilience is lost.

Self-alienation is another explanation for the loss of motivation leading to a 1,1 orientation. An individual who was motivated by some other mode in the past and who was knowledgeable and successful may have been led into various "bad" actions that grated on the conscience. As this erosion of self-worth occurs, such a person begins to rationalize "it's not worth it" to continue the game. The individual eventually withdraws, both mentally and emotionally, finding inaction congenial, until a 1,1 "get by" approach becomes a dominant orientation.

"Burnout" is a phenomenon that may well occur as the challenge of the work experience becomes depleted over time. The activity seems repetitious and second nature, and a hollowness sets in. There is nothing else to replace what may formerly have been very meaningful and satisfying work. The recommended treatment may be rest, relaxation, and a change of pace, but these are only temporary diversions. The real cure is to find new challenges and interests, possibly by shifting into a 9,9 orientation, where the contribution made to the customer is fulfilling.

One of the conspicuous aspects of 1,1 as an orientation that replaces some other previously dominant Grid style is that the person tends to slip into 1,1 without being aware of what is happening. This slippage into an attitude of low involvement, indifference, and lack of real commitment is often rationalized away by the salesperson who is going through the rites and rituals and even parleying the language and discussion of everyday work. However, when this is done, the person's heart is not in it, and it is those missing elements of conviction and enthusiasm which are so critical to effectiveness.

We know from evidence from many walks of life that when a 1,1-oriented person becomes aware of having slipped into the 1,1 corner, this fact in itself may be sufficient to cause the person to bounce out and to regain energy and involvement. However, often it requires a more intense experience with feedback from others to convince the person that this slippage has occurred. Then, with such evidence, the bounce back may be very dramatic indeed.

KNOWLEDGE: PRODUCT, CUSTOMER, AND COMPETITOR

A salesperson with dominant 1,1 attitudes is unlikely to gain more than casual product knowledge. If questioned closely about the product's features, the salesperson might reply, "These are the general details. It's hard for anyone to keep up with the complexity in products nowadays. You can get in touch with our technical people if you need more information." The most this salesperson can be expected to do during the sales interview is reach for a book of technical specifications or read from a product brochure.

This same attitude toward knowledge about a product is found in the area of understanding a customer. Because the salesperson has little interest in the customer as a person, there seems to be little reason for bothering to understand the customer's situation. Once the product has been described, the prospect—who knows the situation best—can use personal background information to determine whether or not it is needed. In any event, the salesperson knows it is the customer who has the final say, and influence does not matter much, one way or the other.

The salesperson realizes that competitors can cut down sales volume but rationalizes that there is little to be done about it. Studying competitors to get to know more about them and their products is not going to change them or make a dime's worth of difference either way. "Why worry? It's better to ignore them."

A customer may want to pose questions concerning the relative merits of the product that the salesperson is presenting in comparison with those of competitors. An uninformed salesperson, unable to field such inquiries, leaves the customer unsatisfied. Additionally, this information void makes it impossible to recognize or to correct false impressions that may have been planted in the customer's mind by a competitor.

PARTICIPATION AND INVOLVEMENT

The 1,1 attitude produces little desire to promote the involvement and participation of a customer in a mutual problem-solving discussion. "If the prospect wants it, I'll make a sale. If not, I won't—and there's not much I can do about it. I provide whatever information I have, and the next move's up to the customer." This sales approach offers the customer an unlimited opportunity to talk. However, the customer is likely to realize that this silence does not represent genuine listening on the salesperson's part, but rather is nothing more than a display of bored apathy.

It is an odd experience to be called upon by a salesperson who has adopted the bombed-out 1,1 approach. This person sits down and speaks briefly, with no enthusiasm whatsoever. The customer has an eerie feeling that a prerecorded announcement is being played and is somehow transmitted via human voice. The message does not catch one's attention, but maybe some use for the product will be gleaned from observation and inquiries made about it. The customer still receives the impression of having been hooked up to some telephone answering service, for the answers are totally unrelated to the questions posed. It soon becomes obvious that a precise answer is not forthcoming—this machine is simply not equipped to give one. Perhaps a promise will be made to refer the customer's question to another source more technically qualified than the salesperson. More often than not, however, that will be the end of this business deal.

The following is a typical short conversation with this type of salesperson.

SP: Would you like to place an order in the meantime?
PC: I just don't know. I really haven't made up my mind.
SP: Well, that's okay, I'll call again some other time.

Although the customer has been involved, it has been in a negative sense, and this, of course, is not to the advantage of the sales representative's firm. The customer, instead, turns to another supplier and ends up buying a comparable product. The 1,1-oriented salesperson probably never even realizes that a sale that could have been made was not.

The 1,1 orientation toward giving help is "Who needs it?" This indifference characterizes the salesperson's numbness and uninvolvement in the human situation and further reduces the interest taken in the customer and the product. The neutral, noninvolved attitude is rationalized: "It wouldn't be appreciated anyway."

COMMUNICATION

The 1,1-oriented salesperson is unlikely to formulate and pose questions. Such a salesperson does not think in terms of what information might be necessary in order to provide a solution to the customer's problem. Rather, this individual is more likely to leave it to the customer to make inquiries, assuming that information will be asked for if it is desired.

1,1-oriented listening is generally inattentive, with the salesperson neither emotionally involved with the product nor enamored with sales technique. Thus, ample opportunity is provided for the customer to talk, but the conversation is tuned out and the sales representative daydreams about other things instead. When the salesperson fails to hear a positive indication of customer readiness to buy, or resistance becomes evident, the immediate attitude is "Well, this one's gone down the drain—there's nothing more to discuss." In other words, the salesperson short-circuits the entire sales interview rather than moving forward in a sound manner.

Interruption is taken as a sign that the customer is uninterested in buying and wants to steer away from the subject. Thus the interview is abruptly concluded. The salesperson's response is to assume that all is lost and to give consideration to the free time that has been provided. "That one didn't take long; maybe I can do some shopping before going to the 11:30 appointment uptown." While dealing perfunctorily with the interruption, this salesperson is mentally putting on a coat and closing the briefcase. It is quite possible that the customer is trying to make a relevant comment about the situation with regard to the use of the product, but this salesperson will never know. Giving up is a self-fulfilling prophecy type of action, and another potential sales goes unrealized.

The 1,1 orientation to emotions is almost a contradiction in terms.

A person who has gravitated into 1,1 attitudes has totally disconnected emotions from the circumstances at hand. No longer is there any interest in taking a risk or in venturing into new situations that might be emotionally invigorating. The salesperson has mentally and emotionally, if not physically, retired.

THE NEW CUSTOMER

Opening

The 1,1-oriented sales representative remains around the periphery of action, and it is often necessary for the prospect to seek this salesperson out. Such a person is passive or neutral and responds to the customer's queries in a minimally factual and noncommittal way, waiting for the customer to take the initiative. In some cases this salesperson tries to appear "busy," not even looking up when the customer appears and hoping in this way to discourage the prospect from making contact.

In this example the salesperson exerts the minimum effort possible.

SP: Here's a brochure describing the product you asked about.
PC: Hmmm . . . it doesn't seem to have very much detail and technical information. I'm not sure I can evaluate the product in terms of what we really need.
SP: Well, it's not up to me. You're the judge of what your company requires.
PC: Perhaps you could get me a technical manual, and I could check out the specs against our requirements.
SP: I'll work on having one sent to you.

The lack of interest in the customer, of conviction about the product, or of enthusiasm for contact leaves the customer with a vague sense of uneasiness and an unwillingness to return.

Needs Analysis

The salesperson's attitude toward prospects' needs is based on attitudes such as these: "When making the first contact, it's a waste of effort to do more than describe the basic facts"; "If customers want to know something, they will ask"; "There's no sense in trying to probe the customer's thinking—the customer's mind is probably made up already." The normal practice is for the salesperson to bypass anything approaching a needs analysis. Discussion is rarely initiated about a product's applicability in terms of how the customer might use it to fulfill particular requirements.

In this example the customer approaches a 1,1-oriented salesperson.

PC: I'd like to see your latest model.
SP: Okay. Here it is.

Thereafter it is up to the prospect to make the next move, and the next, and the next, and the next.

Identifying the Customer

The 1,1-oriented salesperson is relatively unconcerned with identifying the real buyer. The prospect is accepted for what he or she is—a person with whom the salesperson is now in contact. Whether or not this person is the ultimate customer makes little or no difference. This prospect is now in the purchasing situation and must exercise the effort. Reactions are given only when the prospect initiates a needs analysis.

This basic lack of concern is demonstrated in the following conversation between a prospective customer and a 1,1-oriented salesperson.

PC: Pardon me, I'm looking for a cassette tape player.
SP: (Remaining behind counter.) They are on those shelves over there.
PC: Well, this is all new to me. It's for my wife. She wants one to listen to music, and I don't know the difference between one and another.
SP: I really couldn't say which is better; I don't have an ear for music.

It is the responsibility of the customer to analyze personal needs, and the salesperson expects to be told what is desired.

Establishing Expectations

The 1,1-oriented salesperson avoids initiative that might lead to the development of positive expectations. This salesperson sets strict boundaries as to what the customer can reasonably anticipate. In this way the salesperson never has to explain or rationalize in order to appease a disappointed customer.

This way of setting expectations can be seen in the following conversation in which the salesperson is discussing reservations and objections with the prospective customer.

SP: Anything else?

PC: Yes, there is. I've heard they're coming out with some even fancier models in the years to come. Innovations seem to be just around the corner these days. I'm afraid this may be obsolete before I get my money's worth.

SP: Hey, look, I've got no crystal ball.

PC: But what do you think the prospects are?

SP: No one can tell the future.

PC: Well, what do you recommend?

SP: Suit yourself. You're the one to be satisfied.

A customer cannot exactly look back on this experience and say, "I was sold a bill of goods."

Presentation

When receiving an inquiry, a 1,1-oriented salesperson is unlikely to interpret this as a desire by the prospect to see or experience the product. Therefore, responses tend to be strictly literal. "Do you carry X?" for example, is answered by, "Yes, we do." Because the salesperson fails to initiate any further action, the customer is compelled to say, "Do you have it in stock?" The salesperson responds, "Yes, I think we do," or "Let me check." Before the salesperson leaves, the wary customer replies, "Well, let me see it if you find you have it available." Thus, the 1,1-oriented salesperson brings the product forward but does little more. The product itself is shown only when requested.

The following conversation illustrates the lack of preciseness when the salesperson is involved in a presentation to a prospective customer.

SP: Those are pretty complicated questions, and I'm no engineer.

PC: Well, I might want it, but I do need more information.

SP: Well, here's the operation manual. Why not read it and decide on the parts you want?

PC: If I wanted the parts listed right here, how much would that be?

SP: Just add it up and get a total, or, if you really prefer, I guess I can do it for you.

Minimum interest reveals itself in a thousand ways, all of which say, "Check it out for yourself." Even this latter remark is a disinterested way for the salesperson to avoid exercising initiative in the pursuit of a sale.

As indicated earlier, the 1,1-oriented sales representative prefers to lose an order rather than to get into the crack or out on a limb establishing expectations that are later violated. Thus, this person retains a kind of passive integrity. For safety's sake, the salesperson may draw back from making some commitment that is well within the product's, or the company's, capability to perform. "I don't know whether we can guarantee that, I'd have to check it out. Is it important? . . . Oh well, maybe you could ask your engineers what they think. Here are the specifications." Now the salesperson has an alibi in hand, all ready for the future. If a piece of information turns up that the salesperson did not volunteer, the standard response, when the salesperson is questioned about it at a later time, is "But you didn't ask about that," shifting the blame onto somebody else.

Objections

The 1,1-oriented salesperson tries to steer the conversation along an objection-free path, as this is the easiest way to handle the interview. Once an objection is raised, however, the strategy is either to ignore it or to simply go along with it for what it is worth. As far as possible, this sales representative sees no disagreement, hears no disagreement, and speaks no disagreement. As a matter of fact, no disagreement is likely to be felt, since neutrality is the central core of this salesperson's emotions. The calm, placid, patient exterior is not the result of inner peace but comes from being devoid of any emotional involvement and thus is untouched by challenge, contradiction, or any hostility.

When a 1,1-oriented salesperson is dealing with a prospect, the prospect may withhold reservations, doubts, or objections, having already become aware that the salesperson is not responsive and, therefore, "Why bring them up?"

If the customer does raise an objection, the salesperson is likely to downplay it by saying that there is little chance the problem will ever arise. Or, the salesperson may divert the conversation by indicating the need to consult with someone back at the company to get a detailed answer to this "technical" question. When asked what people think about a product or about a problem likely to be encountered in using the product, the sales representative possesses an infinite variety of neutral answers: "They didn't say"; "I haven't heard"; "I wasn't there." When pressed for a recommendation or to express a conviction, this salesperson is equally adept: "It's up to you"; "I wouldn't want to influence your decision"; "Whatever you say"; "I'm no expert." The salesperson who is slick with words may try to double-talk the customer, creating a mirage of terminology—an answer that is not really an answer. "It could be X . . . for the following reasons . . . or it could be Y . . . but I'm not sure which is best." In all these ways the 1,1-oriented salesperson evades disagreement and controversy. When there is a choice between dealing fully with the customer's objection or losing the sale, it is preferable to lose the sale.

The 1,1-oriented sales representative and the prospective customer who is persistent in raising objections might interact as described below.

SP: Of course, there are no exceptions to this guarantee.
PC: What makes it so binding?
SP: Our word.
PC: Well, I don't know about that. I have a friend whose warranty you refused to honor.
SP: Well, all I know is that they tell me it's foolproof.

Another situation demonstrates how the 1,1-oriented salesperson may try to anticipate and avoid objections.

SP: What do you think?
PC: Well, it's okay, but what's your opinion of its quality?
SP: I'm not selling opinions. I'm selling equipment. All I can do is repeat what I'm told. I've been told it's first-rate.
PC: Well, do you agree with them?
SP: Look, I don't agree or disagree. All I can tell you is what they tell me. No more, no less. And they say it's first-rate. I rely on their judgment.
PC: Well, I'm concerned because I read on those comparison reports that it was judged second best.

SP: I didn't know about that. Still, it could be a mistake. But the choice is up to you.

In both of the examples above, the 1,1-oriented salesperson is not involved in an emotional way and experiences no inner contradiction between the company's message and the customer's denial of it.

Closing

The salesperson approaches the closing phase of the interview in a very matter-of-fact way. The closing initiative may be little more than a vague question, "Do you feel like buying it?" If the customer wants it, fine. The salesperson will take the order. In this sense, the salesperson can be viewed as a message carrier, more or less mechanically transmitting the customer's purchase order to the company for processing without adding any personal energy.

Price is never mentioned spontaneously. The 1,1-oriented salesperson may not answer even when the question of cost comes up. By saying something like "I'm not certain, but I think it's on the tag," or "I think it's in the brochure," the salesperson shifts the responsibility for finding out onto the prospect.

If the decision is not to buy, the salesperson's attitude is "Well, okay," or "You can't win them all." To this salesperson it is obvious that the customer had no interest to begin with, so why waste time beating a dead horse? Even if the customer shows some interest but is still undecided, the first "no" is accepted as final. The sales representative leaves an address or phone number and then departs, or the customer is invited to leave with a "Call again."

This lack of persistence in closing is illustrated in the conversation below.

SP: Well, I'm sorry you are uncertain, but I know it takes time to make up your mind.

PC: Thanks for helping, anyway.

SP: It's okay. Come back if I can help.

If the sales interview does extend through to a closing, it may be a successful but not a happy or rewarding occasion. The reason is that the salesperson is without joviality, gives little or no support, and is likely, if anything, to emphasize product limitations and liabilities in order to avoid future conflict with the customer. Salespeople with a 1,1-orientation feel that it is important to avoid creating false expectations that might come back to haunt them.

A 1,1-oriented salesperson is more likely to be successful in browsing situations that invite the customer to lift, feel, turn on, read instructions, and even carry the purchase to the cashier or wrapping desk. "If that is what you want I will write it up."

In this situation the salesperson is of minimum importance and may be called on to do little more than replenish stock, dust, rearrange the merchandise, or simply point the way. Such situations usually involve small ticket items and are likely to be ones that do not merit sales talent or pay more than the minimum wage. Unfortunately, many 1,1-oriented salespersons who are selling helicopters, computer systems, medical equipment, or complex audiovisual equipment have rationalized that they, too, are operating in a sales cafeteria when, in fact, the contributions of the salesperson can make a critical difference to whether or not a successful outcome is reached.

ESTABLISHED BUSINESS

Steady customers are likely to be what the salesperson relies upon for bread and butter. By moving around an established circuit, the salesperson can take periodic orders without making much of an effort.

Maintaining Accounts

The salesperson with a 1,1 orientation tends to gravitate to situations where regular customers provide sufficient orders on a routine basis. Usually, a stable sales volume can be maintained under these circumstances, and as long as the company is satisfied, so is the salesperson. This kind of reliable timetable for contacting established accounts and collecting their orders with minimum intrusion can be quite acceptable to the habitual customer, too. It does not burden the customer with making new decisions. Neither does it occupy time in listening to the kind of sales talk previously heard.

The circumstances where a salesperson has generated a large number of established accounts at an earlier time who are unlikely to take their business elsewhere, coupled with a generous income from these customers, can make it easy for a sales representative to slide from some other orientation into 1,1 attitudes. There is no need to scramble for customers, for the salesperson's income is acceptable or possibly even beyond earlier expectations. This sales representative can be lulled into inactivity without even realizing it, and the company ultimately suffers.

Complaints

A salesperson with 1,1 attitudes has developed ways to remain insulated from being stirred up or from becoming involved in customer complaints. "There's nothing I can do about it, so let somebody else get the grief."

If the customer persists with the complaint, the salesperson may say, "Look, put that in writing, will you? I'll see that it gets to the right people." Nothing more is done, on the assumption that "nature will take its course." Since the salesperson does not become concerned about complaints, they may eventually come to appear unimportant in the customer's eyes as well! If subsequently the customer presses for action, the salesperson says, "Well, okay, I'll follow up on it," but probably does nothing, on the assumption that the problem will eventually go away. Sometimes this happens.

Rush Business

Rush business is risky. The difficulties encountered in trying to satisfy it are, as often as not, greater than the gain in sales volume. The salesperson is likely to suggest that there is no real need for urgency and that the customer can get along until the normal delivery is made. Thus the salesperson defers taking the order and thereby avoids accepting a potentially worrisome responsibility. The problems of others belong solely to them, but the salesperson will agree, if necessary, to take the person-in-the-middle role, relaying the request from customer to company and back again.

Even when delivery may be possible by Thursday, though this is quicker than the norm, the salesperson will say it cannot be done "before the following Monday at the earliest." In this way, it is possible to avoid any risk that something might misfire and violate the customer's expectations.

SELF-MANAGEMENT

Since the 1,1-oriented sales representative is only marking time within the system, there is no stimulation to do more than the basics of what is required. This salesperson tends to be inert, increasing tempo or shifting direction only after a crisis has hit.

SCHEDULING AND TIME MANAGEMENT. I don't need to schedule my activities. Customers contact me, and their requests keep me busy enough.

PROSPECTING. I rely mostly on prospects finding me. When I get time, I follow up on ones that are pointed out.

SERVICING. The business is out of my hands once it reaches the office. The customer will let me know if anything else is needed. If so, I pass the message on.

EXPENSES. I know how my expenses run. It's easier to stay in line than to have to account for special circumstances or exceptions.

SELF-STEERING. I feel no need to review my performance. The boss will tell me what I need to know.[8]

CUSTOMER REACTIONS

Customers want to be satisfied with their purchases, and the sales representative can often make the difference through the enthusiasm displayed. Additionally, the salesperson gains respect by showing the customer how to use a product to its maximum capabilities and by aiding the customer to see the unique merits of the product, or by showing the customer why the purchase is such an excellent buy.

From the examples given thus far it is obvious that the 1,1-oriented salesperson does none of these.

The 1,1 sales strategy is unlikely to be effective with customers, whatever their Grid style. The only exception is when a clearly defined product need exists and no other sales representatives are promoting alternative products through which this need can be met. Unless the customer has a burning desire to buy, however, or happens to be replenishing the inventory at the time the salesperson visits, it is unlikely that the 1,1 approach will result in sales.

9,1

When offering a presentation to a 9,1-oriented customer and confronted with resistance, the salesperson withdraws from any degree of commitment that may already have been made. This effectively prevents any combat between customer and salesperson. The customer's hostile statements have little effect on the salesperson's emotions, but they convey quite clearly the message that "all bets are off." Mentally, the salesperson throws in the towel, saying, "What's the use; this customer doesn't want to buy."

1,9

The 1,1-oriented sales representative is likely to misread the clues in the 1,9-oriented customer's behavior. Rather than accurately interpreting the customer's desire to be liked, the salesperson instead sees the customer as keeping the contact going in order to eventually make a decision. The interview may continue for some time, but it suddenly comes to a halt when a point of indecision is reached. The salesperson will generally leave without attempting to close and may establish a time, place, and date for a future visit.

1,1

When the colorless and bland procedure of the 1,1-oriented salesperson is matched by a customer who lapses into an indifferent attitude toward the purchase, very little is likely to develop. Should the customer's response be partially positive, the salesperson may offer some sketchy information or a few facts.

5,5

The disinterested and mechanical way in which a 1,1-oriented salesperson operates does little or nothing to arouse the curiosity of a 5,5-oriented customer. This lack of interest and enthusiasm does not inspire sufficient confidence to cause the customer to purchase. A possible exception is if the salesperson's product or company is very prestigious. The 5,5-oriented customer is so status conscious that this may prompt a purchase despite the salesperson.

9,9

A salesperson operating in a 1,1 mode can anticipate failure in dealing with a 9,9-oriented customer. Shallow or superficial product knowledge will not impact a customer who is seeking sound solutions based on a thorough understanding of a product's capabilities. However, the customer may in some cases prompt the salesperson away from the 1,1 orientation by a confrontation that elevates the presentation to a more involved level.

SUMMARY

The salesperson with a 1,1 orientation has learned to be "out of it" while remaining in the organization. Though this orientation is not uncommon as a dominant style, it is an unnatural approach in most cases. One is likely to adopt this style or to slide progressively into it when one has accepted defeat or has lost any sense of persistence. The style may involve a no-confidence vote for the product, with the feeling that there is no real hope of selling it against the competitors' lines. Possibly the salesperson has become discouraged by some prospects' attitudes toward him or her as a salesperson and feels trapped in a job that lacks status. To become reinvolved in what happens in the selling situation may lead only to deeper frustration and discouragement.

What is the likely impact on profit of a 1,1-oriented salesperson? The attitude is "I accept the business that comes my way. This is my job; I guess all business is profitable." In fact this salesperson is likely to lose more customers than are gained and to have a trend toward ever-decreasing sales volume. Given a really competitive selling situation, then, the 1,1-oriented sales representative constitutes dead weight —carried by the organization but not contributing to it. It can be a case of all drag and no thrust.

A salesperson who meets barriers and obstacles daily, and perhaps hourly, must be alert to signs of easy recourse to a 1,1 attitude when the path to a sale is not smooth. Frequently, trying alternative ways of viewing the customer's problem, searching for more information from the customer to stimulate different ideas, summarizing so as to find whether an apparent impasse is real, or digging more deeply into the feelings that are being expressed beneath the words—plus other sound ways to maintain a problem-solving orientation—can lead to a successful interview.

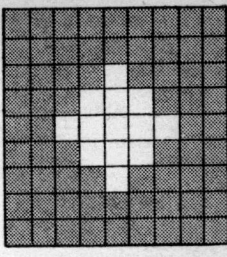

5,5

Status Conscious

The salesperson with a 5,5 predisposition is in the middle. This sales representative is proud of having a realistic outlook and of being a good steady performer who sets and reaches attainable sales objectives. Such a person is not reaching for the stars, striving to achieve excellence in sales performance to create ideal relationships with customers. That, according to a 5,5-oriented salesperson, would be impractical. The justification is "No matter how hard you try, you can only please some of the customers some of the time."

The positive motivation of a 5,5-oriented person is the need for membership, to be popular, to be accepted and "in." A successful 5,5 orientation leads to a salesperson's experiencing a sense of security and well-being. These good feelings may persist even though a person may have just compromised a long-term gain for a short-term convenience, embraced a point of view only because the boss and business associates did so, withheld a vital piece of information to avoid criticism, or winked at a shady practice because "everybody does it." The ability to shift, twist, and turn, and yet stay with the majority, is important to a 5,5-oriented person's style. The motivational motto is "If I think, look, and act like everyone else, but a little more so, I will be a person in good standing."

The negative motivation is to avoid being different, because this indicates that a person's membership is threatened. When this situation comes about, such a person feels left out and unpopular, and experiences anxiety. Therefore, every action and reaction is carefully considered as to its likely effects.

Upon entering the selling profession, the 5,5-oriented sales representative may have read several handbooks or taken courses to find out which were the best selling methods based on past experience—methods long proved by trial and error that could safely be adopted. Possibly the salesperson relies on a company sales manual that recommends certain methods to be followed. Pointers and techniques are placed in this person's sales repertoire after they are modified where necessary to fit personal characteristics. The result is a tried-and-true selling routine.

As a part of this techniques-oriented approach, the sales representative is likely to have built up a repertoire of palaver. Included are up-to-date knowledge of sports and information about local happenings as well as the rumors and stories that are making the rounds, the "in" movies and TV shows and those that are "out," possibly the top ten fiction and nonfiction books, and almost certainly the best-selling records and the Oscar and Grammy winners. All of this is invaluable for establishing and maintaining contact with a prospect by being able to discuss matters of interest on familiar terms. Depending upon the size of the ticket item, all these may be supported by membership in the right clubs, the right church, sometimes even the right political organization.

With this rich arsenal of information and experience to support and maintain the relationship, it often becomes attractive for the prospect to become a customer of a 5,5 prestige-oriented salesperson, who can catalyze the relationship and facilitate the movement of the prospect toward becoming a customer.

When relying on conventional practices, the 5,5-oriented salesperson feels self-confident and ready to handle any customer. Such a salesperson can take the lead and conduct a standard presentation when precedents or past practices dictate the way. But the salesperson rarely modifies standard selling techniques or moves ahead of current trends in the company until a new direction has become well established.

Whenever disagreements arise between the salesperson and customers, compromise positions are sought in order to break the impasses. The sales representative tries to be fair and to get a resolution that is acceptable to each of the parties involved, balancing out and trading off as many different considerations as necessary to reach an acceptable compromise of conflicting points of view. When humor is introduced into a situation, it is of the kind that either sells the salesperson—in terms of increasing the salesperson's acceptance by others—or advances the point of view that is favorable to others.

KNOWLEDGE: PRODUCT, CUSTOMER, AND COMPETITOR

Product knowledge is a supportive rather than a primary selling tool for a 5,5-oriented salesperson. This is a person who knows something about everything but not a very great deal about anything. Emphasis is placed on getting enough information to be in a position to deal satisfactorily with the most frequent customer inquiries. The information is conveyed so as to convince customers that the salesperson possesses a sound knowledge of the product. The sales representative is prepared to talk about the main features and functions of the product but does not think it important to be able to deal with technical aspects and matters of detail in the way that an expert might. One of the ways a 5,5-oriented salesperson rationalizes this superficiality is "Ask me the question you want answered, and I'll get the information you desire." In this way the salesperson can determine just how much information is needed and just how much can be guessed. The product's ability to fit standard situations is well known, but the salesperson is unlikely to venture outside that area or to suggest new and creative ways for customers to use products. For example, if selling a small pocket-size camera, the salesperson gives a good account of photography as a hobby. It probably does not occur to this salesperson, though, that a camera also can be useful in business and industrial applications, such as in making a photographic record of production charts before the entries are changed.

Before contacting new business prospects, the 5,5-oriented sales representative tries to gather some information about them, such as their position in the organization, school background, and social standing in the community. What this salesperson does is to glean information from the customer that will be placed in a file for follow-up. For example, if it is learned that the customer is a business executive, this information is brought out at a later time when it is relevant to the conversation. If the customer is a homemaker, the sales representative then relates to this person in terms of family, children, home, and so on, as opposed to trying to identify other interests that might lead to a sound purchase decision. These kinds of facts are sufficient for the purpose of coming to terms with the customer in the opening stage of the interview. However, they are not enough for readying the salesperson to understand the true nature of a customer's problem and the ways in which the product might provide a solution.

The salesperson attempts to stay informed, at least in general terms, about competitors' activities. However, the 5,5-oriented salesperson avoids derogatory remarks that might have to be defended or justified at a later time. Acknowledging competitors' products with faint praise tells the customer that the salesperson is honest, but it also avoids giving competitors' products a sales boost. Successful or attempted takeovers of this salesperson's accounts by the competition receive attention, but no counteraction is launched against such competitive newcomers. The sales representative keeps track of new prospects whose accounts previously belonged to competitors. Not actively searching for information about the novel, innovative, and creative moves of competitors, this salesperson is satisfied with recognizing and responding to them only when they have become established trends. Thus the salesperson is not in a position to get a jump on competitors but quite often is able to catch up after they have established a lead.

To sum up, it can be said that the salesperson's knowledge, whether of product, customer, or competitor, tends to be shallow. The objective of acquiring such knowledge is to create rapport or to shield the salesperson from exposure to criticism by the customer for being uninformed.

PARTICIPATION AND INVOLVEMENT

The 5,5-oriented salesperson has several clever but tricky sales techniques to get the customer's pseudo participation. One way is to convert declarative statements into questions with which the prospect can be expected to agree. This is evident in the following conversation.

SP: That's a beautiful color, isn't it?
PC: Yes, it's pretty.
SP: Nicely styled, isn't it?
PC: Yes, it is.

Figuratively hand in hand, down a path strewn with "yes-blossoms," the salesperson attempts to lead the customer to a final purchase decision. The proposition is made quite undramatically. It now seems just a matter of routine to answer "yes."

Another variant of pseudo participation through questioning is the "cathedral chimes" technique. Again, the intention is to get the customer habituated to making a positive reply. This time, however, the customer is agreeing to attractive general propositions which suggest that a sound and personally rewarding decision is being made. Note the harmonious chiming effect of the following declarative statements posed as questions: "Mr. Brown, you do *understand* how this service of ours is going to save you money?" (The unverbalized answer, but the one the customer is expected to feel, is "Yes, of course, I do.") "I'm sure you *feel* your company would greatly *benefit* through ensuring the safety of its work force?" ("Oh, yes I do.") "And surely you *appreciate* the freedom from worry that our service would give you and your employees?" ("Yes, yes.") "You would *like* to be out from under such a burden of responsibility as you are carrying at present? Right?" ("Yes, most certainly!")

Another 5,5-oriented way of trying to guide a customer through the use of pseudo participation is to present a boxed-in choice. Two alternatives are given for the prospect's evaluation. But, whichever is deemed preferable, the option has been preplanned to be favorable to the salesperson's end in making the sale. "Which would you like—black or white?"

When a customer's felt needs cannot be matched, either because of product or price, the 5,5-oriented salesperson attempts to bring the customer to an intermediate position. This is the most accepted basis for decision in the buy/sell relationship today. Pseudo participation and involvement quite often are dominated by attempts to reach solutions on product usage, selling price, discounts, and so on, by accommodating differences.

Another aspect of the 5,5 orientation is "I'll scratch your back if you'll scratch mine." This kind of helpfulness promotes continual balancing of the scales, with each party feeling that for propriety's sake something should be given in return for whatever is received. It is more or less on the level of "I got treated to lunch last time so now it's my turn to pick up the check." A classical example of this orientation is exemplified in the following. Certain vendors were publishing special inflated price lists for one company purchasing agent so he could claim savings to top management after supposedly negotiating prices down. This kind of bargaining and trade-out rarely contributes to true effectiveness of selling. In nonbusiness situations its underlying commercial motivation tarnishes the sales representative who utilizes it and leads the customer to ask, "What's the angle?" Through "status" connections for obtaining hard-to-get theater tickets or ringside tables in expensive restaurants, the salesperson expands upon these quid pro quo tactics.

COMMUNICATION

The 5,5-oriented salesperson has a preset agenda of questions that are worked out and arranged to move a prospect indirectly toward a positive decision. The strategy is fixed, yet the tactics are flexible. Thus, the second, third, and fourth questions may very well be on different subjects. The second question asked is a function of the answer to the first. The third question is selected while displaying great interest in the information given in answer to the second question, and so on. However, this "prepackaged" quality can quickly be recognized by customers, who realize that the questions are intended to maneuver them in a planned direction. As a result, customers are unlikely to be aroused to enthusiasm by this type of pseudo-sophisticated, shallow interrogation.

A person listening in a 5,5 way is attempting to pigeonhole each remark heard according to some preestablished system of interpretation. If what is being said can be placed in a particular category, the salesperson then knows what answer to give. The underlying thinking is "Ah, here's *interest.* Now I can start building *confidence,*" and efforts to persuasion are intensified. This kind of listening is good to the extent that it creates a preestablished framework. The major difficulty, however, is that no frame of reference can be so refined as to catalog all the nuances of thought-plus-feelings that characterize the expressions of customers. Each is unique; all are different. Thus, the 5,5-oriented salesperson's restricted scope of listening is likely to lead to answers that, while they may appear relevant, are not completely on target.

The 5,5 way of treating interruptions is to appreciate that customers are often disposed to talk about matters that are not directly relevant to the sales interview. The 5,5-oriented sales representative humors such customers because it is frequently possible to move them to a purchase decision via their own individual byways. So these interruptions are accepted as a detour through which the sales interview must pass in order to get a closing. The interruption is acknowledged by a courteous pause. The salesperson listens to whatever is said and tries to connect it with a preestablished part of the sales presentation. If no connection is evident, the sales representative nevertheless hears the customer out, making some bland remark such as "That's very interesting," and then shifting back to the main road.

5,5-oriented salespeople have a distinctive emotional disposition. They take care to avoid getting out on an emotional limb where anybody could cut it off. This mode of emotional adjustment is conservative, sheltering such people from risk, but also depriving them of the richness of living. It makes these sales representatives seem mechanical and emotionally shallow. This shows through in the sense that emotions are calibrated almost as an engineer might set the controls of a machine to carry out some process. To "fit the situation" these salespeople respond as expected rather than according to true feelings.

NEW CUSTOMERS

Opening

The attitude underlying a 5,5 orientation is that the gateway to a prospect's mind surely opens when the prospect can be engaged in conversation that presents the salesperson as an attractive personality. The 5,5-oriented salesperson conveys a professional air, coupled with a hail-fellow-well-met approach. "Glad to see you. What can I do to help?"

SP: Let me introduce myself. My name is John Smith. Just call me Jack.

PC: Good to know you, Mr. . . . , er, Jack. My name is Elizabeth Brown.

SP: Liz for short, right?

PC: Uh, yes.

SP: It's a real pleasure to know you and to have this opportunity to introduce you to our fine company and its products.

PC: How exactly would you describe your company?

SP: Oh, yes. Thank you for asking. We are the oldest producer west of the Mississippi. Been at it steady for 30 years. So you see, you can count on us for reliability.

The opening phase may include a review of mutual acquaintances or a discussion of topics of general interest, all designed to aid the prospect to move into an easy give-and-take conversation and to feel accepted as a knowledgeable, alert person.

Conversation centers around whatever the customer wants to discuss. Having approximately the same concern for people as for the sale, being reasonably well informed on many subjects, and taking the client's tempo, the 5,5-oriented sales representative gains a reputation for being an easy person with whom to discuss business. The character of the discussion shifts in a subtle way, however, with the salesperson listening in the beginning to pick up the prospect's themes, interests, attitudes, and so on. Following this the salesperson becomes much more participative in the discussion and gears the conversation to conform with these major themes, attitudes, and feelings.

In this way the salesperson sizes up the customer and decides what kinds of selling appeals to use. If a favorable climate is not established or if the customer appears disinterested, the salesperson moves quickly into another sales technique geared to producing customer participation, whether genuine or not.

Identifying the Customer

A 5,5-oriented salesperson usually has been well coached to determine whether the person contacted is the ultimate purchaser or is acting in behalf of someone else. The question "Is this for you?" is a standard feature early in the transaction.

When the prospect is acting in behalf of another person, the sales representative seeks to make contact with the third party, albeit indirectly, by asking, "Do you think this is what your boss is looking for?" The intermediary is used as a sounding board to discover the real customer's felt needs. When doubts are expressed, the sales representative may invite the person being dealt with to bring the real purchaser into the situation or may offer to visit the ultimate purchaser. If this does not strike a chord, the person is dealt with as an intermediary. "Why don't you test this out with your boss? I'm sure it will be just the right thing."

Needs Analysis

The basic 5,5 assumption is that the customer's felt needs or expressed needs are the ultimate point of departure for needs analysis. The best chance to make a sale is to find out what the customer feels or thinks is needed. Being alert to clues in what the customer is saying may identify particular tendencies, interests, and emotions to which the salesperson can appeal. The salesperson adopts the prospect's frame of reference in understanding these needs. Even when the salesperson realizes that the felt need, as expressed, is not the real need, challenging the prospect is resisted and thus having to convert a felt need into an exploration of a real need is avoided. In practice, this means that within the felt-need framework, the salesperson aids the customer to sharpen, deepen, broaden, and clarify the characteristics of this felt need.

Then the salesperson attempts to match a product to what the customer seems to want. The 5,5-oriented salesperson does not try to assist the customer in diagnosing the problem, which would lead to the best decision, but rather develops a skill in sounding out the customer in order to provide what he or she claims to want. A "cafeteria line" of products is presented to meet the customer's expressed needs. This cafeteria catalog or line is likely to be remarkably similar to that of competitors, and price tends to be "what the traffic will bear." Every experienced salesperson has had a customer whose expressed needs were not the best expression of actual needs. When the purchase decision is based on felt needs rather than real product needs, customers often become dissatisfied, realizing that the product was not what they were really after.

The following conversation between a salesperson and prospective customer demonstrates this approach.

SP: What can I help you with today?

PC: I am about to leave for a vacation, and I need a good camera. I would hate not having great pictures to remember the trip.

SP: Did you have anything particular in mind?

PC: Not really. I don't know much about cameras, but I suppose I need one of those sophisticated models to get really good pictures.

SP: Well, we certainly have some good ones to choose from. This one here has all the latest features, and look at all the optional equipment it offers.

PC: It's quite attractive. And very compact.

SP: Beyond that, you'll notice that this camera is made by the company specializing in the top of the line.

PC: What's the price on this one?

SP: Oh, it's most reasonable. Only $239.

PC: But that's way out of my reach!

SP: Oh, well, then let's look over here. These are made by another company and, maybe it's hard to believe, they have the same qualities of optics, focusing, and speed. The only reason that they are cheaper is because the user is required to do a little more manually. Still, they are at the top of their line. I believe this will suit your needs to a T.

This customer, unless there is sufficient time to develop skill in using a sophisticated camera, is unlikely to be able to take good photographs on the vacation. What probably would best suit this customer's needs is just a good quality, simple camera that is easy to operate. The salesperson has disregarded the fact that the customer is a novice and has responded to the felt need that a complex, sophisticated camera is the answer.

Establishing Expectations

A 5,5-oriented salesperson has a variety of ways to whet the prospect's appetite and in this way to stimulate a readiness to sign on the bottom line. This appetite whetting is done by keeping things somewhat nebulous prior to moving in for a "yes" answer. For example, if the customer desires exclusiveness, the salesperson says, "You'll never come upon another one like this!"

If the customer's needs are for prestige and status: "This is recognized worldwide as the Cadillac of the line."

If the customer wants quality, the 5,5-oriented salesperson will extoll the product's virtues:

SP: It is attractive, isn't it?

PC: Yes, but how does it stand in terms of quality?

SP: Our customers are experts, and they like it. The testing laboratories say it's good, and the engineers rate it number one.

PC: What do you think about it?

SP: Well, I hate to brag. It might sound like a hard sell. But our products are really top-notch.

PC: Is that your personal opinion?

SP: I agree with the engineers, our customers, and the testing lab, of course. All of them speak well of it and so do I. The evidence is all here.

PC: But this national study put it in second place.

SP: Oh, there are always differences in opinion, you know.

PC: But these were documented facts saying the engineering was slightly deficient and that the product didn't stand up as well under vigorous use.

SP: Just picky little points. Let's just say it's one of the top two. But you'd never punish it like those testing laboratories do anyway, and it's probably still number one when operated under normal use.

Here the salesperson brings in other customers and the testing laboratories as backup references to boost the customer's confidence in the quality of the product.

Sales Presentation

Tricks, gimmicks, techniques, humor, speeding up, slowing down, and cooling off are the tools a 5,5-oriented salesperson uses to keep interviews and presentations moving along at a good, steady pace.

The salesperson avoids showing a single product if there are several versions available, each doing the same job with small distinguishing features. This way the sales representative avoids pushing one and offers the prospect the apparition of exercising choice. A fixed routine of chatter points to common features of all and distinctive features of each. In this way the customer is aided to develop a preference for one over the other. "These two models both do the job you want done. Which do you prefer? This one is round and painted green; that one is square and colored blue. Which fits your setting better?" Should the customer answer "neither," the salesperson says, "We also have the model in yellow, red, and white, and I will be pleased to show these to you."

A 5,5-oriented sales presentation tends to be stereotyped, following a standard sequence along previously rehearsed points. These are presented in a way that lacks thoroughness and depth. They imply indirectly, rather than emphasize through flat statements, whatever merits the product possesses. The presentation is calculated to engage the prospect's interest and to occupy the prospect in answering leading questions. The expected result is that by the time of closing, the prospect will have been introduced to and agreed with all the desirable qualities in the product. All these are in the forefront, for the question-and-answer process makes it difficult for the prospect to concentrate on possible limitations or deficiencies on the product. The salesperson's motto is "Accentuate the positive and eliminate the negative."

The lack of product knowledge may show through dramatically at this point, particularly if the product is technical.

SP: Here's the equipment and here is an example of the finished product. Really terrific, isn't it? Mindboggling . . .

PC: Can I see it work?

SP: Well, I'm no engineer, but thank goodness I don't need to be. They've simplified it down to nothing.

PC: Let's see it work.

SP: Okay. All you have to do after you plug it in is to hit the start switch. Like this. Wups! Wonder what went wrong? Let me reverse the plug and see if that works? Nope. Golly, what's wrong? Where's the manual? Okay. Here's where it tells how to troubleshoot. I've not had time to study this, but it won't take long. Could you come back, say, in 30 minutes?

PC: Okay. If I can make it, I'll try.

SP: Good. If I can't figure it out, I'll have the best engineer in the business in here to demonstrate the operation and use of this fine product.

Here the salesperson was caught short by lack of thoroughness in the product knowledge area. It is doubtful whether this salesperson will ever take the time to learn the complexities.

The salesperson has a well-marshaled list (sometimes supplied by the company) of high-status product users who can always be referred to by name and quoted during an interview as the basis for building the prospect's confidence. Name-dropping is one of the primary tools of influence.

If only one model is available, i.e., a standard contract, the 5,5-oriented salesperson describes its basic characteristics but also emphasizes its distinguishing features relative to competitors' products, pointing to the positive features of the model being offered, without specific reference to the competition.

The salesperson anticipates some of the risks of promoting customer hostility and seeks to avoid them by exerting as little pressuring and pushing as possible. The salesperson also avoids "giving in to a customer." Thus, while not likely to attempt to justify an unreasonably high price, the sales representative is reluctant to make any adjustments in the buyer's favor that would have sales margins below the level known to be acceptable to those who judge sales performance.

A 5,5-oriented salesperson respects the truth but exercises flexibility in seeking and interpreting what the truth is. While what is said is correct, what is left unsaid or what is implied may lead to conclusions that are not fully justified. Thus, the sales representative is careful to toe the line on "What I actually said"—when all that was said was truth, but not all the truth was said. When confronted with the dilemma of making an invalid statement as opposed to remaining silent, the 5,5-oriented salesperson is very conscious of "how things look on the record," "what's in the sales brochure," or "never saying things you can't back up"—all 5,5-oriented admonitions. Whatever the "sins" are, they are all sins of omission. This legalistic concept of integrity ensures that the statements made are true while providing plenty of legroom for the customer to draw unjustified implications and for the building up of customer confidence that is not entirely realistic.

There are several ways to arouse doubt and uncertainty, especially about a competitor. Truth, for example, is embedded in faint praise. The sliding yardstick approach of "Theirs is good, but ours is better" is another way of accomplishing the same thing. Direct criticism of the competitor's product is avoided in making comparisons, but the salesperson cleverly utilizes praise in the sales pitch. As already mentioned, there is the sin of omission. This may occur when a limitation in the competitor's product is heartily acknowledged, but a comparable limitation in the salesperson's own product is played down. Additionally, when the customer points out a positive feature in a competitor's product, this is berated and termed insignificant.

Subtle exaggerations within a framework of truth are also characteristic of this style. The salesperson implies rather than says directly that the product will perform beyond its actual capabilities, especially if the customer is unlikely to utilize it beyond normal limits. Another way to create an exaggeration is to leave a misunderstanding uncorrected, particularly when a customer, eager to have felt needs fulfilled, assumes that the product is more useful than it really is. When the customer ultimately becomes disillusioned, the salesperson accepts no responsibility for the misconceptions. In the most notorious instance the sales representative says, "I never claimed that it cures cancer." Otherwise, the usual statement uttered with sincere regret is "I'm so sorry, but it just didn't register with me that this was what you expected from our product."

Bluffing is another way to shade the truth. This occurs when the sales representative becomes committed to doing something in the hope that the goods can be delivered, yet where there are realistic doubts about the possibility of doing so. Having made the commitment, the salesperson tries to live with it by taking the steps necessary for bringing about the result. This kind of a bluff is also found in the 9,1 orientation, but the difference is that a salesperson exploiting the 9,1 bluff "moves hell and high water" to deliver and in this way may avoid being held accountable. By comparison, the 5,5 attitude is to have a bundle of excuses ready when confronted, and if these are unacceptable, to seek reacceptance through profuse apologies.

A customer's reaction to 5,5-oriented bluffing tactics, once aware of them, is likely to be "You have to take everything with a grain of salt." The customer soon learns to discount whatever the salesperson says and to listen to every remark for the unspoken word or phrase.

Objections

The 5,5-oriented salesperson conveys an air of self-confidence to the customer. Convictions are never expressed clearly enough to be proved wrong. Since options are kept open, the customer feels the transaction is flexible. Recognizing the risk of promoting hostility, this salesperson is ready to shift if resistance is conveyed by a customer. In this way the salesperson avoids being placed in jeopardy of conflict, and convictions do not become polarized.

Rather than dealing with objections according to the customer's frame of reference, the salesperson seeks to introduce consideration of some benefit that is of sufficient size to balance out and leave a residue of positive attitudes against the stated objection. Then, it is hoped, the prospect will say, "Well, I guess my objection is really not very important in the light of the total circumstances," and in this way the 5,5-oriented salesperson has successfully overcome a stumbling block toward an affirmative decision.

The 5,5-oriented salesperson is ready to acknowledge that a perfect fit is a rarity indeed. The salesperson also feels that a fairly close approximation to what the customer wants is a feasible possibility. After all, there are many ways of making an approximation almost a perfect fit.

Although the sales representative may suggest that an objection is partially justified but not wholly so, an attempt is made to promote a positive attitude by indicating the better features of the product that compensate for any limitations that have been identified. If the customer raises two or more objections, the salesperson may write these down on one side of a sheet of paper and then develop a longer list of reasons why the customer should buy. The suggestion, whether spoken or not, is that the customer's objections have been "outvoted." Or the salesperson may suggest that while the product might not meet all the customer's requirements, it does satisfy the essential ones. Another gambit is to try to sandwich the objection in between two positive features, pointing to a positive quality. In this way the significance of the objection is reduced by the positive attributes with which the salesperson surrounds the recognized limitation.

The following conversation reveals how such a salesperson deals with a prospective customer to gloss over conflict inherent in expressed objections.

SP: This guarantee is acknowledged to be foolproof. They say there are no exceptions.

PC: What makes it so binding?

SP: Our word for over 95 years.

PC: I have to take exception to that. I know a person whose warranty you refused to honor.

SP: Well, you can never interpret anything literally. There's a little stretch in every promise. But still, it's rare when we don't make good.

A customer's questions are not simply brushed aside so as to continue the presentation. Rather, the salesperson has a bank of pat, rehearsed answers and reveals them when appropriate.

Another way of trying to meet an objection without dealing with it directly is through bargaining. This may involve a side deal, throwing in a little "something extra" to balance out the situation if the customer will accept the limitation and make the purchase. This attitude of trying to compromise, bargain, and trade off with the customer to gain acceptance of the product without resolving the objections is based upon a general 5,5 disposition. In essence, it calls for settling for what you can get rather than going after what is sound from the standpoint of solving the customer's problems in a objective way. The 5,5 motto is "A half loaf is better than none."

Because of a high reliance on the tried-and-true presentation, this salesperson is particularly vulnerable when vigorously probed by the customer. When this technique is punctured, the sales representative is likely to be unable to recoup because there is no prepared response to cope with the unique situation.

Closing

Sales seminars, books, tapes, and bulletins continually caution about the number of sales lost because the salesperson failed to ask for the sale. When decision-making time draws near, this salesperson usually knows the appropriate time to "pop the question." In terms of smiles, a positive mental attitude, a direct nod, good humor, constant recall of benefits, and so on, this salesperson overflows with enthusiasm when it comes to asking for the sale. For those using a 5,5 strategy, the excitement in terms of the pending sale literally makes the adrenalin flow. Every known technique "comes on stage" as the salesperson strives for a positive purchase decision. Failure to ask for the sale is a weakness of many sales representatives in general, but not for 5,5-oriented salespeople, who derive security from "successful" formulas revealed by colleagues.

The salesperson has a mental checklist of steps to go through during the presentation calculated to bring about a successful close. Many of its features are based upon gaining the customer's acceptance through suggestion. These include appealing to pride in ownership or the reputation of the company, or building ego by suggesting that status in the eyes of the community will be elevated as soon as the purchase becomes known. It has been suggested that many computers and executive jets have been sold with this as a significant basis for the decision. Many times such generalities are enough to satisfy the customer at the point of purchase even though dissatisfaction may arise later at the point of use. This brings out another facet of the 5,5-oriented salesperson—short term, bird in the hand.

The salesperson is patient and willing to take the time necessary to get a positive result. All the techniques in the book are utilized to influence this outcome, including the silent-treatment technique, the assumptive technique, the seed-planting technique, the use of rhetorical questions that confirm the answer the salesperson wants the purchaser to say out loud, and a mixture of twenty-seven other prescriptive closing techniques.

If the customer is carried through to closing, the 5,5-oriented salesperson's outcome is likely to be successful and carried off with a great deal of hoop-la. This becomes evident in the salesperson's eagerness to compliment the customer on an excellent purchase, the soundness in reaching it, and the deep enjoyment or the reward that will be derived from having exercised such solid decision making. This unadulterated use of positive reinforcement coincides with the need many people experience to be accepted by others as reasonable and thoughtful people who have exercised good judgment. A critical difference is that the salesperson's reinforcement strategies constitute a selling technique rather than an expression of genuine conviction that the customer's solution-seeking or decision-making behavior has truly been sound. The customer, having left the buying situation and beginning to reflect on the purchase, even though satisfied with it, is likely to develop a sense of uneasiness. This customer may become distrustful of the salesperson's integrity, wary about being engulfed in further interviews.

Price is introduced early in the presentation in order to get the prospect accustomed to the terms. The hoped-for outcome is that this conditioning process will give the customer a valid expectation with regard to the expense involved in buying the product. If this is not the case, the salesperson may need to add that "because of inflation this price is likely to be advanced without notice," or "a product of this quality will never be available on these terms again in our lifetime."

If the formula-based presentation does not produce the expected results by the time closing comes around, the salesperson is likely to become less tentative, pushing all the visible "hot buttons" that might induce the customer to buy. While high-pressure techniques are still avoided and prophecies of doom are not indulged in, subtle remarks are inserted about how the customer runs the risk of losing everything if a negative decision is made. If it appears that the customer is about to break off the interview, the salesperson ventures some follow-up feelers: "Please let me contact you after you've had time to think about it." Or "I'm disappointed because I've seen so many people benefit from this product. Perhaps I could introduce you to. . . ." Or "I see that you are very busy so I won't take up any more of your time today. But I *would* like to stop by next week and discuss it some more."

The following conversation is typical of the 5,5 approach to closing.

SP: I'm sorry you are uncertain, but I know it takes time to make up your mind.

PC: Well, thanks for your help.

SP: Don't mention it. Sometimes prospects want a little more time and will return to take another look, so I'll be on the lookout for you in a few days. I feel you will really want this once you've had a chance to think about it.

Salesperson makes a follow-up phone call at a later date.

SP: Just thought I'd keep in touch. Have you thought about it? Want me to wrap it up?

PC: No, I've reconsidered . . .

SP: If it's the price, I am sure we can work out a discount or something.

PC: No, I've made up my mind, but thanks anyway for calling.

ESTABLISHED BUSINESS

The 5,5-oriented salesperson usually does not take established accounts for granted but, rather, actively nurtures them, yet without pressing too hard.

Beyond the value of keeping in touch for maintaining the account, casual friendships with a constant exchange of information, rumors, and so on are in themselves quite satisfying. When appropriate, advantage is taken of club memberships—luncheons, afternoon golf, tennis matches, a drink in the clubroom—in order to cement an account into place.

Maintaining Accounts

One way of maintaining accounts is through regularly scheduled visits to respond to any expanded sales opportunities that may have developed. A second way is to focus the customer's attention on something new and different during each successive sales contact. The customer remains interested, never quite knowing what will be introduced next.

Even though some of the new details are trivial, the 5,5-oriented salesperson exaggerates their importance in order to maintain interest. By keeping in touch, the salesperson is reassured that an account is progressing satisfactorily. These initiatives have no direct connection with the product or service but may involve a tidbit of information, a suggestion about vacation, a new way of thinking about the business situation, or any useful background fact the salesperson may have learned from another customer, whose anonymity is preserved. All this is geared to keeping the customer on the line by introducing fresh elements of interest. These contacts are more than "touching base." They are used to seek further business from the customer, who comes to depend upon the salesperson's eyes and ears for the latest gossip regarding what is new.

Complaints

The 5,5-oriented salesperson keeps alert for complaints from established accounts, realizing that failure to deal with them can have an adverse effect on steady, continuing business. Often standard procedures have been worked out between the salesperson and customer for dealing with the more common kinds of complaints. These may work well, keeping the customer's product satisfaction at a reasonable level. In the absence of established procedures, a 5,5 way of dealing with a complaint is to reinterpret it in a different context so that, looked at from another perspective, it does not seem as important as it had previously appeared. When complaints are lodged that cannot be answered, accommodated, or compromised, the 5,5-oriented salesperson tries to mollify the customer with profuse apologies that communicate a sincere desire to solve the customer's problem.

When a complaint cannot be dealt with in these ways, the 5,5-oriented sales representative may try to adjust the difference. For example, if a commitment is made to deliver 1000 units and these units are held up due to manufacturing difficulties, the salesperson might try to soothe the complaining customer by delivering the absolute minimum number needed to keep things going for the time being. Returning to the organization, the salesperson doubles the customer's order and then permits Production to bargain down to the minimum number promised the customer. In this way an adjustment is reached that reduces the customer's frustration. This in turn mollifies the Production people, because they have beaten the sales representative down to a smaller amount for the priority shipment. From the 5,5 angle this is an all-round "workable" solution to a complaint. It does not solve the fundamental problem of why a promised delivery is not met, but it does bring an accommodation and adjustment of the difference into play with which everyone can live.

Rush Business

If the company can meet rush business without inconvenience, the 5,5-oriented salesperson is more than pleased to take orders, emphasizing a readiness to give customers special attention. If the company cannot easily adjust to rush business, the approach to the problem is similar to that illustrated in the previous section. It involves compromising and accommodation during which the salesperson seeks to move people toward an "equilibrium" level. This means that the customer will receive more than the Production or Distribution people initially indicated they could release, but a lesser amount than the customer at first considered essential. Through this kind of bargaining, the customer's needs are at least partially met, yet the salesperson avoids being charged with putting unreasonable demands on Production. No one is entirely satisfied, but no one is left completely frustrated. More importantly, the risk of exposing this customer to aggressive sales competition is reduced, though of course not entirely eliminated.

SELF-MANAGEMENT

When it comes to self-improvement, a 5,5-oriented salesperson seeks middle positions, wanting neither to lead the pack in innovation nor to be out of step in the sense of doing less than others are doing. Direction comes from falling into step with what colleagues are doing. An eclectic attitude is deemed most reliable, as a potpourri of approaches are considered a safer bet than one in-depth problem-solving approach. If others have found that something works, this salesperson uses it too, but always with minor adjustments to personalize it. Routine and regularity add to feelings of security that actions are consistent with what others expect.

Here are typical 5,5-oriented attitudes toward self-improvement.

SCHEDULING AND TIME MANAGEMENT. I schedule my activities in order to achieve a steady level of performance without pushing too hard. I ease the pressure on myself by adopting an orderly routine.

PROSPECTING. I follow through on most leads I get and create my own from lists and statistical documents. I step up my prospecting whenever it appears I'm falling behind.

SERVICING. I represent the customer to my company's internal organization. A customer is entitled to fair treatment.

EXPENSES. I usually keep my expenses within policy guidelines. At times, additional expenditures may help me capture sales opportunities.

SELF-STEERING. Frequently self-appraisal helps me identify where I am out of step.[9]

CUSTOMER REACTIONS

The 5,5-oriented salesperson is really controlled by a customer's actions and reactions, because of "flexibility" in accommodating to the customer more or less regardless of Grid style. The selling tempo is usually paced in accord with the customer's mood of the moment, moving along rapidly when the customer is ready to go and slacking off when the customer is showing doubt. The customer becomes the salesperson's metronome. This agent's finely tuned ability to use "techniques," coupled with a personal approach to integrity that permits certain details to be left out that might be disadvantageous to making a sale, oftentimes causes a customer to be trapped into commitments made without full awareness of the facts or, for that matter, without even having the realization that a commitment has been made.

Customer reactions to 5,5-oriented sales techniques vary. Sometimes this salesperson's strategy succeeds, particularly with customers who are in a hurry or for some reason are distracted and unable to concentrate fully on the criteria for making a sound purchasing decision. Almost all prospects who come close to being persuaded can be swayed by subtle suggestions at one time or another. There is also a strong likelihood, however, that customers who encounter this salesperson are alert to making the best use of their time as well as their own company's purchasing dollar. Many times all the customer has to do is to detect a false note in the salesperson's presentation and certain suspicions are aroused. Watching and listening ever more closely, the customer soon begins to see through the surface film of illusion. If the salesperson and the product are not instantly rejected, the customer continues a display of self-defense by thinking of objections to put this smooth sales technique out of kilter.

9,1

To a 9,1-oriented customer, a 5,5 sales presentation has a hollow ring. Lacking real convictions, it is unconvincing. The salesperson's knowledge, as evidenced in the presentation and in responses to questions, is not sufficiently deep to give the full confidence that this customer needs to feel that a sound return on investment will be gained. Objections are parried and deflected rather than being handled with factual answers expressed strongly and in a way that wins approval.

In order to "fight," a 9,1-oriented client needs something to push against. The 5,5-oriented salesperson is so flexible in position taking that a shift can be made on a moment's notice. This defensive mechanism allows the salesperson to avoid polarizing issues. Even here, though, a customer who feels trapped or victimized by the agent's technique may still take an aggressive stance. The 5,5-oriented sales representative's inclination is to continue with a tried-and-true routine, attempting to stay on the predetermined track and to overcome interruptions and objections when they occur. Some of these are simply ignored, and to others the answer is "yes, but . . ." The agent tries to forestall future objections by expanding the presentation to answer possible questions in advance. This continues up to the point when the customer expresses dislike for the proposition, becomes impatient and openly hostile, and finally terminates the interview, possibly with a dodge like "Let me think about it" or a flat "No go."

The salesperson's moderate energy and enthusiasm and the gimmicks that characterize the 5,5 technique are not likely to move a 9,1-oriented customer out of the 9,1 Grid style. The salesperson does not level with the customer in a way that encourages a buying attitude.

1,9

The 5,5 approach is more likely to be successful with a 1,9-oriented customer, because there is much in it to please and little to arouse anxiety. The presentation is exciting to this customer and so elicits a positive response. The customer wants to say "yes" and to avoid saying "no" and therefore is most likely to respond affirmatively to the salesperson's queries. Although the salesperson may not fully satisfy the customer's desire to be liked, the customer will probably move positively toward the closing. Difficulties for this salesperson begin when the definite time for closing arrives. Although the customer has indicated "yes" all along, there may now be an unwillingness to proceed. Rather than saying "no," the customer simply tries to defer the decision. In this way, the 1,9-oriented customer avoids being blatantly negative but still avoids a final "yes" decision. If the salesperson presses forward at this point instead of accepting excuses, it is quite likely that the customer will make an affirmative decision to buy. However, if expectations are not fulfilled later on, the customer feels let down, hurt, and disappointed.

1,1

The salesperson is quick to recognize the key difference between customers with 1,9 and 1,1 orientations. Whereas the 1,9-oriented customer responds affirmatively to the programmed questions of a 5,5 presentation, a 1,1-oriented customer responds with grunts or well-aimed silence. Rather than taking this silence as an indication of "zero interest" and becoming discouraged, the 5,5-oriented salesperson continues the presentation, closely following a number of closing techniques. This customer is easy to deal with and a joy to sell, because both salesperson and customer respond to the same kind of signals. The customer's lack of interest in deep product knowledge fits the sales representative's superficial level of research. Most of the sales pitch appeals to needs that do not exist for the 1,1-oriented customer. The customer's desires, which are formulated in conventional terms, tend to be consistent with the salesperson's tried-and-true presentation technique. Questions asked by a 5,5-oriented customer are not so deep that they challenge the salesperson's rather superficial knowledge. The customer finds nothing abrasive in the presentation, and the salesperson moves at a tempo harmonious to the prospective customer.

5,5

This salesperson's approach is most natural and successful with a 5,5-oriented customer. Because this customer comes into the purchasing situation with a prestige-centered orientation, and since the sales representative is tuned to respond to this need, the two individuals often work well together and really "hit it off."

9,9

The 9,9-oriented customer typically finds the 5,5-oriented presentation unconvincing, unless the product or service is seen as solving a real need. Usually, the customer wants more facts about the product, more logical connections between the facts to support the salesperson's claims for the merits of the product, and more information about the relationship between the product's capabilities and the customer's needs. Generally, the 5,5-oriented salesperson is unable to provide this detailed information.

As the presentation unfolds, it is quickly punctured and interrupted by the customer in an effort to uncover the salesperson's true depth of knowledge and possession of facts. Interrogation by a 9,9-oriented customer is not intended to be destructive. It is a constructive attempt to illuminate and thus create a better understanding of the strengths and weaknesses of the sales representative's presentation. In this way the salesperson is able to gain a better comprehension of the customer's true situation and the extent to which a particular property will fulfill the expressed needs.

Upon being subjected to this customer's problem-solving search, the sales representative quickly demonstrates a high level of incompetence. The salesperson operating under 5,5 assumptions finds it difficult to deal successfully with a 9,9-oriented customer, even though the opportunity for a successful outcome is quite good, particularly if the salesperson takes the customer's lead and gathers the relevant facts and information required for an insight-based decision. Since 9,9-oriented customers bring enthusiasm and commitment to a purchase, their way of participating in the interview and the nature of their questions invite more openness and candor on the salesperson's part and greater clarity in specifying what the product can and cannot do, its reliability, the conditions in which it will be used, and so on. The salesperson who responds to the customer's initiatives shifts from a 5,5 dominant style into a 9,9 backup.

SUMMARY

The 5,5 salesperson is not charged with high energy and promotes illusions rather than arousing enthusiasm for what the product can really do. The presentation does not genuinely involve the customer. The conviction and commitment it evokes may be strong enough to produce a sale, but being somewhat illusory, these tend to vanish afterward. The 5,5 approach is often effective, however, particularly in moving highly reputable products when a customer desires personal prestige or where there is a clear need for the product.

A 5,5-oriented salesperson wants to build up prestige and to avoid being labeled as odd, different, or unusual. It is important to be a good salesperson in the eyes of customers and of bosses and other sales personnel. By respecting corporate traditions and norms, supporting the status quo, and avoiding behavior that might be viewed as deviating from established norms, this salesperson gains the kind of reputation that provides a career path to security.

It can be expected that a 5,5-oriented salesperson will put the same degree of emphasis on profit as the company does and use price structure closely as a guide. The attitude is "Reasonable profit is built into our price structure and is necessary for company stability. Although I try to maintain price levels, I can't always keep customer goodwill and realize a profit at the same time." However, the salesperson is likely to try to increase sales volume by applying a double standard toward price structure. For example, new business with a low profit margin may be accepted. In this way sales volume can be increased, profit levels kept constant, and total dollar savings increased. Thus only a slight degree of drag is introduced into the system when customer pressures are high. The overall sales result to be expected from a 5,5-oriented salesperson is likely to be that of maintaining present profitability levels, but not much more than that. The salesperson works to keep a fair share of established accounts and to replace lost accounts with new business.

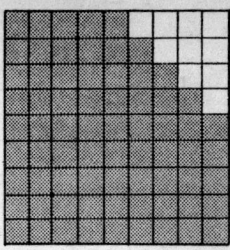

9,9
Solution Seeking

The salesperson with a 9,9 orientation places high value on reaching sound sale-and-purchase decisions with customers. The primary concern is in helping the customer reach a purchase decision based on reason and logic that feels right *and has the highest probability, in the long run, of proving right.* The purchasing decision is usually reinforced by positive emotions at the time it is made. During the discussion leading up to it, the salesperson does not attempt to persuade the prospect with emotion-directed appeals in the spirit of the moment. The salesperson wants to work with the customer to find out how a product or service can best contribute to satisfying the customer's needs or to resolve existing problems. Needless to say, the transaction must also be sound in terms of the sales organization's objectives and marketing policies. This is "solution selling," because it satisfies the customer while advancing the objectives of the corporation.

The positive motivations of 9,9-oriented

sales representatives lead them to act in ways that indicate they *care* for people. These motivations contribute to self-fulfillment through making a genuine contribution. Basic to such contributions are actions taken to study markets, to learn technology, and to keep abreast of new laws. Standards of excellence are adhered to as one measure of contribution. This means that personal integrity and ethical considerations are held as basic criteria of decision making. Such decisions convey a sense of caring, because the customer is considered important and customer satisfaction is ensured. The 9,9-oriented salesperson embraces challenging goals, exercises diligent effort, and stimulates creative solutions to difficulties encountered in selling. The involvement with the interests of customers, including meticulous attention to facts and detail, is all part of the sales representative's demonstration of caring, as indicated by the willingness to contribute to the customer's problem solving or solution seeking. As a result, the salesperson's personal sense of fulfillment is enhanced.

The avoidance of selfishness characterizes the negative motivation. Selfishness reduces a 9,9-oriented person's self-esteem because one person's gain is another's loss. Therefore, selfishly motivated behavior, putting one's own vested interests ahead of the client's interests, is avoided. Examples include committing or promising more than one is capable of delivering, pursuing less than full follow-up, and not taking steps to thoroughly diagnose, identify, and rectify real barriers to effective selling.

It is characteristic of the 9,9-oriented salesperson's dealings with customers to listen for and seek out ideas, opinions, and attitudes that differ from his or her own. The 9,9 focus is on the quality of thinking and its essential validity, regardless of whether it represents a personal view or a customer's view or emerges from their interaction. The salesperson is a real starter in the sense of initiating action as well as following through. Customers and others tend to pick up a sense of confidence that their needs are important to the sales representative.

The more subjective elements of people's behavior—their feelings, attitudes, and fluctuating emotions—are recognized as essential ingredients of human experience and thus part of any sales interview. Emotions cannot be kept out of a sales interview, nor can they be kept separate during any phase of it. They are part and parcel of any purchasing decision and can either facilitate good results or block a sound decision, depending on how they are handled. Whenever a conflict of ideas and emotions arises between the salesperson and the prospect, the reasons are identified and the underlying causes resolved by working with the other person to gain insightful understanding into the facts and feelings that are involved. 9,9-oriented salespeople rarely lose their temper, even when stirred up. Their humor fits the situation and is not used as a weapon or a lever or as oil on troubled waters; rather, humor is utilized to illuminate and clarify a situation.

KNOWLEDGE: PRODUCT, CUSTOMER, AND COMPETITOR

Heavy emphasis on selling fact-based solutions is one of the key features of a 9,9 sales orientation. Product, customer, and competitor facts are data to be considered together.

Recognizing the persuasive power of knowledge, a 9,9-oriented salesperson builds self-reliance by acquiring expert knowledge of the product. This is accomplished through continuous study, analysis, and inquiry regarding the qualities of the product itself, taking every opportunity to consult with technical specialists who design and manufacture the particular product.

The sales representative stays well informed with regard to established customers' experiences in using the product. As a result, there is little need to rely on others to support a sales interview. On the occasions when others must be referred to for special product advice, the need for information usually relates to new or innovative applications that involve a technical understanding beyond what can be expected of a person whose primary job is selling.

Since customers are people who have problems for which the product may provide solutions, the salesperson makes an effort to know and understand each customer's situation. Product knowledge is conveyed *after* finding out how the product might benefit the customer being interviewed. In the process, the salesperson becomes informed about whatever alternative products and services the prospect has considered or tried.

The 9,9-oriented salesperson also comes to know more about the customer as an individual. *The emotions of a customer,* as well as the customer's objective situation, *are facts to the salesperson.* The capacity to respond to interests, desires, and aspirations is an asset for the salesperson with regard to knowledge about the customer. The quality of response reflects the quality of a salesperson's concern for a customer. To encourage a speedy purchase decision by appealing to feelings and aspirations that a salesperson knows will not be satisfied by the product is only to create the likelihood that the customer's expectations will be violated after such a purchase. Many apparent shortcuts are unsound and counterproductive in terms of results. In these circumstances the salesperson's loss—in terms of future business—may be greater than is apparent from a consideration of one customer's disappointment. Disgruntled purchasers often counteradvertise salespersons and the products they represent.

The 9,9-oriented salesperson avoids creating these consequences and actively works to eliminate them as possibilities. The main concern, both for the customer and for the quality of the sales result, leads the salesperson to check and make sure that the customer's expectations as to what will be gained by purchasing are realistic.

In pursuing these unified concerns, the 9,9-oriented salesperson may frequently come to understand the customer's problems or needs even more clearly than they are understood by the customer, who may not see them as objectively as an outside observer. The interview that evolves is a situation in which two people are deliberating about how one of them can best use a product and about what is the best choice between alternative versions of this particular product.

The 9,9-oriented salesperson realizes that competitors are offering solutions to the customer's problems, too. Thus, in order to compete successfully, the sales representative aims at understanding competitors' products thoroughly and comprehensively. In reading through trade contracts, the salesperson seeks out what experiences other consumers are having with competitors' products. This may be accomplished by experimenting directly with a competitor's product and by dismantling, examining, and reassembling it in order to understand manufacturing and operational characteristics. Additionally, the salesperson stays informed about established customers' experiences with a product. The sales representative's company may take responsibility for analyzing the more expensive and complex products of competitors and then circulate useful information. The benefit from gaining this kind of knowledge is that it enables the 9,9-oriented salesperson to deal factually and analytically with a customer's inquiries at a time when the customer is trying to get an idea of how the salesperson's product compares with the competitor's.

Often a customer begins to think comparatively about "this product versus the other product" during a sales interview. The customer may feel that there are not enough data to make a good evaluation of both products, and the salesperson is the only source from whom needed information can be drawn. The customer may ask a question, even if skeptical about the validity of the response. In effect, the customer is applying a test of authenticity to the salesperson. If a customer wants to compare competitors' products, the salesperson is prepared to comment objectively on the relative merits of each, with comments or conclusions being supported by facts, performance data, and logic. If the customer detects a substantial bias against a competitor's product, it is likely that there will be a correspondingly biased slant against the salesperson.

This is by no means to say that the salesperson adopts the attitude of a scientist making a cold comparison. In presenting various perspectives, the salesperson is acknowledging that the prospect *is* going to make comparisons, either during this interview or at some other time before making a decision, and that these comparisons are likely to be pivotal in the purchase decision. The salesperson is in an excellent position to set up the kind of comparative framework that the customer can use. While doing this, the sales representative demonstrates the advantages of the product without berating the competitor. This kind of open-minded objectivity lays a foundation for building the prospect's confidence in the salesperson and the product.

Why is so much emphasis placed on comparison of one's own products with those of competitors? The answer is apparent when you step into the customer's shoes. As a customer, your needs are best served when you can make a choice from a variety of products presented by several different salespeople. This range permits you to compare and choose, with your final selection made from a range of comparable products, a spectrum of prices, and an array of servicing provisions. The mental attitude of a salesperson, whose interests are served by your purchase, is understandably different from your mental attitude. But salespeople should not consider their own attitudes to be the rule of life. If a salesperson unwittingly assumes that you know the product well, that you *should* be eager to select this product and disregard the competitor's, that you are unconcerned about the relative prices of competitive products, or that you are not comparing servicing arrangements with those offered by competitors, then the salesperson is living in a false world of hope, not reality. Consequently, the salesperson is less likely to be effective during the interview and to bring about a successful close than if a continual alertness to differences were maintained.

The primitive, unreasoned inclination of many salespeople, then, is to reduce a customer's opportunity to compare products. The natural inclination of a customer is to try to increase the possibilities of comparison. Some salespeople want to restrict comparison in order to avoid the negative results—in terms of fewer sales—that the customer's wide-ranging consideration might provide. The customer, on the other hand, wants to increase comparison opportunities in order to have a stronger basis on which to formulate a purchasing decision.

The 9,9-oriented sales approach does not rest on the assumption that it is necessary to keep a set of blinders on the customer to induce acceptance of a product in preference to a competitor's. Instead, the assumption is that when a customer can be assisted to compare products in a sound and valid way, the salesperson is in a stronger position to gain confidence and respect. The sales representative is also more likely to forward the product against the background of "silent" comparisons the customer is usually making.

This is not to be interpreted as meaning that people are mostly "fact, data, and logic" oriented, rarely making purchasing decisions that are influenced by status considerations or emotions or other subjective factors. Most purchasing decisions are weighted with heavy status and prestige rationales, more subjective and emotional than factual and reasoned but, nevertheless, no less important. In the final analysis, perhaps the majority of purchasing decisions are triggered by an emotional feeling of "This is what I want," based on subjective factors. The

9,9: SOLUTION SEEKING 125

salesperson should acknowledge and respect these needs just as much as other needs that are based more on facts.

The point to be made is this: Decisions that are based on fact and reason are more likely to be durable and rewarding than those that are based solely on impulse and emotion. Over the long term, they tend to provide continued satisfaction as the product is used and its suitability is confirmed. There is less disappointment as the first glow of ownership recedes. A 9,9-oriented salesperson is reluctant to make a snap close of the sale based solely on a customer's speedily heightened emotions and impulse to buy, preferring to keep the decision open a while longer so that data and logic are fully acknowledged. Often, added intellectual appreciation reinforces the customer's emotional desires. The result is a stronger sale and an increased likelihood of a steady and improving account. If the purchase is made merely on a basis of unreasoned enthusiasm, without a good appreciation of how the product can precisely fit needs and wishes, the customer may easily become disillusioned with it later and blame the salesperson. Thus, being able to combine deep product knowledge with a sound understanding of the prospect's situation, the 9,9-oriented salesperson is uniquely capable of forwarding a product in a positive and constructive way.

The attitude of openness and candor that typifies the 9,9 sales orientation can result in a lost sale if it becomes obvious to the salesperson and customer alike that a competitor's product is obviously better in answer to a problem. This does not mean that a 9,9 sales orientation is harmful to a company's interests. Indeed, if the product is not competitive with another in terms of satisfying a particular type of need, the salesperson and the company should realize this. They are then alerted to the situation and can take the necessary steps to improve their competitiveness in this field.

PARTICIPATION AND INVOLVEMENT

The key to a 9,9 approach to selling is in integrating two basic concerns. One is a genuine concern on the part of the salesperson for creating sound, profitable, and continuing business for the company. The other is for ensuring that the customer makes the kind of purchase that most closely approaches a problem-solving or need-satisfaction level. There is no contradiction between these two concerns—rather, they become one, providing a unified and authentic professional approach.

9,9 is *the* selling approach that rests on stimulating the participation and involvement of customers. Closing begins only when there is a genuine meeting of minds. Understanding and agreement between salesperson and customer are reinforced by feelings of emotional validity—that the purchase decision is right.

How does this kind of understanding between the customer and salesperson come about? The salesperson acts as a leader and sets the pace with a general attitude that creates a climate of give-and-take. This is done by exploring with the customer what the actual requirements are and how best these can be satisfied within the limits acknowledged by both parties. Limits include the product characteristics and budgetary restraints set by the customer, among others. Within these limits or boundaries, there is an area where a sound sale-and-purchase transaction may be reached, satisfactory from the point of view of each party. Involvement for both parties is at its peak when the customer arrives at a purchase decision that truly satisfies realistic needs.

The 9,9-oriented salesperson approaches the customer with objective facts and data concerning the product, combined with a responsible attitude toward using it. In addition, this salesperson is prepared to contribute any and all imaginative powers that can be brought to bear. The sales representative probably does not present all facts at the beginning of the interview, because product facts, by themselves, are not useful until they can be related to a customer's real requirements. Neither are facts withheld as an interview proceeds. Instead, the customer has full access to the salesperson's "data bank." Quite often effective participation and involvement are achieved by moving from abstract to concrete levels through the use of selling aids—pictures, examples of use, graphs, and charts that organize an otherwise complex array of statistics and support straightforward conclusions.

The other side of participation and involvement is that the salesperson needs information from the customer concerning the latter's unique situation and requirements. Therefore, the salesperson seeks active customer participation from the outset. It is likely that they will soon be working together in a give-and-take discussion that can result in genuine customer-salesperson consensus. Whatever the initial reservations, the customer will respond to the salesperson's keen commitment to participation and involvement with growing participation and involvement. The consequences are that the customer becomes both intellectually and emotionally involved in making a sound purchase. In this way, the consensus reached between salesperson and customer is based on a genuine partnership in arriving at a mutually beneficial transaction. It begins as a selling-purchasing relationship but is likely to endure and to generate future business.

From the standpoint of being helpful, a 9,9-oriented salesperson gives someone assistance that otherwise would be absent. Possibly it is not something the recipient would miss if it had not been given. But the key is that a person is acting both because there is an opportunity to do so and because a contribution can be made to another person's situation. The contribution in itself is its own reward. There are no strings attached. This helpfulness may be commonplace, such as simply passing along some new information that puts the recipient in a stronger position to understand some situation or event. It is valued because the recipient recognizes that it was unnecessary for the sales representative to provide it. It adds to the customer's understanding, and the customer knows there is no obligation. The same applies when there is a very large contribution, such as aiding the recipient to seize an important opportunity that would not otherwise have been apparent. It is only possible to be helpful in this way when the person giving the help has a high concern for aiding other people to be more effective, for strengthening them, or for making them "fuller"—more complete as persons.

The salesperson, not being entrenched in the same situation as a customer, may be able to see the total situation in a clearer way than the customer, who confronts the circumstances at short range. Sometimes the greatest help that the salesperson can give is no more or less than a deep and genuine interest in a customer's problem. It is a relief for the customer to be able to talk it over with someone who is sympathetic and unbiased. It is better still when the salesperson helps the customer to think the problem through and to see the outlines of its solution.

This is particularly so when the sales representative is concerned about understanding the customer's situation and does so through advanced preparation. In addition to normal product sales and service matters, the salesperson may be well situated to assist in unexpected ways that are quite separate from the product's potential contribution. These are helpful initiatives from the salesperson's side but are not motivated by the "making a sale" consideration. Nevertheless, important gains can be realized. The salesperson's positive interest in the customer is shown to be constructive, not self-seeking and devious. This is what builds confidence and trust and increases the salesperson's credibility with regard to the product.

The giving of help is undoubtedly one of the more subtle and significant matters in any human relationship. One should be aware of the personal motivation for doing so and of the likely negative consequences if it is done for the wrong reason. Equally, a salesperson should be clear as to the possible reciprocal benefits of giving help for sound reasons—both from the recipient's point of view and from the salesperson's.

COMMUNICATION

How does a salesperson with a 9,9 orientation go about acquiring the kind of information that is so vital to an effective selling relationship? Prior to asking questions, this salesperson begins by expressing what is already known about the customer's situation in order to acquaint the customer with the salesperson's level of understanding. Confidence in the salesperson is increased because now the customer knows where the salesperson stands. Then the salesperson asks questions, letting the customer know *how* it will help to have the answers sought. It takes only a few extra words to answer the customer's implicit "Why?" beforehand. Additionally, the product can be best explained if it is described in terms that make it most rewarding and relevant to the customer. The 9,9-oriented salesperson is building a foundation of trust and confidence.

The *manner* of approach reinforces what the salesperson *says*. One thing being communicated is that the customer is respected as an individual and is not viewed simply as just another cipher. Other unspoken messages are that the customer's ability to think is appreciated and that the information conveyed is valued and will be used during the interview. The questions are not being asked as a gambit to soften up the customer by encouraging discussion. By being open with respect to intentions, the salesperson is creating in the customer an emotional readiness to accept the salesperson as an honest and genuine individual and to respond in kind.

The prime ingredient of 9,9 listening is the salesperson's knowledge that the essence of thought and feeling is never fully captured in words. This sales representative knows that words are less than perfect tools of communication. When the customer expresses any questions, reservations, or objections, it is important that the salesperson gain a genuine understanding of the customer's nature and circumstances. For this reason, the 9,9-oriented sales representative is likely to repeat, not in the same words that were spoken but according to his or her understanding of those words, the question or inquiry made by the customer, so as to verify it. In this way the salesperson can be assured of truly understanding, to the fullest extent possible, what the customer has in mind. By doing this the 9,9-oriented salesperson is in the best position to be able to answer any questions, according to the needs of the speaker, frequently summarizing an issue to ensure that they are still on the same wavelength.

The 9,9-oriented sales representative's receptivity is objective. It is unlikely that what is being said will be screened or distorted by mingling personal views with the customer's in such a way as to misinterpret or attach undue emphasis to certain aspects of the conversation. This salesperson is able to keep personal feelings separate so that they do not affect the capacity to hear objectively.

A 9,9-oriented salesperson understands and respects human relationships and appreciates that life is more than logic. While life should be guided by sound reason, it is nevertheless felt through emotions. The 9,9-oriented salesperson wants to help the customer constructively to find solutions to problems but also realizes that a customer has unique needs, emotions, feelings, and frustrations. All these may pull conversations away from the straight path of logic. The salesperson sees such departures not as unnecessary detours but rather as part of the complexity of human life.

Whatever the reason for an interruption, the 9,9-oriented salesperson has respect for the customer's feelings. The interruption may not seem to bring out any new and important information bearing on the subject of the sales interview, but it is certainly important from the customer's standpoint. So the salesperson feels that it is significant to understand why the customer interrupted at a particular point. Taking this kind of diagnostic attitude, the salesperson is in a sound position to appreciate the customer as a person. Comprehending how and what the customer thinks, and the underlying reasons for such thinking, is of background value in aiding the salesperson to see how the product might be presented so as to make it most understandable to the customer.

A 9,9-oriented salesperson does not attempt to keep customers always on the subject. To be irritated at apparently aimless meandering or by disconnected statements that seem to have no bearing on the topic of discussion is only to lose the deeper possibilities that a sales conversation presents. An interruption can be a key to gaining and holding customers' attention. Accepting interruptions conveys to customers that their thoughts, ideas, opinions, and feelings are acknowledged as important in the discussion, and this influences the purchase decision.

9,9-oriented emotions are valid responses to situations that are being viewed from an objective perspective. A 9,9-oriented person experiences emotions of antipathy toward those responsible for injustice, emotions of affection for those capable of responding in a like manner. The plight of people who are uninvolved and withdrawn is felt, and the conservative, emotional, "playing it safe" attitude of the person whose emotions are always in the middle is comprehended. Situations that are wrong are challenged and situations that are right acknowledged because 9,9 emotions are a trustworthy source of judgment. They provide a self-confident basis for coping constructively with situations across the whole spectrum of people encountered.

9,9: SOLUTION SEEKING 131

NEW CUSTOMERS

Opening

The 9,9 strategy is one of gaining access to the customer's feelings. When the salesperson meets the customer and asks, "What can I do to help?" an open invitation has been extended for the customer to present needs, interests, or problems. Where it goes from there is determined by how the prospect responds. The goal is first to understand the problem or need. For instance, the salesperson might open by inquiring whether the customer is acquainted with the product, has had any experience with it, or knows of others who have used it. In this way, the salesperson samples and tests the customer's degree of understanding so as to correct it if there are misconceptions and to avoid repetitiveness in the presentation.

The following is an example of the 9,9-oriented approach to opening with a prospective customer.

SP: Thank you for making the time available.

PC: You're welcome. What is it that you wish to discuss?

SP: This month our company is bringing onto the market a significantly new approach to servicing the standard units. We anticipate a heavy demand for this service.

PC: Why?

SP: My firsthand knowledge is through field contacts where high interest has been shown. This squares with what other people have reported to headquarters. We are convinced that the service we intend to provide meets a clear need.

I wanted to describe this new service to you because if you decide to go with it, it will significantly influence the number of potential customers in this area.

The size of your account will provide a base from which we can build personnel requirements in order to supply a larger demand.

In this sense you are a priority prospect, but, of course, the real issue is the contribution this service can make to your organization. I realize that our bringing the service into this market area is only of secondary interest to you.

PC: Well, it does sound interesting. I'd like to hear the specifics of your proposal.

This kind of opening conveys to the customer that time will be well used. The customer feels that it will be possible to make a sound judgment rather than a decision under conditions of incomplete understanding.

If the customer appears indifferent or reserved during this initial exploratory period, the 9,9-oriented salesperson seeks to understand the barriers to establishing an open business relationship. The salesperson might say, "After I've had the opportunity to present the facts, if you are still uninterested, at least we will both know that your disinterest is founded on logic and understanding. This is something that I can appreciate, but I would like to have an opportunity to establish what your reservations are, rather than simply assuming that we can't really provide you a useful product or service." The prospect may be stimulated to run a mental check on his or her current situation. The salesperson has not only stated a position but has also given the customer an opportunity to pursue and, it is hoped, to satisfy needs and desires in the discussion that follows. It becomes apparent to the customer that this salesperson is not trying to gain dominance. Nor is the approach indirect or coaxing. What the salesperson has to say is both purposeful and authentic, setting the keynote of frankness for a productive discussion.

What can be seen in this 9,9-oriented attitude is a high concern for the sale integrated with a high concern for people. The salesperson is alert to the individual needs of new prospects. Therefore, each initial contact is pursued in the same high-quality, optimistic way. From the beginning, the sales representative's confident (but not cocky) attitude impresses the customer with the salesperson's degree of knowledge. The 9,9-oriented salesperson gets down to brass tacks quickly, but only when it is felt that the customer is ready to focus attention on the real problem to be solved. Thus, speed in getting to the essentials is not accomplished in an abrasive way, but rather is achieved by aiding the customer to concentrate on the problem at hand without worries or doubts about the qualifications of the salesperson. The sales representative begins to develop an information bank as to the customer's needs and objectives by demonstrating a sincere interest and encouraging the customer's active involvement and participation. A customer is usually quick to discover whether a salesperson is acting in the customer's best

9,9: SOLUTION SEEKING   133

interest or whether the real aim is to make money at the customer's expense.

Identifying the Customer

The salesperson seeks to clarify early in the presentation whether the person being dealt with is a prospect or a representative of the real customer. If the person is a representative, the salesperson utilizes this intermediary as a resource for understanding the ultimate buyer's needs. If it is determined that the felt needs, as expressed by the intermediary, are not the same as the real needs of the ultimate customer, then the salesperson may seek a conference with the true decision maker. If this cannot be accomplished, the salesperson then takes the attitude of "Here is a description of what we can do for you. If you decide we are in a position to help you, I hope you will be back in touch."

Needs Analysis

The basic assumption of a 9,9-oriented salesperson is that the felt needs expressed by a prospect may not be the real needs. Whatever the case, the customer is still respected and not brushed aside or disregarded. This salesperson's objective is to help the customer distinguish between felt and real needs if a true difference exists.

The salesperson works to quickly establish an open give-and-take relationship in order to facilitate exploring real needs. The relationship is centered upon a collaborative effort, assisting the customer to understand what the salesperson has to offer and aiding the salesperson to understand what the customer truly needs. This results in an informal, spontaneous kind of interaction that is not person oriented or product-centered but is problem solving and need satisfying. This can be expressed as "I understand what you are saying. But what you might really want to consider as an alternative is the second option I mentioned."

The following conversation reflects the give-and-take between a 9,9-oriented salesperson and a prospective customer.

SP: Welcome. I'm Mary Smith.
PC: Hello. My name is John Turner.
SP: What can I do for you?

PC: Well, I'm not sure. I'm looking for something.

SP: Okay. Why don't you describe what you need and I'll see what I can do.

PC: We are looking for new supplies, and I wanted to explore the capacities and characteristics of your company.

SP: I'm glad you dropped in. I would appreciate knowing a little more about your interests in developing a relationship with a new supplier, and also what you already know about us. Then I may be able to provide some more useful information.

PC: I know the usual things, Dun & Bradstreet data, your advertising, and some of your customers. However, we have advertised for bids and you have not come in. Why is that?

SP: That's a good point. Our growth has been rapid and sound; we've avoided taking on more than we could chew in order to avoid a decline in quality or reliability. We've seen your ads, but only now are we in a position to respond.

PC: Why now and not last year?

SP: We've recently brought a new plant on stream and ironed out the bugs. We did not want to commit beyond what we could deliver. We now feel we are servicing all our contracts at a high-quality level. With this new plant, we have the capacity to serve a larger market in a first-class way. If you've got time, I'd like to arrange a plant visit, then you can get a better picture of us and our capabilities.

PC: That sounds good. We need a new supplier who can meet our needs.

SP: It would help me to know your requirements more precisely so I can determine how we might assist you in the soundest possible way.

This is the beginning of a solid relationship that is open and aboveboard and in all probability will grow into a sound business venture.

Establishing Expectations

The underlying assumption of the 9,9-oriented salesperson is that expectations established in the customer ought to be realistic and therefore unlikely to be violated at a future point in time. For this reason the salesperson works with the customer to explain all aspects of the product's availability, performance, delivery, service, and so on, and at the same time to ensure that this information is fully understood. This does not mean a salesperson overemphasizes product limitations, but

9,9: SOLUTION SEEKING

it does mean that objectivity and realism are maintained wherever limitations do exist.

The following conversation exemplifies the way in which a 9,9-oriented sales representative seeks to create valid customer expectations.

PC: It's unfortunate that you don't have it in stock. What can you promise by way of delivery?

SP: The best answer I can give you on that is from invoices which show the time lapse from ordering to delivery during the past 5 weeks. The average time is 4 days, the longest 6, and the shortest 3.

PC: That sounds reasonable. But can you promise that something won't change? History doesn't always repeat itself, you know, and I don't want to be the one to pay for it.

SP: Well, "promise" is a bit strong. I'm often in contact with the factory, and I feel sure the same conditions will prevail next week as have been for the past several weeks. Furthermore, if anything does change I'll give you my word to let you know right away.

PC: I expect that's about as much as I can ask. Okay, go ahead and order it for me.

Once the salesperson has gauged the customer's knowledge and dealt with any initial reservations, the interview can develop into a more detailed examination of the product and how it may contribute to solving the customer's problems and needs. The salesperson seeks to expand the customer's knowledge and understanding of the product and to deal with essential issues. These are considered based on their relative importance in terms of relating product facts to the customer's own situation.

Sales Presentation

A 9,9-oriented sales presentation is quite different from those previously discussed. A basic assumption is that the sales presentation is not a pitch, but an interview. Another is that the salesperson should already be clear about the customer's problem or needs as the basis for organizing the presentation. A third is that facts, data, logic, and evidence are key factors in bringing about a positive decision. Fourth is the view that customers are thinking people whose concerns and doubts should be dealt with respectfully.

What is a 9,9-oriented sales interview like, given these four assumptions? If, during the opening, it is discovered that the customer is not well informed about the product, the sales representative may begin by spelling out in a general way the benefits that can reasonably be expected from a purchase. The salesperson continues to aid the customer by defining and specifying aspects of particular problems that can be satisfied or solved with this product. The salesperson then describes the product in a way that correlates its functions with the customer's requirements. As the interview proceeds, the salesperson listens and questions so as to extend knowledge of the customer's situation and thus gain deeper understanding of how the product might provide the greatest benefit.

The 9,9-oriented salesperson is realistic. Product knowledge identifies the outer boundaries of the product's usefulness. Possible misunderstandings are anticipated and corrected during the interview by probing to ensure that the customer's knowledge is at a satisfactory level.

This kind of selling is a two-way street. It is versatile in the sense that the interview "fits" the needs and problem-solving requirements of the customer. This is achieved by actively involving the customer in the interview. As the customer comes to see the merits of the product, enthusiasm and conviction mount into a purchasing decision.

Acting on 9,9 assumptions, the salesperson seeks to gain the customer's participation and involvement at the same time as the product is being introduced. The presentation is not in the monotonous lecturer-to-listener form that many salespersons apply based on their faulty "description first, persuasion later" assumptions. There are many ways in which participation and involvement can be accomplished. One is for the salesperson to ask the customer certain questions—not of a temperature-taking variety, but questions that evoke responses that will result in greater involvement of the salesperson in the customer's situation. 9,9-oriented salespeople are ready and eager to develop firsthand understanding of the situation while increasing the customer's direct experience with the product. They enthusiastically probe, analyze, and project themselves into situations. As collaboration grows, they actively experiment with customers to see how their product can best be employed. This is far more than desk-level demonstration. It is experience by experiment in a situation of use. Here the salesperson is qualified

9,9: SOLUTION SEEKING

by knowledge of product and customer to speak with conviction as to how the product can function to provide a solution to the problem.

There are other natural and positive ways in which participation and involvement can be brought forward. One means is to enable a prospect to see, hear, touch, feel, handle, or try on the product, test it for size, or interact with it in other ways. As this is done, the 9,9-oriented salesperson introduces thoughts and ideas that help the prospect to understand feelings as they develop. As an understanding of the product itself and of the feelings toward it increases, the customer is building a rational basis of respect for the product. The customer can consider personal requirements and needs on a factual level and determine whether or not the product meets them. Emotions serve to support this understanding. Thus, the customer is fully and naturally committed. Evaluation is not tinged with skepticism that might have resulted under conditions of rhetoric and pressure. The salesperson has aided the customer's understanding, and the customer has become convinced based on evidence. A readiness to purchase has been established.

Give-and-take exchanges lead the salesperson to a realistic understanding of the prospect's needs, a restatement of which constitutes the beginning of the presentation as seen in the following.

SP: The problem you seek to solve (or need you wish to satisfy) can best be solved with an automatic sprinkler system, activated either by smoke or heat, which can deliver a certain number of gallons per minute in a designated area of space. Additionally, you have special problems related to the shape of several rooms such as the conference room and large spaces such as the research library and cafeteria. I know you want to keep the dollar expense per square foot down. Does that pretty well cover it?

PC: Yes, I think so.

SP: We have three alternatives then. Two are within your maximum, and I'd like to present these first. The third one is somewhat higher, but it has many valuable features, some of which we might be able to incorporate into the less expensive versions. We have mock-ups of the three different kinds of installations. First, I'd like to demonstrate how heat or smoke triggers them. Then we can examine the degree of saturation the units provide and the speed with which they complete their work. Any questions before we take a look?

PC: Not at the moment. Why don't you go ahead?

SP: Okay, I'll show the least expensive unit first. Let me solicit your collaboration in a little experiment that will illustrate how these work. Here I have a match, a stopwatch, and a pad. The way to get a firsthand feel of how this operates is to ignite the material located in the middle of the floor. Don't worry. You'll have time to light it and get out of the room. Now take the stopwatch and note elapsed time before the detector is activated and the nozzle begins to flow. This unit does not have an audible warning signal.

We have a duplicate room where we can test the speed with which heat activates this same detector. Carrying out an experiment like this takes very little time and provides you with concrete information on how the various systems work as well as allowing you to assess their capabilities. Repeating the same experiment with the second unit allows you to make a comparison of reaction time between the two. You might note that they both produce the same amount of water. Now the third unit is even more sensitive, providing a higher water volume and simultaneously activating an audio system in a location in the guard area which is coupled with a visual signal designating the precise location of the fire.

After the three systems are demonstrated,

SP: Now that you have seen the range of possibilities of all three lines, what do you think?

PC: Unit one would seem to meet our needs for large areas, while unit two appears best for those parts of our facility filled with flammable materials. Do you have any statistics pointing out the optimal unit for various areas?

SP: Yes, indeed. By the way, the third unit is particularly valuable for any area which houses highly valued records or equipment.

Without carrying the example any further, the problem-oriented, solution-seeking character of this situation is clear. Facts and data are acquired and insight into options is gained by virtue of a collaborative experience in which the customer is actively engaged as a participant in the experimental comparison.

Some products do not lend themselves to direct tryout or firsthand experience during the sales interview. For example, the product may be a "one-of-a-kind" machine that can be tested only after it has been delivered and installed. It may be a long-term service that cannot realistically be "sampled" during the interview. There are many ways of arranging for the customer to participate and to become involved other than to have been there in person. The salesperson can describe options that will enable the customer to visualize the product's use. The experiences of others who own the product or make use of it can be invaluable. The salesperson does not refer to others in a name-dropping way to suggest the prestige of the product. Rather, the description of how others use it aids the prospect to experience it to some extent, thereby coming to know more thoroughly what the product is like. Where possible, the salesperson arranges visits to users and tries to be with the customer during these visits. While the customer is seeing and hearing how others utilize the product or service, new ideas are being introduced that can increase personal involvement.

Objections

The kind of participation and involvement that is central to establishing a creative interplay between thoughts and emotions comes to the forefront in the area of objections. The 9,9-oriented salesperson's attitude toward objections is one of the most significant attributes that can lead to a valid sale and a satisfied customer.

Almost invariably customers raise doubts and reservations when viewing the product for the first time. The salesperson recognizes this fact and accepts it at face value. Opportunities are created for the customer to express and discuss misgivings, particularly in the early phases and also throughout the interview. The salesperson knows that if these are not brought out, they are likely to persist and to influence the customer's thinking and feelings adversely. When these doubts are expressed openly, an opportunity exists to respond to them and to remove them as barriers to forward progress.

There are several kinds of reservations. Some are the result of a lack of information. Initially, the customer may be hesitant to reveal objections, wanting to get a better idea of the kind of person being dealt with before leveling. If the salesperson has a tendency to suppress disagreement, the customer will not feel safe. Quite likely the customer will simply withhold objections, looking for an opportunity to terminate the interview. The 9,9-oriented salesperson openly invites a customer's queries and comments whether favorable or not. The salesperson seeks to understand the customer's views, asking supplementary questions to clarify any misconceptions. Only then is the salesperson in a position to provide the necessary information to the customer so as to dissolve initial objections and to gain support for the product.

Other objections may be based on misinformation about the function, quality, usefulness, and other attributes of the product. The salesperson who invites the customer to participate in examining the product creates opportunities for finding out what these misunderstandings actually are. Misinformation can then be replaced with valid information to remove the objection.

Sometimes unstated objections are founded upon reservations and doubts rooted solely in the customer's feelings. The customer may be quite unaware that emotions are affecting personal objectivity. By inviting the customer to express feelings about the product and listening attentively to what is said, the salesperson may come to understand what is bothering the customer. For example, the product may be the scapegoat of a customer's strong general prejudice against a whole class of items—the customer may object to a chemical product or treatment because it is considered "artificial." Even in this instance, however, a customer's initial reactions can be replaced with the enthusiasm of emotional involvement if the true objection is pinpointed at the outset. A salesperson can deal with such illogical and emotion-based reactions calmly, providing facts within a structure of thinking that allows the customer to gain better insights into what the product can and cannot do. If the salesperson is genuinely trying to bring out the customer's reservations and objections for discussion—rather than looking for ammunition to win arguments—the customer will usually recognize this honest motivation and respect the salesperson for it. Generally, people do respond to authentic attempts by others to understand their points of view. This in turn often helps them to respond constructively when new information is presented.

The following illustrates a 9,9 approach to dealing with reservations and objections.

SP: Do you have any other questions?
PC: Yes, there is one. Isn't it likely to be out of date within a year or so? Innovations are coming so fast that a better piece of equipment

9,9: SOLUTION SEEKING 141

is likely to appear before I'd get any use out of this one, don't you think?

SP: That's quite possible. The rate of obsolescence seems to accelerate each year.

PC: Then perhaps I should postpone making a decision. This is a once-in-a-lifetime choice for me.

SP: I know you like this product, and I'd like to see you have it, but I certainly respect your feelings. However, I wonder if the situation won't be the same next year? Then you put it off and put it off, never experiencing the enjoyment that you want.

PC: That's a good point.

SP: The fact is that changes are gradual and evolutionary, and they are both major and minor. Several years pass between *major* innovations. This particular equipment contains the latest technology, suggesting that it won't be significantly improved on for some time. Minor changes will be numerous, but a major innovation will probably not be justified for a good number of years. So the risk/enjoyment ratio is very likely to be in your favor.

When a customer's objection is based on genuine and valid points, the 9,9 approach is to acknowledge the objection and then openly explore realistic possibilities for dealing conclusively with it. This may involve probing in order to get to the root of the customer's thinking. More often than not, when an objection or disagreement is discussed candidly, one of two things may occur. Either it turns out to be less important than it first appeared, or creative ways can be found for having the product or service modified to correspond more fully with the customer's real needs.

This way of openly confronting conflict promotes true understanding and respect between salesperson and customer. It provides the best method for achieving a sound basis of resolution of points of disagreement. Emotions and feelings are brought out into the open, permitting those that are barriers to be eliminated and replaced with enthusiastic convictions and commitment. Selling a customer in a way that results in having expectations violated is avoided. Of course, it may take longer to reach a 9,9 consensus than it would for a 9,1-oriented salesperson to overwhelm and crush an objection. However, the 9,9 approach is time-conserving in the long run. By permitting people to resolve their disagreements after examining the facts, data, and reasoning, a true meeting of minds can occur. This is an authentic problem-solving approach where the salesperson is as committed to fulfilling the customer's needs as the customer is interested in making a sound purchase.

The 9,9 orientation is based on an assumption that valid ends have a greater likelihood of being reached when valid means are employed in approaching them. Thus, integrity is basic to the 9,9 orientation. Truth is sought through openness and candor, acknowledging existing limitations.

Where statements involve interpretation and judgment, the 9,9-oriented salesperson feels no reluctance about giving a personal point of view. In this way possibilities that may not be subject to verification can still be voiced. But notice is given to the listener when a statement is fact-based and when it is a subjective interpretation. In this way the customer knows what statements involve facts and what statements involve opinions. Thus, the customer can weigh the predictability of a statement and interpret it accordingly.

Closing

The 9,9 approach to closing is often a foregone conclusion to the purchase because reservations and doubts have been identified, discussed, and resolved along the way. The closing may contain a number of distinctive features. One of these is summing up. This is not the loaded machine-gun summary of benefits that many salespeople employ; nor is it a bald statement of pros and cons that leaves customers feeling right back where they started. The 9,9 orientation to summing up aids the customer to crystallize thinking and to weigh the decision in the light of all major points previously developed. The salesperson helps the customer reach a positive decision because the decision can be considered and confirmed in a totally integrated context. The last issues discussed may be the most vivid in the customer's thinking, but they are not necessarily the most significant.

Another feature is active checking with the customer on all points to ensure they are well understood and to permit the customer to pose any additional inquiries. Although further reservations and doubts are not encouraged, the customer is provided the opportunity to identify ones that may not yet have been expressed. Finally, a 9,9-oriented

9,9: SOLUTION SEEKING   143

salesperson can be expected to express convictions and enthusiasm about the benefits that the customer can anticipate from making a positive decision.

> **SP:** We've concluded that the product is what you're after, that the price is competitive, that warranty considerations offer the necessary protection, and that we can deliver against your requirements. Are there other considerations or questions we haven't given needed attention?
>
> **PC:** No, that about covers it.
>
> **SP:** Well, if you are satisfied, then let me wrap it up.
>
> **PC:** No, don't just wrap it up, write it up. I'll have someone here Tuesday around ten to accept delivery. Thanks a lot. It's been a pleasure working with you.

The salesperson avoids increasing the pressure if a positive decision is not reached at this point. Instead, strong interest is shown in understanding the customer's reasons for not closing. This is not for the purpose of knocking them down. Rather, the salesperson seeks to gain a fuller understanding of these undisclosed barriers that are blocking the customer's positive decision. This can aid in anticipating similar problems with future prospects. It may yield valuable information to transmit back to the company so that real problems in the product's performance, quality, or pricing can be dealt with and solved. Finally, this kind of exit interview or debriefing provides a good basis for a later return call that can make a difference in sales effectiveness. The prospect's situation may change or the salesperson may have a different product or terms on which to negotiate, and a good exit feeling can open the door to future business.

Research and experience support the conclusion that sales interviews conducted in a 9,9-orientation are most likely to pass through the various steps in the sequence and to reach a successful closing. When easy rapport has been established, the result is a friendly give-and-take, which quickly leads to a needs analysis. The needs analysis penetrates the expressed needs and identifies the real ones that underlie the prospect's motivation to buy in the first place. The presentation is functional in the sense of matching product characteristics to real needs and finding an ideal or optimum fit. Objections, reservations, and doubts are invited, identified, and resolved, with pricing brought into the presentation along the way so that it is not an obstacle at the end. Nothing beyond simple mechanics remains to be completed at the point of closing, and these matters are carried to conclusion in a congenial atmosphere of mutual satisfaction. The salesperson is pleased to have contributed to the customer by facilitating a sound purchase decision. The customer is pleased because personal convictions about the purchase are self-reinforcing.

ESTABLISHED BUSINESS

When the interview has been brought to a successful closing, an excellent foundation has been laid for repeat orders and expanding business. The 9,9 orientation with its knowledge-based and problem-solving character impacts customers in a way that makes them responsive to future sales possibilities. The customer is likely to summon the salesperson when confronted with a problem for which the salesperson's product may supply a solution.

Maintaining Accounts

A 9,9-oriented salesperson can be expected to do several things to maintain established business relationships. One is to keep in touch with the customer on a regular schedule. The frequency of visiting by phone or on a face-to-face basis is determined by analyzing the customer's situation and estimating when there is a likelihood of new orders. The salesperson also follows up to check on possible dissatisfactions or reservations that the customer may feel but has not yet raised. In this way difficulties can be spotted early and steps taken to correct the situation. Another way of maintaining accounts is to arrange for special contacts and visits whenever new developments become evident or whenever there are changes in company products about which the customer needs to know. In maintaining the relationship in these ways, the salesperson reduces the risk of the customer's being taken over by competitors and increases the possibility of expanding business with established accounts.

Complaints

Complaints are a warning signal to the 9,9-oriented salesperson. Unless there is knowledge of them and they are dealt with promptly and effectively, they can grow into deeper customer discontent. This sales representative is prepared to take action immediately. No matter how small the complaint may appear, the salesperson realizes that it may not seem small to the customer.

The salesperson meets with the customer as quickly as possible after a complaint has been voiced. The customer is encouraged to describe the problem and to express feelings and opinions as to what he or she thinks will alleviate the situation. Where the product's or the company's performance is at fault, the salesperson frankly acknowledges this, making it clear that the customer's openness is appreciated. Using product knowledge while staying within the limits of personal technical ability, the salesperson outlines the best way of righting the situation, checking it out with specialists in the company and reaching agreement with the customer on what should be done. Follow-up ensures that the necessary corrective actions result.

Rush Business

Rush business is both a hazard and an opportunity. It offers the possibility of increasing sales volume. The hazard, however, is twofold. On the one hand, when a customer's expectations cannot be met, competitors who are able to satisfy the need may usurp this business. The other danger is that while it may be possible to fill rush orders as a means of getting a sale, the expense to the sales organization of doing so may make the effort unprofitable.

Thus the 9,9-oriented salesperson probes to understand the necessity of a rush and to see if there are other ways to handle the situation. If there are no other ways, the salesperson discusses the problem with Manufacturing or Distribution to see whether or not it can be handled, and if so, in what manner. Sometimes rescheduling of deliveries can be arranged without causing inconvenience to other customers. In any case, the salesperson stays with the problem until the customer is satisfied or until the possibility of serving the customer has become unrealistic. This may mean going out to find an emergency source of supply, often resulting in no personal profit to the salesperson. The customer is aided to think through requirements in advance in order to anticipate needs and avoid rush orders in the future.

The information exchanged between salesperson and customer leads to realistic and valid expectations. It is straight shooting. There is no hesitation on the salesperson's part to promise delivery. But this salesperson will estimate and state clearly, on a realistic basis, how much certainty or uncertainty there is that delivery is possible on the target date.

SELF-MANAGEMENT

Self-management is an apt description of the 9,9-oriented salesperson, who possesses the skills of setting personal selling objectives and applying energy in result-oriented ways. Thus, this salesperson is capable of autonomous action. Because the orientation is a problem-solving one, not only can self-direction be maintained but the salesperson is also alert to changes in situations that call for shifts in direction.

An unsuccessful closing is not taken as a personal disaster but is reviewed for actions that might have been taken or not taken that could have meant the difference between success and failure in this instance. Having a learning-oriented attitude, the salesperson reviews each failure as well as each success, carrying out a critique of why the effort went well or why it did not. Critique is the most important form of learning that a salesperson can engage in, and when done well, lack of success with one prospect may provide a source of insight as to how to achieve better results with the next. This is the source of the resilience that characterizes the 9,9-oriented salesperson.

The 9,9-oriented salesperson has an experimental attitude, continually searching for ways to strengthen strategies that work well and to discover new ones by trying to solve the unknown or to comprehend what is not understood in each selling situation. Feedback from customers is used, both in the ongoing selling situation and in a later critique of efforts, to aid this salesperson to learn from the experiences of both strong and weak features in the presentation and approach.

SCHEDULING AND TIME MANAGEMENT. I put effort into scheduling my activities in terms of sales objectives. In this way it is possible to perform all my responsibilities, and emergencies are rare.

PROSPECTING. Prospecting is vital to sales growth. I see every customer as a gatekeeper who can open the door for new business. Existing customers are analyzed for the categories they represent, with effort concentrated on new contacts in the most favorable categories first.

SERVICING. I see that my commitments are met and top service is provided. By following through with the customer, I try to anticipate servicing requirements. The customer has paid for sound treatment, and continued satisfaction increases the strength of the account.

EXPENSES. The expenses under my control are essential in doing business, and my integrity and prudence provide guidance as I incur them. Full value in terms of sales results should be realized from the money I spend.

SELF-STEERING. I improve my skills and increase my professional contribution by analyzing reasons for failures as well as successes.[10]

Many products of today are so complex that it has become impossible for a single salesperson to represent them in a comprehensive way. This is particularly so when customers' needs involve systems concepts, such as in advanced process control, traffic and transportation, research and development, and in defense-supply industry contexts. Conversely, a very large company's purchasing agents and the potential users of the products or system may be specialists as well. In view of the possible size of the total sale, both supplier and customer companies may find it most convenient to negotiate an overall purchasing contract or set of contracts. This is done after the whole range of products or the entire system has been presented by a team of specialist salespersons and considered by a team of specialist purchasing agents.

This kind of situation calls for *teamwork*. It entails cooperative effort by two or more salespersons who, together and jointly but not separately and individually, possess the full capability for representing the total product. On the purchasing side too, integrated knowledge and a coordinated approach are essential. Aside from benefits obtained from comprehensive and large-scale selling and purchasing, much useful operational knowledge can be shared and new insights gained. Specific 9,9-oriented team selling skills are not dis-

148 GUIDEPOSTS FOR EFFECTIVE SALESMANSHIP

cussed here. However, the character of teamwork is more fully analyzed in other publications.

CUSTOMER REACTIONS

A 9,9 sales orientation has the greatest likelihood of achieving positive consequences with customers of any Grid style. This is because 9,9 assumptions provide a valid basis for getting a fit between the salesperson's product and the customer's real needs. The approach is to work with every customer in a 9,9-oriented way and thereby to enjoy the probability that 9,9-oriented buyer reactions can be elicited, regardless of the customer's "natural" Grid style.

9,1

A high concern for the customer's problem appeals to the 9,1-oriented customer's objective of making a good purchase, although this customer is likely to find that the salesperson cannot be pressured into unjustifiable concessions. Being open and aboveboard, the 9,9 orientation does not arouse suspiciousness, or if this is already present, it tends to reduce unwarranted fears of being "taken." The salesperson is responsive to the 9,1-oriented customer's objective of "getting the most the traffic can bear" and to defensive posture toward making a purchase decision. It is anticipated in advance that this customer will act in a provocative manner and have negative, skeptical attitudes.

Thus, the first point of entry is to develop trust by providing general background knowledge. The salesperson begins by introducing some easy questions of a sort that do not suggest any pressure on the customer to admit ignorance. The purpose is to capture interest by first stimulating the customer's thinking. Queries and negative reactions provide the salesperson with various clues as to what additional information is required in order to adequately comprehend the possibilities in a situation. Next the salesperson elicits descriptions of what the customer hopes to accomplish and any problems that might be anticipated in the transaction. At this point the salesperson is in an excellent position to proceed deeper and to start putting the "nuts and bolts" together. By getting the customer to compare knowledge and desires simultaneously, the salesperson develops a basis for making sure that the customer's expectations are in concert with realistic possibilities.

It is rare for a 9,9-oriented salesperson to place a customer in the position of fighting back or to allow a win-lose battle. However, if this occurs, the 9,9-oriented approach is to find out the real reason for the resentment and to work for a solution that prevents it from becoming a problem again. In these ways the 9,9-oriented salesperson helps the 9,1-oriented customer to become convinced as to the soundness of a decision that meets personal desires and needs.

1,9

Because it is predicated on understanding the customer's situation and has a high concern for the customer, a 9,9 sales approach meets the 1,9-oriented customer's desire to be liked. The salesperson quickly senses the risks that are inherent in a swift and easy closing. The customer's trust and respect for this sales representative are increased as a result of being involved in a sound purchase decision.

Rather than starting with a knowledge-based presentation as might be done with a 9,1-oriented prospect, the salesperson begins by probing the 1,9-oriented customer's desires as a means of gaining a deeper understanding of needs and wants. The salesperson might anticipate finding that the customer's desires are based more on emotions than on realistic assessments. The task then is to supplement the customer's knowledge and to identify these unrealistic expectations, thus ensuring that expectations are well grounded. Customers are in a position to make more complete and definite decisions when the salesperson's approach provides facts and data in the logical and persuasive way characteristic of a 9,9 orientation.

The salesperson communicates friendliness by not making an issue of the customer's lack of thoroughness and thus not embarrassing the customer. The difficult point is that a 1,9-oriented customer is prepared to listen and accept whatever information is provided. So the salesperson needs to test continuously to make sure that the customer is not past the point of saturation—that there is a true comprehension of what is being said and that each additional point is being related to what has been explained previously.

When 1,9-oriented customers have made a definite decision, they are not pushed to "go along" just because the logic is reasonable and expectations seem realistic. Involvement and participation are used to arouse their interest and to develop genuine convictions. In this way, the 9,9-oriented salesperson can readily bring 1,9-oriented prospects into agreement, based on confidence and a genuine understanding of evidence.

1,1

The 9,9-oriented sales approach has the likelihood of activating a different backup style in the dominant 1,1-oriented prospect and stimulating an interest in the transaction that would otherwise be dormant. Efforts to overcome 1,1 apathy are manifest in the way the salesperson works with knowledge and enthusiasm to discover what might create a spark of interest on the part of the customer. Initial inquiries are briefly phrased and aimed at eliciting some yes-or-no answers to determine whether pickup is occurring. The objective is to activate a definitive response or to locate a foundation of understanding to build on in order to successfully complete a sale.

5,5

The 5,5-oriented customer is responsive to a 9,9-oriented salesperson because the customer is treated as a person worthy of diplomacy and respect. The salesperson is not oversolicitous but provokes the customer's readiness to participate and to be involved. Being knowledgeable about competitors' products, the salesperson steers the customer's interest into thinking along problem-solving channels, ferreting out real needs and desires. The 9,9 approach is to convert the prospect's customary reliance on reputation and prestige into a greater readiness to consider innovative and creative solutions. When prospects can see how a positive decision fits their actual needs, tentativeness changes to a sound basis for action. The salesperson adds confidence to this by aiding the customer to gain insight into how the sale will take shape and how the net result will meet personal desires and give true satisfaction.

9,9

The greatest personal reward from selling for the 9,9-oriented salesperson is success in a transaction with a 9,9-oriented client. The approach clicks immediately with such a customer. Not only is the interview geared to responding to the customer's needs, but it is conducted on the basis of facts, data, and logical reasoning. Efforts are made to ensure that the customer's expectations about the transaction are realistic and valid. From then on both customer and salesperson become consultants to one another as to the soundest actions to take. The salesperson's order of presentation follows valid principles for creating conditions of customer involvement and participation in problem solving, with a successful outcome being the most likely result.

This salesperson possesses great strength through the logical use of in-depth knowledge of the product and competitors, in conjunction with the orientation to sell solutions that fit the customer's needs. The importance of realistic expectations regarding what the transaction will or will not accomplish is equally clear to both the salesperson and the customer. Both search for a basis of creating realistic and valid expectations, knowing that this is the foundation for making sound decisions. Reciprocal attitudes make participation and involvement a natural process of give-and-take, making it easy for the salesperson to discuss limitations openly and without fear that this discussion might itself be a reason for a negative purchase decision.

Versatility as a 9,9 Characteristic

What are the implications of adopting a 9,9 orientation toward every customer contacted? Does this kind of solution selling restrict a salesperson, extinguishing spontaneity and stereotyping behavior? Is this salesperson an idealistic "saint with a sample case?" No—a 9,9 orientation opens new doors to becoming more versatile, creative, and individual-centered in one's sales approach.

This is because solution selling within the 9,9 orientation gives a salesperson such versatility. By thinking in problem-solving terms, the sales representative is more likely to get on the same wavelength as the customer and to do so quickly.

The process of formulating issues in terms of alternatives and options, and weighing the pros and cons of each, increases the likelihood that a "best-fit" solution will be found. Gearing the presentation to facts, data, and logic promotes more realistic expectations of the consequences of a purchase decision. Conducting the interview as a two-person participation-and-involvement situation increases the probability that the consistent appeal to the customer's logic and profoundest self-interest can resonate with personal emotions and feelings.

All this generates a customer's respect and increases appreciation for the salesperson's competence. The result is that customer confidence is heightened and any doubts that might lead to reluctance to purchase are reduced. The greatest versatility, then, comes from 9,9-oriented solution selling, which opens up more situational variables to examination, produces a deeper, more valid human contact between salesperson and customer, and gears a sales presentation to need-fulfilling performance rather than the creation of hopeful illusions that would later be followed by disillusion.

Another aspect of how to increase the possibility of 9,9 problem solving between salesperson and customer can now be pointed out. It has been repeatedly observed that most customers have a wide range and variety of Grid style attitudes that can influence their personal behavior in different situations. This means that almost anyone can operate under a 9,9 problem-solving orientation should the right circumstances be created. Thus, the conclusion is that a salesperson should try to maintain a 9,9 sales approach because, other things equal, it is the approach most likely to produce greater sales effectiveness. With this approach, the salesperson stands a good chance of being able to lead the customer into adopting the same orientation. Then their two attitudes complement each other to the advantage and benefit of both. The salesperson has the greatest likelihood of effecting a sale and the customer has the greatest likelihood of making a sound purchase when the action of each is based upon convictions that are reinforced in a 9,9 way.

Therefore, in comparison with other Grid styles, a 9,9 orientation has the greatest likelihood of achieving positive sales results. This is true with customers who may themselves be oriented to another of the Grid styles. There is a simple reason for this. 9,9 assumptions provide a valid basis for structuring a transaction to the client's real needs. It is the sizzle in the 9,9 solution that satisfies the customer, not the noise that surrounds the sale.

SUMMARY

The 9,9-oriented salesperson keeps in perspective the complex and subtle factors that enter into ensuring that a sale is profitable. This sales representative does not automatically assume that nothing should be allowed to stand in the way of an order, as is likely to be true for a 9,1 orientation, or that nothing is too much for a customer, as a 1,9 orientation might suggest. Rather, the attitude is "My business is satisfying consumer needs while making a profit for my company. When I must put something before the profitability of a transaction, all related factors must be considered very carefully. My objective is profitable selling with full customer satisfaction. This is in the best long-term interest of my company, my customers, and myself." The salesperson is constantly striving to upgrade the product that is being purchased by established accounts, as well as to maintain the profit margins on sales. In this way sales volume can be increased, dollar volume of earnings improved, and profitability heightened.

All things considered, then, it does appear that a 9,9 orientation runs the fewest risks, particularly when viewed in a long-term perspective. It brings the greatest possible benefits of expanded sales volume and customer satisfaction from both new and established accounts.

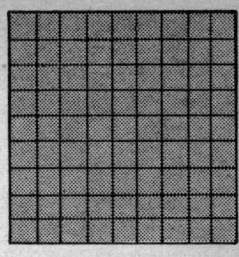

MIXED THEORIES

8

The basic sales orientations, along with the deceptive facades that we will encounter in Chapter 9, constitute the major approaches found in salesperson-customer relationships. There are, however, a few special cases that involve more than one theory. These include a reliance on two theories at the same time or in quick succession, or shifting from one theory to another to another, depending upon the circumstances being encountered with the customer. Since none of these involve shifting from dominant to backup, they should be studied as major orientations to selling.

PATERNALISM AND MATERNALISM: TWO THEORIES SIMULTANEOUSLY PRESENT

This orientation combines two basic Grid styles into one. The 9,1-oriented direction is in the interest of seeing to it that the customer buys what is needed and does not make a mistake. The 1,9-oriented aspect is in the feeling of love and affection for the customer and simultaneously in the desire for the customer to return love and affection in exchange for the strong and "correct" guidance that the salesperson asks the customer to accept.

The paternalistic or maternalistic orientation is of importance because it "locks" reluctant customers in, obligating them to make purchases even though they may prefer not to do so. Paternalism and maternalism are considered here as equivalent, as the same. The apparent difference is more superficial than real, and the only significant distinction is that paternalistic salespeople are usually men while maternalistic salespeople are usually women.

How a paternalistic (or maternalistic) salesperson puts a lock on the customer is not difficult to understand. The hard-driving salesperson knows what the customer needs. Furthermore, this knowledge is based upon a true understanding of the problem confronted or the need that the customer wishes to satisfy. The salesperson insists that the customer buy the product without bringing the customer to a sound understanding of why, yet not in a coercive, hard-sell way either. Rather, it is in the sense of "father knows best" or "you must take this for your own good."

Customers sense that the paternalistic (or maternalistic) salesperson has their own best interests in mind. It is this feature that makes it so hard for a customer to resist the strong recommendations of the salesperson. Yet the customer may resent being treated like a child, without a will of his or her own. The buildup of resentment is greater under this orientation than with any other. The reason is that the customer wants to exercise independent thinking but is "not allowed" to do so. All the opportunities from which the customer might have gained deeper insight into the situation are blocked in advance. The only option available to escape this paternalistic prison may be for the customer to buy and leave rather than to resist and stay. Being sold in this paternalistic manner is resented even more than being forced into purchasing from a 9,1-oriented sales representative. The reason is that a customer can fight back when being pushed around by a 9,1-oriented salesperson; however, to fight back against a paternalist is to fight against what seems to be one's own best interests. Resentment is stored up inside because it cannot be expressed.

The customer is unlikely to return once out of the paternalistic selling relationship. This is due to the fact that the customer wants to avoid getting trapped into the same untenable situation again.

TWO-HAT APPROACH: TWO THEORIES IN QUICK SUCCESSION

Two-hat selling also combines a 9,1 with a 1,9 orientation, but in a different way than the paternalistic approach. The salesperson sells according to a 9,1 orientation of "all work and no play," really pushing to get the sale and overwhelming the customer if necessary. Once the sale is completed, the salesperson's interest shifts 180 degrees away from the product and is focused instead on the customer. The customer becomes the center of intense personal interest, with the salesperson inquiring about home, family, vocational and avocational interests, vacation plans, and other such topics. Any or all of these subjects are brought into discussion in a genuine and heartfelt way. The customer is no longer a customer but a person toward whom the salesperson feels warmth and affection and from whom the salesperson wants love and approval.

The salesperson has shifted from a 9,1 to a 1,9 orientation, not as a backup but as the second phase in the sales relationship. This can even happen at some point along the way when the salesperson has decided that there will be no closing. The 180-degree shift occurs as if the sale had been completed. In either case one hat is worn during the sales presentation—that is the 9,1 orientation. The other hat is worn after the sales transaction has been completed or abandoned—that is the 1,9 orientation.

Some customers bask in this kind of treatment, feeling that the salesperson's appreciation of them is the result of their sound decision, whether this is to buy or not to buy. The salesperson feels the need to behave in this way in order to avoid having the customer leave unsatisfied, for this would result in the salesperson experiencing feelings of rejection. Such emotions in turn lead the salesperson to experience guilt for having been too pushy. Utilizing this 180-degree shift, the salesperson is able to pacify any developing feelings of remorse by establishing a warm and responsive atmosphere through the use of a 1,9 orientation.

Whether the salesperson's approach is paternalistic (or maternalistic), or of the two-hat variety, thoughts and feelings for the customer as a problem-solving, need-satisfying, or decision-making person are distorted. The salesperson is neither a consultant nor a facilitator, and is not engaged in a collaboration with the customer as the customer seeks to make a decision. In the case of paternalism, however, few customers (except possibly those who buy from a 1,9-oriented sales representative) feel gratified at the kind of treatment they receive. The opposite may be true with regard to the two-hat approach, however, with many customers feeling gratified at the warm and generous treatment when the presentation is over.

The salesperson operating from either of these points of view sees the customer as a purchaser and as a human being, but not in the integrated way of a 9,9 sales orientation. By comparison, the 9,9 orientation provides information as to how the salesperson sees the customer and works with this customer in such a way as to create a relationship premised upon mutual trust and respect.

STATISTICAL 5,5 (SITUATIONAL SELLING)

Still another theory needs to be introduced. It is the contingency approach, better referred to as statistical 5,5 and often spoken of as situational selling.

When a statistical 5,5-oriented salesperson deals with customers, how they are treated is contingent upon the way the customers present themselves. If the customer seems to be suspicious and defensive, the salesperson reacts in a 9,1 way, often with the result of provoking antagonism or a fight. To be tough with a tough customer is more important than making a sale. If the customer's orientation seems to be in the 1,9 area, the salesperson approaches this person from a 1,9 orientation, acting like a warm and loving human being, following the customer in preference to exercising leadership. If the customer does not move the discussion into a consideration of the product, the salesperson does not do so either, and the conversation may range far and wide. However, the salesperson does not wish to be seen as pushy by a 1,9-oriented customer and therefore lets the customer take the lead, preferring to lose the sale rather than come on strong.

If the customer is in a 1,1 orientation, the salesperson adopts this orientation as the basis for handling the situation. If the customer asks no questions, the salesperson offers no information. If the customer appears disinterested, the salesperson avoids any show of concern. Thus, a statistical 5,5-oriented salesperson dealing with a 1,1 customer may be seen as not caring one way or the other, and the sales interview may be of short duration indeed.

When dealing with a 5,5-oriented customer, the statistical 5,5-oriented salesperson takes the lead from the customer but now is prepared to play the political game and to talk about community events, sports, or whatever topic the customer introduces. The statistical 5,5-oriented salesperson, in other words, prefers to be known by the customer as one who is well informed and well situated rather than as a person who goes for the sale.

When approached by a 9,9-oriented customer, the statistical 5,5-oriented salesperson quickly adopts a problem-solving or needs-analysis orientation that helps the customer develop the information necessary for making a sound decision. The statistical 5,5-oriented sales representative prefers to be seen by this customer as one who really knows the product thoroughly and is ready to discuss objections to it and its inherent characteristics. This is in preference to being seen as a person who abandons these values in the interest of making a sale.

The statistical 5,5-oriented salesperson, in other words, adopts an approach to the customer that is contingent upon the perceived characteristics of the customer, jumping around the Grid in order to match the sales approach to what is seen to be the dominant characteristics of the customer. In this way, the statistical 5,5-oriented salesperson is seen as all things to all people and may be seen by colleagues or the sales manager as highly successful with some customers and highly unsuccessful with others.

The situational selling approach is popular because it is seen to be flexible and offers the salesperson a lot of legroom. However, the Achilles' heel of the statistical 5,5 approach is that it sacrifices a basically sound selling relationship for whatever may appear acceptable at any given point in time. It does so by unwittingly allowing the customer to be the leader. The salesperson, who should be an expert, abandons that role in preference to following the lead of the customer.

The option is for the salesperson to use the sales situation as an opportunity to lead the customer through thoroughness, data, and logic, introduced under conditions of mutuality and respect, to develop the kind of conviction essential for making a purchase based upon full understanding.

SUMMARY

Three different combinatory or mixed sales theories have been described.[11] These are approaches to selling that rely on more than one theory simultaneously or in quick succession, not in the sense of dominant and backup, but in the sense of relying equally on two or more theories as the basis for establishing a dominant approach.

Paternalism (maternalism) rests upon a 9,1 orientation to push for a sound decision, but the salesperson does so in the best interest of the customer, in this way being concerned with earning the customer's love and approval. The two-hat theory couples the 9,1 and 1,9 orientations from the standpoint of pushing the product in a 9,1-oriented way but at some point in time, either when a sale has been locked in or when the prospect of making a sale has been abandoned, shifting 180 degrees and showering great interest on the customer as a person. The reason for this may be a need to assuage feelings of guilt at having pushed too hard. Having shown oneself to be a warm and loving person, one can then feel that the hardness of the push in the initial phase was not resented by the customer because tensions were washed away in the latter phase.

The statistical 5,5-oriented salesperson relies on all theories on a contingency basis, which leads to situational selling, the approach utilized premised upon what will match the customer's dominant attitude.

Thus, a 9,1 orientation is matched to a 9,1 orientation on the part of the customer, and so on through the other dominant Grid styles.

None of these approaches to selling is Machiavellian. All are authentic and no deception on the part of the salesperson is involved or intended. Rather, it is the salesperson's direct assumption that this way of dealing with a customer is the best all the way around.

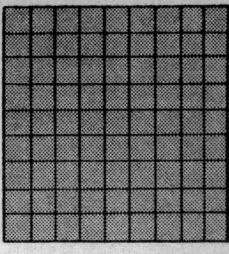

ON BEING DECEPTIVE

Many sales representatives are straightforward, but others are intentionally deceptive and manipulative. This kind of salesperson is a facade strategist, working from behind a false front.

Some sales companies have buildings with a facade. Maybe this front appears to be fully integrated with the rest of the building. There may be no special ornamentation to give the entire building a grandiose appearance. But the front of the building, as you may be able to see it from above or behind, gives a false impression of the character of the whole structure. Looking down from above, you may see a one-story building lying behind a three-story facade—what looks like a palace from the front looks like a barn from behind. Such a facade may intrigue the customer to enter. This is a relatively harmless deception. No one is hurt, and once inside, the customer can walk around and deal with people as they are.

A personal facade is something else

again. It is carefully prepared but no less phony. Appearances, expressions, words, actions, and deeds are all part of a facade strategy. The primary motivation is trickery, with the facade serving as a front for concealing true intentions.

DIFFERENCES BETWEEN A GRID STYLE AND A FACADE

The pure theories of the 9,1; 1,9; 1,1; 5,5; and 9,9 orientations all share a basic attribute. They arise naturally from the particular sets of assumptions that salespeople adopt. The person who employs one or more of these strategies is doing so based on the belief that this is how one should be performing as a salesperson or because it has become second nature. Although the consequences of this behavior may not be consistent with what was anticipated, this behavior is nevertheless genuine. There is no counterfeit involved.

A facade, on the other hand, is a cover for deception, intrigue, and trickery. When a selling facade is used, the goal is to achieve, by indirect or roundabout ways, a sales result that, it is thought, would be unattainable if actual intentions were revealed or if pertinent facts and issues were confronted. Thus, a facade builder tries to avoid allowing real intentions to appear on the surface. The approach is manipulative and devious.

Certainly there are tactics and "sure-fire" sales techniques that numerous sales representatives use as tools of their trade. Salespeople who have adopted 9,1 and 5,5 orientations are particularly attracted to such techniques, but they are used as tools and gimmicks in order to extract a purchase decision. There is a basic philosophy of honest purpose underlying them. They are not based on subterfuge.

KEY FEATURES OF FACADES

A general feature of any facade is that the facade strategist avoids revealing personal thoughts and feelings. However, the customer is given the impression that the sales representative is being open and candid. There is little or nothing in what is said or done that prompts the customer to probe or question motivations, for they seem quite obvious. Yet the customer is deceived by a facade, failing to recognize the salesperson's true intentions.

The reasons why people employ facades are as varied as their underlying intentions. However, there are two principal motivations that serve as the underpinnings of any facade. The one most widespread motivation for utilizing a facade is a drive for mastery and control over people. You might think at first that this refers to a 9,1-oriented salesperson who does not want to appear blatantly domineering when face to face with a customer. However, the authentic 9,1 orientation is to prove oneself through *visible achievement*, usually in terms of high sales volume. Of course, salespeople with 9,1 attitudes sometimes have a tendency to lose sight of this higher objective and to get sidetracked into proving themselves by winning an argument with a customer. But 9,1-oriented sales representatives are open and honest with respect to intentions, desiring above all else to win. In contrast, the facade builder's goal is private and personal. This person derives satisfaction from controlling and influencing people and events without their knowing it. High sales volume may be attained as a by-product of these manipulations, but this is not of real interest as it is for the authentic 9,1-oriented person. The facadist is power-hungry and finds enjoyment in "working" others on a ventriloquist/dummy basis.

A second category of facade motivation is related to the aim of being accepted and respected by the people with whom one associates. Here, also, the facade strategist masks true intentions. For example, this person may assume a "tough guy" facade that resembles a 9,1 attitude of thorough-mindedness so as to camouflage personal intentions. The actual motivation remains hidden.

The facade utilized may or may not be consistent from one time to another. Tactics may shift from one situation to another, depending on what is thought to be workable. The surface of a facade often has a 9,9 or 5,5 appearance; less frequently it shows itself as 9,1; 1,9; or 1,1.

Cloaking True Intentions

There are many ways in which a facade strategist can hide true aims and intentions. One is simply to avoid getting into in-depth discussions with a customer, keeping the conversation at a surface level. Then there is less likelihood that the facadist will be asked to state clearly his or her exact position. Another way of hiding is to remain passive to some factor that is noticed in the situation, such as would be done by a 1,1-oriented salesperson. The difference between the two is that the facade builder takes the information and thinks about how it can be used. This seeming passivity is only superficial; the customer is not alerted that the salesperson is onto something. If the customer were to realize this, it would run counter to the facade builder's principle that "unshared knowledge is power at my disposal for manipulation" and might inadvertently reveal that the salesperson's aims differed from those of the customer.

A third way is to speak to a customer so as to reflect the expressed opinions back without the customer's noticing that the salesperson's opinions and attitudes are not being revealed. Similarly, reacting to a question with a counterquery can serve to deflect a customer probe. A fourth way involves the salesperson's giving a reaction, but what the customer usually receives is a set of impressive-sounding half-truths that are phrased so as to gain favor. Still another way of cloaking true intentions is by telling an outright lie. This is not done rashly; the salesperson manages to lie in a way that is difficult to detect.

Building and Maintaining a Reputation

The facade builder not only avoids revealing intentions but also works hard to create a positive reputation as a cover for deceptive practices. Reputation building is a matter of speaking and acting consistently when in public and of connecting oneself with everything that is generally esteemed to be "good." A positive reputation serves the purpose of inducing people to favorably interpret all of one's actions as long as none of these actions is startlingly at variance with the rest. This gives the facade a quality of smoothness and polish. The likelihood is increased that actual motives and ways of operating are not recognized. In this way one can appear to have integrity, as others are unable to see behind outward appearances to sense what really lies beneath.

Writers since Machiavelli have suggested how a reputation may be used to control, master, and dominate. The reputation is built around virtue, good deeds, and subscribing to popular causes. Many well-respected people are engaged in helpful community activities, having no ulterior motives.[12] The facade builder joins in and gets to know them, sharing the goodwill and working to bestow honor on all who excel. By this means, the facadist becomes identified with excellence. Benefit can also be gained from praising others—a tactic that will be examined in more detail later on.

Another cover-up is to express lofty convictions and socially valued ideals. Genuinely humanitarian people speak and act in this way, and so, ostensibly, does the facade builder. Surface behavior frequently cannot be distinguished from that which is motivated by valid intentions. As impressive social and church connections are strengthened, it becomes possible to use the names, activities, and business or official functions of well-respected persons to bolster personal actions. By joining these kinds of community activities, the facadist finds that many entry points with prospects also become available that otherwise might be closed doors. Therein lie the facadist's true intentions. When the facade builder can name-drop or enlist the support of opinion molders, the scope for undercover work to further personal ambitions has been widely extended.

Whatever tactics are being used, the purpose in facade building is the same: to ensure that others perceive the salesperson's aims as genuine and honorable when, in fact, they are devious and manipulative. When customers and others have sufficient confidence in the facadist to relax their usual vigilance and omit normal precautions, they are susceptible to the salesperson's influence. In this way the facadist gains personal authority or sales results on a disproportionate scale to actual competence and contribution.

Motivating and Controlling Customers

The facade strategist recognizes two principal ways of motivating and controlling other people. A demonstrated concern for the other person, with expressions of approval or praise for what is being expressed, is a positive way of exerting influence. Criticism, or any other way of speaking or acting so as to reduce self-esteem, is a negative and punishing form of motivation. A deceptive salesperson is carefully selective in using these two options and the alternatives within each.

The clever use of praise is a key factor. A friendly concern may be read into the close attention and unqualified support given to the customer's point of view, with a readiness to discuss any general topic that the customer brings up. However, in the 1,9 orientation the concern is genuine. A 1,9-oriented salesperson is interested in people, liking them and wanting to be liked by them. The facade strategist wants to use people. "You can catch more flies with honey than with vinegar" is a well-known adage that fits the thinking of the facade strategist.

The facadist is lavish with praise and approbation. Compliments make the customer feel important and build up self-esteem. The person who has been made to feel praiseworthy also comes to like and admire the salesperson from whom the praise originated. Praise buys influence over the customer, and hence, a sale. It is an exchange: the customer is made to feel good and responds. Whether there is anything *deserving* of praise is an irrelevant question to the facadist. But this type of salesperson knows that the praise should, to some degree, be discriminating and therefore is careful not to go too far, for this might endanger credibility. The pertinent question is "How far is *too* far?" and there is a clear idea in dealing with each customer of the limit beyond which praise would be detected as obvious flattery. In all things, the facadist avoids being obvious. By the same token, care is exercised so as not to be led astray by flattery from others.

Showing concern for the other people's needs and respecting their opinions is a more subtle form of influence than is direct praise. To a deceptive salesperson, it is important throughout the sales interview to come across to the customer as one who is genuinely interested, both in the customer as an individual and in what the customer has to say. Ways in which this is done vary from being a good supportive listener, who grunts approval on cue, to never suggesting that the customer is in error, to avoiding arguments or any hint of opposition. As one facadist has said, "I make it a point to find out what customers are most interested in so I can ask questions and get them to talk. In this way, not only do customers tend to be put in a positive frame of mind, but they also feel important. Because of this friendliness toward me, customers are more likely to buy later on." The facade strategist need not risk incurring customers' dislike by correcting them on some matter. Mistaken opinions can be used, in a number of subtle ways, to bring customers under control. Like a judo expert, the deceptive salesperson uses the other person's errors as opportunities. On the surface, there is an appearance of sympathy for the customer's ideas and opinions. To a customer who assumes that the salesperson is well intentioned, these manifestations of concern will probably have overtones of a 9,9 or 1,9 orientation.

Extensive manipulation can be carried out under the cover of a 1,9-oriented facade. One pattern that is relatively simple and easily recognized occurs when a salesperson initiates and fosters a social relationship, apparently for no other reason than liking the person involved. The real purpose, however, is to achieve a hidden aim. For instance, on a social visit, there is general conversation ranging across several topics, including the other person's health, family composition, retirement plans, and so on. Only after the salesperson feels fully accepted as a friend, maybe days or weeks later, is the real subject broached, which is to make a sale.

This kind of 1,9-oriented facade seems to derive its motivation from a fear of offending. To reduce this fear, the salesperson has taken out an "insurance policy" of personal acceptance—paying the premium by being nice—as a cover for true intentions. In Asia this facade is labeled "long toes." Extreme sensitivity to the thought of being rejected or "stepped on" has driven the salesperson to establish a personal relationship as the setting within which to realize true aims.

When a 9,9-oriented facade is being employed, all aspects of the Sales Grid style except integrity are present. Data are presented objectively, the customer is brought into participation and helped to analyze and define requirements, and a product or program is satisfactorily fitted to them. Within the interview situation there has been full candor, and consensus has been achieved. But there is something outside of it that is hidden from the customer.

For example, representatives of an insurance company may call on a prominent citizen. They explain that their company has not previously written policies in this city or state but is now beginning to enter this market. They present and explain their programs. From the personal data provided, they draw up sample proposals for a comprehensive coverage that the customer lacks at present. The customer may check these over and perhaps is favorably impressed. The premium rates might appear advantageous in comparison to what would be quoted by any other company operating in the area, and coverage and benefits are equal or superior. The representatives state that they have been authorized to write a very limited number of policies at reduced premium rates in this initial phase of new business development. The customer signs on the dotted line, and the representatives leave, suggesting that the customer recommend their company to friends. It is a spontaneous, casual gesture on the customer's part to say, "Sure. I'll be glad to."

What the sales representatives have not stated is that the customer was selected as a target person to be signed up and thereafter utilized as part of the company's sales promotion campaign strategy in the region. From now on, the customer's name will be put before every prospect who is likely to be impressed. It will be implied that this customer is a well-satisfied policyholder and, implicitly, one who endorses the soundness of the company and of every deal that its salespeople negotiate.

To the facade strategist, negative forms of motivation appear dangerous. Criticism of any aspect of a customer's situation, even of a competitor's product that has been purchased or is being considered, is ruled out. For example, under one school of thought a person may justifiably feel critical yet should not directly criticize another, because people are seen as emotional rather than logical. Criticism can easily ignite the emotions, setting off the "powder keg of pride."[13] The suggestion, then, is that direct criticism is too dangerous for an individual to play with if friendships are to be formed and influence exerted on others. By abstaining from criticism, one avoids the negative reactions that could ensue. The tacit deception is of no consequence.

The manipulative feature here is that all facts and opinions that might be unpleasant are withheld. When this is done, the person to whom these facts and opinions could have proved instructive is misled.

Acting with Initiative and Perseverance

The facade strategist acts with initiative and continues to pursue the objective until success is ensured. Contrary to superficial appearances, the facadist is tough-minded, acting quickly when there is an advantage to be gained. Becoming sentimentally involved with people is avoided, even though feigned interest appears real. Rather, people are used to make alliances that are easily and quickly set aside as the occasion demands. By staying uninvolved, the facadist is not likely to have conflicting motives and can concentrate on the end to be attained. Obstacles are seldom deterrents. If one approach does not succeed, the facadist draws back and then tries another tactic until the objective is realized.

In a like manner the facade strategist is not daunted by difficult selling problems or by stresses the customer may impose. Yet this salesperson is not closed-minded and responds to new facts and new opportunities that might provide additional leverage. Inwardly, the facadist is not likely to be restricted by respect for company rules and traditional practices, as full observance of these may often limit the range of opportunities. However, when it is advantageous, the facade strategist personifies and upholds the status quo.

Thus, in building and maintaining a personal facade, the salesperson:

1. is lavish with praise and approbation
2. demonstrates a concern for people
3. avoids direct criticism
4. never gives up, but knows when to withdraw so as to launch an attack from another direction

In these ways the facadist avoids antagonizing customers and others and stimulates their willingness to go along.

REASONS FOR USING FACADES

Deceiving Others

A few of the ways in which facade builders screen off their personal motivation from customers and others have been illustrated. Control and mastery of customers can be achieved through persuasion and acceptance. The salesperson knows it is not practical to coerce customers. However, in effect, the facadist uses people as if they were nonhuman objects, setting them up for processing or brushing them aside when they are in the way. The facade serves the purpose of disguising these manipulations.

The rationale for this is that the facade builder believes that personal objectives would be unattainable if the approach utilized were open and honest. To the extent that power is pursued and there is personal pleasure in manipulating others, the means chosen for gaining these ends appear to be the only ones practical. Most people would recoil if they knew of these intentions and would oppose any efforts made by the salesperson. The facade permits selection and pursuit of personal goals, privately screening them from outside observation so as to prevent resistance—which would reduce power—from developing. The important thing to note is that the facade strategist's rationale for this conduct is the attainment of "super power" or super sales that he or she believes can be gained in no other way. This belief influences the whole approach and everything the salesperson does. It is a central assumption that is as potent in governing personal behavior as any of the assumptions that undergird the various Grid styles.

One reason for building up and maintaining a facade is that facadists do not value mutual trust between themselves and customers. Still, the appearance of trustfulness is important. Through creating an impression that candor, helpfulness, and honesty are central to their approach, facadists can more easily achieve their personal goals. On the plane of social ethics, the consequence is that shortcuts are taken to reach the desired end. The facade strategist is not governed by commonly accepted rules for maintaining social morality.

Another occasion for facade building is when one strives to

achieve a sales goal that is thought to be beyond one's intrinsic capability and skill to accomplish directly. By employing a facade to hide tricky and deceitful maneuvers, the facadist can gain the objective being strived for. The end sought justifies the means used for reaching it.

The tragic aspect is that if these assumptions were different—if the facadist believed that excellent sales results could be achieved and personal ambitions satisfied through straightforward selling effort—energy and resourcefulness would most likely guarantee success. Admittedly, some facade strategists get a distorted thrill out of "living dangerously" and achieving by complex maneuvers what could have been reached by a direct approach. But there are relatively few of these. Most of the salespeople who have adopted deceptive selling strategies lack confidence in their own abilities and are often just deceiving themselves.

Self-Deception

Facade-type behavior sometimes appears when the underlying motivation is unknown even to the salesperson. The individual may literally be unaware of putting on a front. Not only are others deceived, but the salesperson is also a victim of deception. Psychiatry and clinical psychology have described these tricks of the mind, where personal motivations are unclear and cannot be identified or described to others. If directly confronted with these self-deceptions, the individual denies them. *Rationalization* is one way of doing this—the person is quick to provide plausible but untrue motives for personal conduct. This is nothing more than blatant self-deception. The individual may *project* personal motives, arguing that all salespeople have to trick their customers into purchasing something. Another example occurs when a person *compensates* for failure in one area of life by striving to demonstrate success in another area.

Facade-type behavior may be caused by any of these factors or by a mixture of them. To complicate matters further, the behavior may contain components of the pure theories as well. Presence of the latter only adds to the subtlety of the person's self-deception as well as to the deception of others.

SUMMARY

A sales facade may be adopted by a person who seeks to mask pursuit of personal and private goals. Insofar as observable behavior appears well intentioned and true motivation is hidden, the individual is likely to be seen as selling in a 5,5; 9,9; 1,9; or 9,1 orientation, or as adopting a mixture of different Grid strategies. Since tactics vary in order to take advantage of the opportune situations and of people's weaknesses, it may be difficult to identify the facade builder without tracking the person's activities over a period of time. The utilization of facades to cloak intentions constitutes a personal barrier to the achievement of 9,9-oriented relationships with both customers and colleagues.

Facade strategists can be highly successful, but they are a potential Achilles' heel to both customer and company. The lack of integrity inherent in a facade means that the company is being represented to customers by a salesperson who lacks trustworthiness. This aspect of behavior is likely to lead to shady deals that can have a tremendous boomerang effect when customers and the company eventually discover the facade builder has been taking advantage of them.

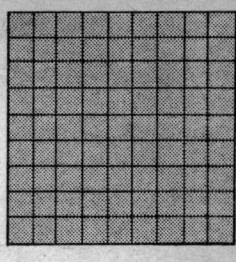

SELF-DEVELOPMENT

10

You completed a Grid mirror early along the way, in Chapter 2. What you saw can now be analyzed and interpreted in terms of the Grid theories that have been presented. First, you may want to reexamine the ranking you made at that time and to adjust it now that you have a more thorough understanding of the Grid in your own sales role.

Next, use Box 4 to aid you in summarizing your rankings to answer the question "What Grid style is most typical of you?" Start with the Thoroughness Element. Copy your ranking in row 1. Copy your ranking for the Involvement Element in row 2, and so on. Then add up the total in each column. The column with the largest number represents your dominant Grid style, the next largest your backup Grid style, and so on.

BOX 4 Summary of Personal Rankings

Element	Grid Style				
	1,1	1,9	5,5	9,1	9,9
1 Thoroughness	C1___	E1___	A1___	D1___	B1___
2 Involvement	A2___	B2___	C2___	D2___	E2___
3 Convictions	D3___	C3___	E3___	B3___	A3___
4 Conflict	A4___	E4___	D4___	C4___	B4___
5 Energetic Enthusiasm	C5___	B5___	A5___	D5___	E5___
6 Resilience	A6___	D6___	E6___	B6___	C6___
Total	___	___	___	___	___

EVALUATING YOUR GRID STYLE

How do you see yourself? Are you oriented in the 9,9 direction? Or is the 9,1; 1,9; 1,1; or 5,5 orientation most characteristic of you? If your answer is 9,9, is that the real you?

This question about the frequency with which people see themselves in the 9,9 orientation can be answered by examining empirical data. People have looked at themselves in the Grid mirror just as you did in Chapter 2. Then they have attended a Grid Seminar involving numerous learning activities. In one of these activities, participants study the Grid and then test their knowledge of it against the understanding of other participants as well as against objective criteria. Each participant is provided with a more in-depth understanding of the Grid in this way. Colleagues offer feedback with regard to the dominant Grid style they observe in each person's behavior during the week's discussions and problem-solving activities. Then the participants reexamine themselves in the Grid mirror and describe what they see to be their dominant and backup Grid styles. The fact is that participation and learning in a Grid Seminar results in a shift in perception as to how people see themselves.

Overcoming Self-Deception

As is shown in Box 5, a large shift in style, particularly with respect to the 9,9 Grid style, occurs between the first self-assessment and the second. Prior to the Seminar, 83 percent of the participants see themselves as 9,9 oriented. After completing the seminar and looking into the mirror again, only 33 percent consider themselves as acting in a 9,9 orientation.

There are several explanations to account for this 50 percent reduction in self-deception:

1. Better understanding. A more thorough comprehension of the concepts makes it possible for a person to be more objective.

2. Self-deception. When looking inside oneself, one is likely to misjudge what is found there. People generally look at their intentions. Often these intentions are good and may correspond in an abstract sense to a 9,9 orientation, but individuals are unlikely to see their true behavior, which may be, and often is, different from and contradictory to intentions.

3. New data. When people receive feedback as to how others see their behavior, they often learn new things about themselves that they previously had not recognized. With this new information, they gain a more objective view of themselves.

Based on these data, this chapter on self-development takes the point of view that only one in three readers is likely to be selling in a 9,9 manner.

The next question, "What do people want to be?" can be answered by data gathered in the following way. After completing Grid Seminars, many thousands of participants answer this question by examining personal values as well as cultural practices, indicating what they think the "soundest" Grid style is, the most effective backup, and the next most effective. Their evaluations are shown in Box 5 in the right-hand column. Almost universally, the 9,9 orientation is endorsed as the best Grid style, 9,1 and 5,5 tie for second place, and 1,9 and 1,1 are ranked last.

This chart indicates that many participants deceive themselves into believing they are selling from a 9,9 orientation, but under close self-scrutiny, the majority realize they are not. The second implication is that almost everyone thinks this would be the best way to conduct personal relationships.

Thus it is evident that the majority of salespeople think the soundest sales strategy is a 9,9 orientation. This can be tested against sales results that are obtained in actual selling situations, where real life can be studied under experimental conditions. These selling experiments include a four-sequence activity. Participants acting as customers buy from salespersons selling different brands of the same products. The experiment is designed so that a customer chooses one of two competing salespersons from whom to buy. Then, in a double diagnosis, salespersons identify Customer Grid styles, and customers identify Salesperson Grid styles. The activity ends with a critique session in which successes and failures of salespersons are analyzed. A second selling experiment takes place the next day. Yesterday's salesperson becomes today's customer and vice versa. Summaries of results and the data that are gathered point out the key aspects of success.

The data permit measurement of the effectiveness of each of the Grid styles. As shown in Box 6, based on data from approximately 10,000 participants in both public and in-company Seminars, 61 percent of the successful sales are made by salespersons seen by their customers as selling in the 9,9 orientation. The next most effective style is the 5,5 orientation. Where one of the two competing salespersons is seen as oriented in a 9,9 way and the other is not, the 9,9-oriented salesperson makes the sale in 94 percent of the instances. This suggests that other Sales Grid styles are rejected when the customer compares them with 9,9-oriented solution selling.

BOX 5 Reactions of Grid Seminar Participants to the 9,9 Grid Style

Percent responding	What Is Your Grid Style?		What Is the "Best" Grid Style for Sound Human Relationships?
	Before Grid Seminars	After Grid Seminars	
100			99.0%
75	83.3%		
50			
25		33.3%	
0			

Reviewing the 9,9-Oriented Sales Style

Before dealing with the issue of how people can change, it is useful to review the major properties of a 9,9 orientation as a Sales Grid style.

The viewpoint of a 9,9-oriented salesperson is that when a purchase is being considered, the customer has a problem to solve or a need to satisfy. It is necessary to define desires and to relate these desires to means by which they can be satisfied. What the customer desires may involve intangible, subjective factors as well as material objects. The means to attain the desires include financial as well as product considerations. Because of the changing nature of most of these variables, the total customer problem is unique at the time each sales interview takes place. It is unique not only for sales interviews with different customers, but also for successive interviews with the same customer. A 9,9-oriented salesperson is committed to selling solutions to customers' problems or needs. For these reasons, the 9,9-oriented sales representative:

1. has expert knowledge of the product
2. gains an in-depth knowledge of the customer
3. keeps well informed of competitor's products and strategies

BOX 6 Sales Success by Grid Styles

Grid Styles	Percent of Sales Made by Grid Style
9,9	61.0
5,5	23.5
9,1	8.1
1,9	6.6
1,1	0.8

4. is ready to compare competitor's products objectively with his or her own

5. samples and tests the customer's knowledge during the opening to assess where to begin and where to correct any misunderstanding the customer may have

6. gains the customer's active participation and involvement in the sales interview

7. sees the customer's thoughts and emotions as a whole needing to be integrated within the sales interview

8. tries to identify underlying reasons when conflict arises and works them through to common understanding

9. conducts the interview as a problem-solving discussion

10. creates opportunities for the customer to express and discuss objections early and throughout the interview

11. summarizes the discussion as the basis for moving toward a close

12. helps the customer to make a reasoned purchasing decision

13. shows a strong interest in understanding the customer's reasons when closing is unsuccessful

14. keeps in sound contact with established accounts

15. treats the prompt and positive handling of complaints as of utmost importance in maintaining an account

16. deals with rush business in a versatile but customer-satisfying way

17. keeps personal integrity constantly in the forefront through open-

ness and candor, by providing facts, data, and logic, and by creating valid expectations

18. plans and schedules activities in terms of sales objectives

19. prospects by treating every customer as a gatekeeper and by continuously analyzing market characteristics and potential

20. sees that service commitments are met with top-grade service provided

21. controls expenses to get full value in terms of sales results from the money spent

22. conducts self-critique to discover the causes of failures as well as of successes

23. uses the profit logic of a private enterprise society to guide selling actions

24. gives help that is over and above the business requirements of sales contacts in a free and spontaneous way

Thirty years ago people often said, "Life begins at forty." But in the era of the 1980's you're over the hill at thirty, according to the "now" generation. What is meant is that most people have become complacent, stuck in their ruts, and, as a consequence, unable to change significantly after reaching thirty. Whether life begins at forty or stops at thirty has nothing to do with bones, muscles, nerves, and blood. It has everything to do with a person's point of view. An individual can get crusty and dead from the neck up at twenty or can be lively, creative, enthusiastic, and growing professionally at sixty.

DEVELOPING YOURSELF THROUGH COMPARISON LEARNING

Learning is essential for change, so it is important to know more about conditions that are favorable for bringing about personal improvement.

Conditions are favorable for learning whenever a person can make comparisons between two or more things. Then similarities and differences can be examined, the reasons for them analyzed, and a determination made of which of the two is better in terms of relative merit.

When you see similarities and differences, understand the reasons beneath the surface, and can evaluate them on a "degrees of good and bad" basis, you are then in a position to plot a course of action for how to get from where you are to where you want to be.

Now take this concept of how learning occurs and apply it to changing your Grid style, if that is what you want to do, or to strengthening the one you have. First of all, the Grid itself provides the basis for a series of comparisons. In many different ways, as you have read this book, you have been comparing a 9,9 orientation with the other styles of behavior. You can see the similarities between the 9,1 and 9,9 orientations. One is that both have a high concern for making a sale. A 9,1 orientation disregards the customer as a unique and distinctive individual, while a 9,9 approach appreciates the customer as a person for whom the salesperson should have the utmost respect. This is the key difference.

1,9 and 1,1 orientations also are similar. Neither of them has much concern for making a sale, but a salesperson with a 1,9 attitude enjoys people whereas the 1,1-oriented salesperson is indifferent to them. Thus there are similarities and differences here, too. A 5,5-oriented salesperson, in comparison with all others, shares some basic similarities but some very important differences. In some respects, this sales representative approaches a 9,9 orientation, but the major difference is that this style is shallow and mechanical rather than deep and committed. This is the fundamental basis for comparison.

Step One: Compare Grid Positions

To start strengthening yourself you should possess a clear understanding with regard to Grid concepts. Here is how you can test yourself. Take some particular selling situation that you now have, and write down what the 9,1 attitude toward that selling situation would be. Then move on and describe the 1,9 attitude. What would be the 1,1 reaction? How would a 5,5-oriented salesperson think about the situation? Finally, picture the 9,9 approach to dealing with it.

Taking your own statements, you might then want to switch back to parts of this book that are related to the same or a similar selling situation and test your statements against the text. You might want to change some and refine others. You will find that writing statements in this way will aid you in diagnosing various ways of seeing a selling situation and therefore in dealing with it. If you will do this from time to time, you will find that it continues strengthening your understanding of the Grid. It will help you in self-diagnosis, because you will be able to see alternative ways of dealing with the situation—ways that differ from your present approach.

Step Two: Compare Your Attitudes with the Grid

You can compare and analyze similarities and differences among these five major orientations, but, of course, there is something far more important if you want to change or strengthen yourself. This involves comparing your own attitudes with those of the Grid and seeing which Grid orientation corresponds most closely with your own. This will tell you where you are. Come to your own conclusions as to why you are there and then decide whether this is where you want to be. In making your decision, it is helpful to analyze which Grid styles are not at all like you. This is important because it will tell you something about your aversions. Once you understand what it is you dislike, you very well may want to ask yourself if you act poorly with customers who represent in their Grid styles the Grid style you reject in yourself. This aids you to see why some customers bother you, and you can discover new ways for working more effectively with such customers who represent aspects of behavior you dislike. The chances are that once you understand your own feelings and actions, you will find it possible to be more constructive and positive in working with your customers.

Step Three: Choose Your Ideal Grid Style

There is still another way you can use the Grid as the basis for self-development. It involves identifying the Grid style that fits you best. This is the one that you think would be ideal as the most effective way of selling. Go even further—identify the soundest backup you can adopt and the type of situation that would impel you to use it. Knowing the Grid description that currently fits you best, as you have been operating, and knowing the Grid style that would be best in terms of effectiveness provide the basis for you to set development objectives for yourself. In making this comparison between the actual you and the ideal you, you will be able to see what it is you do that is sound and what it is you do that is not. It also increases your awareness of what it is you do not do that you would need to do if you were to act in a truly sound way.

Assume that you selected the 9,9 orientation as the ideal, for this is the most likely possibility. No matter how sound any particular Grid style you chose might seem to be, it is realistic only insofar as it is workable. 9,9 is a practical, problem-solving approach which you are probably capable of adopting and to which most customers can respond favorably. However, there are situations where a 9,9 orientation—or any style you adopt as the soundest—may be unworkable. Your skill in selling under this approach may be insufficient. In a particular interview, the behavior of your customer may be such as to obstruct completely your chosen approach. Your soundest selling style may be unworkable because of certain characteristics of your product or because of some of your organization's policies and practices. In situations such as these, you have no choice but to move into a backup strategy until you see an opportunity to return to the dominant style that you have found to be the soundest under most conditions.

The real test in self-development is learning to increase the versatility with which 9,9 solutions can be implemented, so that it seldom is necessary to adopt backup assumptions. You may also find ways to initiate and take part in constructive discussion and improvement of your company's product and its marketing strategies.

Step Four: Compare Your Selling Strategies with Other Salespersons'

Look now into another basis for comparison and see what else you can do for your own self-development. In many situations there are other salespersons, either ones with whom you compete or colleagues who are selling the same products. Use the Grid to analyze them in your own mind. What are their strengths and weaknesses; what Grid styles do you see in those who are least effective; what conclusion does this lead you to? Can you see behavior in those who are most effective that is different from your own and that, if you were to adopt it, would give you even more strength? Do you see behavior in the least effective salesperson that you see in yourself—behavior that you need to change? Another thing you can do here is to reverse the mirror. Give this book to your sales manager or to sales colleagues—to people who have had a chance to observe you being governed by your present attitudes toward selling. Perhaps they have even watched you perform in sales situations. Ask them to read the book, inviting them to place you somewhere in its pages and to jot down notes where they would put you on the Grid. After they have done this, sit down and let them give you feedback on your Grid style. This is an excellent basis for comparison because you can then evaluate what they think of you against what you think of yourself. This kind of comparison is particularly important because it gives you another person's point of view; it can increase your objectivity.

Step Five: Ask Your Spouse or Best Friend to Evaluate You

You can also do this kind of data gathering about yourself by giving this book to your wife or husband or best friend. Your spouse or best friend undoubtedly knows you as well and perhaps better than anyone else, in terms of what turns you on and what turns you off, what you will accept and what you cannot take. Ask this person to read the book and then to return to Chapter 2, picking out paragraphs and elements that are most typical of you. You can gain a great deal of good understanding of yourself through another's eyes. Incidentally, those who are married may find that this has some very good effects on their marriages. Many people have found the Grid a useful way of analyzing how husband and wife exert influence on one another and also how both act with regard to children. This can be very important to you beyond your interest in selling.

Step Six: Compare One Customer with Another

As another basis for comparison, study and compare one customer with another. In this way you get to know your customers in Grid terms so that you can see what it is in them that increases or reduces your own effectiveness. When you see this clearly, you are in a position to work more effectively with a customer's Grid style.

In conclusion, you will be well rewarded by comparing, analyzing, evaluating, and drawing conclusions as these relate to what you should or should not do as a basis for your next steps in development. This is a truly sound basis for self-development.

EXPERIMENTING WITH AND CRITIQUING YOUR SELLING STYLES

Although making comparisons, drawing conclusions, and setting personal objectives is necessary and desirable, it is not enough. You must also act upon your self-recommendations and then study the consequences. Did your new actions do what you wanted them to do for you? Did they produce good or bad results? Why? Much learning comes from critiquing yourself, but you can only critique your actual behavior if you experiment to produce actions that can be studied. Therefore, design personal experiments that you can carry out; conduct the experiment, critique it, evaluate it, and plan next steps.

In designing your own selling experiments, it is important to learn from the feedback that you receive from the customer. Depending on your natural Grid style, you may initially respond to a customer's feedback in one of several ways that are at right angles to learning. By being able to recognize adverse reactions, you are in a better position to take self-correction steps to take advantage of this valuable steering device.

9,1-oriented salespeople have little or no use for customer feedback. This is because they have developed the conviction that they already know everything they need to know, and the purpose of interacting with customers is to sell—not to learn. If a customer thrusts feedback onto a 9,1-oriented salesperson, it is most likely to provoke defensive reactions. These salespeople justify their behavior by insisting that they are only doing whatever is necessary for survival in the "dog-eat-dog" world of selling. To admit that a customer can criticize and be right reeks of failure. Because of this attitude, 9,1-oriented salespeople are likely to repeat the same mistakes endlessly and literally not learn from experience.

A 1,9-oriented salesperson is supersensitive to feedback, both positive and negative. This person basks in the warmth of positive feedback for the reason that it signals acceptance and approval, which provides a 1,9-oriented person with the security that is so essential for a positive self-image. The opposite holds for negative feedback from the customer. It is received as though it were punishment. Negative feedback activates dreaded feelings of personal worthlessness and repudiation.

Here again we see that the feedback is received not from the standpoint of what can be learned from it but from the standpoint of whether it means acceptance or rejection. Accordingly, a 1,9-oriented salesperson is also likely to be a slow learner and to fall into the same traps repeatedly. The exception to this is that a 1,9-oriented person is more likely to "dodge" situations that have been punishing in the past and in this sense to learn to stay out of situations that have previously caused rejection. This learning is not to solve the problem that created the rejection but simply to avoid rejection by escaping from situations that have produced it in the past. This kind of learning limits the 1,9-oriented person's effectiveness because it reduces the areas of interaction that are available for working with customers.

A 5,5-oriented salesperson does take advantage of feedback from a learning perspective. What is taken from feedback are clues that the salesperson's behavior may in some way be different, unique, or "out in left field." Since the 5,5-oriented salesperson seeks to find the middle ground, the information that feedback can provide is of value because it signals how behavior should be shifted in order to make it more acceptable to the majority of customers.

It is almost a contradiction in terms to imply that a 1,1-oriented salesperson learns from feedback, for the simple reason that a 1,1-oriented person is not motivated to learn one way or another. Since the goal is to exert minimum effort, feedback—whether positive or negative—is likely to be disregarded.

A 9,9-oriented salesperson concentrates on feedback, both from the standpoint of using what is learned from the customer for problem solving and from the standpoint of evaluating it for increasing personal effectiveness. The 9,9-oriented attitude toward feedback is that it is an invaluable source of information about what the salesperson is or is not doing that is having beneficial or detrimental effects. Only by "reading it" is the salesperson able to gain insight into ways of improving effectiveness. Reactions by customers are evaluated for what the salesperson is doing that is positive in terms of constructive results or what is limiting effectiveness. In either case, positive actions are reinforced by feedback and negative actions are identified and focused upon in such a way as to reduce them.

A sound way of learning from experience is to design an experiment so that it provides a basis for comparison. Take, for example, two comparable selling situations. Apply your characteristic approach in one of them; this is your control condition. Apply your new strategy in the other; this is your experimental condition. Having conducted the experiment, study the results from each. Did the experimental condition produce better or poorer results than the control condition? Why? What is the implication? Was it a poor experiment? Was it a good experiment you had difficulty in carrying out? Was it a good experiment that failed to give the results you expected? Once you can answer these questions, you are in a position to repeat the experiment in order to develop skill in applying the new strategy in comparison with the old, or perhaps in retaining the old approach while combining it with others. Then you can design additional experiments.

Just a few words of caution are necessary. Think each experiment through carefully. Do one at a time, and be thorough. Continue treating customers as customers, not as laboratory specimens.

DEVELOPING AND STRENGTHENING YOUR RESILIENCE

Over a period of a day or a week you conduct a number of sales interviews. You meet with prospects whom you think to be potential customers. You open and go through your presentation with enthusiasm. You do your best to involve the customer and to bring about a purchase decision that gives lasting satisfaction. Still, the customer turns you down. You go to your next appointment. Again you do your best, but no sale results. You check over what you have been doing and how each customer has responded to you. You cannot find any major flaw in your approach—an approach which, until recently, was achieving sales results. You make your next call and again emerge with no sale. Is it just one of those days, or are you going stale? Thoughts like these revolve in your mind, along with the awareness of the amount of commission you could have made but did not. How will you feel as you go to your next sales interview appointment after three, four, or more successive failures?

What do you do? Watch yourself carefully, for here is a point at which many salespersons take an emotional nosedive. They ensure by their own actions that the first few unproductive interviews are followed by a long sequence of resultless meetings with customers. They are all churned up, classifying themselves as losers, with feelings of impending doom. These emotions can have many negative effects, often in combination. Although the next prospect has neither knowledge of nor collusion with any of the previous interviewees, the salesperson may go in to the interview convinced of the need to sell harder than ever before and win this one if it is "the last thing I'll ever do." Switching to a backup that is far more crude and ineffective as a selling approach than the approach normally used is a strategy commonly employed. The salesperson may be so tense as to forget vital details in the presentation and and be unable to convey to the customer any clear concept of the product. Or the sales representative may lose interest and merely go through the motions. Agitation or despondency colors the salesperson's attitudes and gives the customer an unfavorable impression. All these consequences lessen the likelihood that a sale will be made during this interview, and even more, during subsequent ones. Tomorrow can only be worse.

Keep in mind that there are many reasons for a "no sale" that are outside of your control. Prospects may not want to purchase despite your very best selling efforts. Remember that an interview with one customer is something entirely separate from an interview with another. These considerations can help you avoid the kind of downward spiral that has been described. It is natural for people to expect that hard work will receive its reward and to feel unsettled when one, two, and then three successive efforts bring no result. Yet factors that are beyond your control and that tip the balance against the customer's purchasing can and do sometimes occur in several successive sales interviews, their random nature being mistaken for regularity.

This is not to suggest that successive turndowns should always be attributed to bad luck. It is important to critique each selling performance and to make the necessary changes that will increase your effectiveness. You do this best by remaining calm and examining what the problem may be. If no problem is detected, it is perfectly logical to attribute the lost sale to the "random or undiscovered" causes and to continue with your usual style of selling, with emotions held in check. Continue to keep a lookout for what might still be undiscovered (not random) factors that are working against the achievement of sales. This is resiliency—the ability to maintain energetic enthusiasm in the face of apparent failure. It is a test of your steadfastness in pursuing goals when things are not falling in place as you might wish them to do.

The matter of learning from experience also relates to the issue of resilience. The reason is that every new sales contact is another fresh start, a new opportunity to test one's effectiveness skills and to learn from them. With this basic attitude, a salesperson is eager for new sales contacts, and this sense of enthusiasm for selling is what permits a 9,9-oriented salesperson to avoid complacency, burnout, indifference, and boredom.

GETTING THE BIG PICTURE

Now to return to the beginning. One of the ultimate tests of a salesperson is that of selling an article or services to a customer during their first encounter. There is an even stiffer test, however. Can the individual follow up with more sales the second, third, and fourth times around, enjoying the benefits of a strongly established account?

If you now understand yourself and your customer better, the chances are you will be more successful, initially and in repeated contacts. In human as well as financial terms, you may find your efforts more rewarding. Considering the issues specifically on a business-logic basis, the greatest reward would appear to be that of helping individual customers, or the company that is purchasing, to get full satisfaction from your product. Real satisfaction comes from using the product, not from hopes that were raised beforehand or from any kind of comforting assurance later on meant to compensate in words for what a product does not provide by itself. Real satisfaction, then, is determined—for better or for worse—during the sales interview, when the customer comes to understand fully either what the product is going to do or what it cannot reasonably be expected to do. After a purchase has been made, satisfaction consists in seeing these expectations fulfilled. A salesperson is, in effect, the manager of the customer's expectations. By what is said, the sales representative can introduce valid or false expectations into the customer's mind. By what is not said—in explanation and comment or as an inquiry to test the customer's understanding—the salesperson can allow misconceptions to continue, which result in disillusionment after a purchase.

The expanded repeat business that comes directly through a satisfied customer's reorder or by favorable comments made to other potential purchasers is the essence of progress for a salesperson and the company. Many salespeople verbally subscribe to this principle but abandon it to take advantage of a quick and easy sale. Only one style on the Grid keeps it consistently in mind and backs it with action.

There is a final reason for suggesting that a 9,9 orientation is a strong and effective basis for building selling relationships. This reason is found in human ethics.

The community gives its endorsement to open, candid, straightforward, fact-based, logic-oriented, and problem-solving human relationships. Where these exist or are growing, the society itself is on the upgrade. These are the values that should undergird the conduct of business in a free and open society. To the degree that selling and purchasing are based upon a 9,9 orientation of mutual understanding and respect, sales representatives and their customers are acting in ways consistent with the ethics of a sound society. Each is making a personal contribution to strengthening the social fabric. In the final analysis, what is good for you is good for the company you represent and good for the customer that you and your company serve.

EFFECTIVE SELLING

Summary and Implications

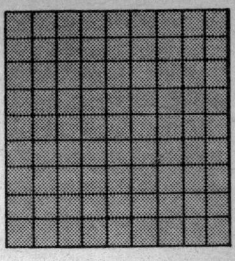

Now you have an appreciation of the Grid as a framework for thinking about yourself as a salesperson. The final step is to summarize how the Grid concepts apply to the moment-to-moment interactions between a salesperson and a customer.

This book has tried to answer the many questions implicit in the selling relationship. Some questions are more important than others, and these were singled out for special examination. The first was "What are you selling?" You might have thought this an unnecessary question. However, how you answer it is pivotal to the success of your selling efforts. This is so because it leads you to evaluate your preparation, including your knowledge of your product, your competitors, and your customer knowledge. These are important in shaping the basic relationship you establish with any and every customer.

The subsequent questions concerned you and the customer as a two-person encounter: How do you gain access to the mind of the customer whose attention you already hold? What are the tactics of your interview? How do you deal with reservations, doubts, and objections? How do you listen? What questions do you ask? What about emotions? In other words, how do you communicate with the customer?

Finally, what are the key human motivations in the contacts between you and your prospect? To answer these questions you examined how the customer's participation and involvement make a significant difference in the readiness to purchase. Other issues are how your way of dealing with customer objections moves you toward or away from a buy decision, and how your integrity impacts on the readiness of a customer to buy. Later in each chapter, the focus was on strengthening established accounts and responding to rush business. Selling profitably, keeping control over your company expenses, and other matters also were dealt with in terms of the Grid assumptions that salespersons hold.

YOUR SALES APPROACH

Your sales approach is reflected in your answer to the question "What are you selling?" The answer to this question may be self-evident to you, but it is not that simple. There are several possible answers. By keeping this question in perspective throughout the book, you noticed the differences between various sales approaches that either heighten or reduce selling effectiveness.

One answer is that you are selling products (9,1). Your job is to get the product into the customer's hands. If the customer needs it, this is a bonus benefit. You want to move the product, regardless of what the customer's requirements may be.

Another is that you are selling yourself (1,9). When you have done so, you hope your product is bought too. This is person-centered selling —acting in ways that you think will increase your charm. It tends to lead to cultivating warm and approving feelings for and from the customer as an end in itself.

A third answer is that you are selling nothing; the product is selling itself (1,1). When customers can figure out that the product matches their needs, sales are made. This view of yourself as a salesperson leads you to be passive and unobtrusive, an order taker or a receipt giver.

The 5,5 answer is that you are selling both—some of the product and some of yourself. You attempt to present the product and yourself in an attractive light by using showmanship and conventional selling techniques.

There is a fifth answer. You are selling solutions (9,9). These solutions satisfy customer needs and wants. They solve customer problems; they provide genuine benefits. Aiding customers to understand their problems and the product is part of selling a solution. Presenting the benefits of a product in a sound and constructive manner is another part of selling a solution. Being genuinely respectful of customers as thinking persons who are fully capable of exercising judgment is another part of selling a solution. Acting toward the customer with utmost integrity is still another condition of effectively selling solutions.

Again, "What are you selling?" is perhaps the single most important question you must answer. Your sales strategies are defined and determined by your answer. To the degree that your concept of what you are selling becomes sound, your selling effectiveness is bound to increase accordingly.

Why not answer the question right now? Peel off the veneer and examine your fundamental attitude as you look at the customer. What have you *really* been selling? Is this what you should present to the customer as the basis for sound solution selling?

KNOWLEDGE OF YOUR PRODUCT, COMPETITORS, AND CUSTOMERS

Product Knowledge

A salesperson is an expert when he or she knows the product inside and out and the benefits customers can expect from it. The process of the product's construction and how it functions are understood. The range and applicability of its uses, its quality and reliability, and the limits beyond which it is unlikely to function properly are important, can be described, and oftentimes can be competently demonstrated.

Being an expert, the salesperson has the confidence that goes with it. This is what is meant by "knowledge is power." With extensive product knowledge, the salesperson is in the best possible position to sell customers on the basis of facts, data, logic, and reasoning—the 9,9 approach. This means that the salesperson designs a presentation that is powerful because it is valid, and this is what transfers the confidence of the salesperson's convictions to the customer. It also places the salesperson in a position to respond in a constructive and problem-solving way to customer queries. From a longer-term point of view, it contributes something else of even greater importance. Because the salesperson knows the product so thoroughly, there is the maximum likelihood that what the customer buys will satisfy the need or provide a sound solution to whatever problem it was that the customer wanted to solve through buying in the first place. Buyers assume that the salesperson knows more than they do about the limitations or defects of the product. When buyers are dissatisfied, they are likely to assume that the seller deliberately withheld some of the facts. This reflects upon the integrity of the salesperson.

Knowledge of Your Competitors

Preparation and thoroughness in knowing your own product and knowing your customers is certainly important, but it is not the whole story. You could be on top of your own situation, but from the standpoint of the bigger picture, you could be like an ostrich with its head in the sand. Knowledge of competitors in many circumstances may be of equal significance and value to your sales success. Knowledge of competitors is not limited to technical information about their products or services; it includes being well informed as to their total marketing and sales techniques.

Why is it so important?

In any selling situation, you are competing with others, either actually or potentially. Though you may not see your competitors, you can rest assured that other salespeople are always waiting in the wings, prepared to compete with you for any potential customer who has not yet been landed. Furthermore, every steady account that you have already established is a prospect for your competitors—who know it and are thinking about you, because their established accounts are among, or should be among, your prospects.

The natural tendency for salespeople is to identify with their own products. That means you sell yourself on your products. Positive attitudes toward your own products are likely to make competitors' products appear less attractive to you than they do to a typical customer. Therefore, you are more likely to ignore them or give them short shrift, and it becomes more difficult for you to see the significance of gaining and maintaining competitor knowledge. A typical attitude is "I know that my product is the best. Why waste time learning about a competitor's? My success depends on how well I represent my own."

It may happen that a prospect, while listening to you—and reflecting on what is known of your competitor's product—will realize that the purchase should be made from your competitor. The reason for this is that customers naturally want to compare things as the basis for making decisions. A comparison frame puts the customer in a position to see the pros and cons of each of several competing products. It provides the opportunity of making the best choice from a spectrum of alternatives. You may be in a position to assist your prospect to make such comparisons, even when, without your knowing it, the customer has already begun to do so. Your contribution will be to aid the customer in relating to the facts more objectively than if you ignored the influence of possibly existing prejudices.

Knowledge of Your Customers

Product and competitor knowledge is indispensable, but even these are not enough to ensure effective selling. For peak sales effectiveness something else, equally important, is required. It is customer knowledge. This means knowing the customers in the sense of being informed of their problems, needs, and values. It is unlikely that you can aid customers to see the benefits available to them through purchasing your product if you don't know what the benefits to them would be. An understanding of the customer's business situation is part of the information you need. More than that, you need to understand how each individual customer is thinking and feeling about that situation.

Some of this knowledge may be available to you as a matter of preparation before you come into contact with the customer. Some of it can only be developed as you two interact. This is why two aspects of your behavior can strongly influence the results you get. One is listening, not simply for words or how to dislodge an objection, but to truly understand the person and his or her situation. But passive listening is not enough, because even the customer may not understand what the real problem is. You may need to aid the development of this understanding—to get a better definition of the problem before the customer is in a position to buy. This means that you need to be skillful in getting the customer to answer your questions in ways that can result first in your understanding the problem and then in your being in a position to forward your product as a way of solving the problem. This is one reason why so much attention has been placed on the dynamics of participation and involvement in the relationship you create with your customer. Fundamentally, selling is a customer-satisfying process, not a goods- or service-producing process. Sometimes the sales force, the people in business who are closest to the customer, lose sight of this fact. How complete your storehouse of information is, and how much emphasis you place on understanding your customer's needs and values as the basis of selling, will give an indication of your *actual* degree of concern for customers.

You know that most people vary in the thoroughness with which they prepare themselves, whether for making a management decision, for taking a university examination, for going on a vacation in an unexplored area, or for dealing with a customer. How thoroughly you prepare yourself is a big factor in your effectiveness. You might assume that the quality and thoroughness of preparation is related to a person's intelligence. Certainly, smart people learn more easily and grasp facts more quickly than those of lesser intelligence. But as an explanation for preparation and thoroughness, the "intelligence" answer is likely to miss the deeper point. A person's preparation and thoroughness is more probably rooted in the product, competitors, and attitudes toward customers than in the capability for understanding. Innate personal capacities set the outer limits to what you can do, but your attitudes make it possible either to reach your fullest potential or to miss it by a wide mark.

You might want to look back at your reactions to the Thoroughness

Element in Chapter 2 for clues to your own attitudes toward being prepared.

PARTICIPATION AND INVOLVEMENT

A major consideration in this book has been the human dynamics that go on between you and your customer. This can be viewed first in a general way against the larger backdrop of the social scene. Significant changes are occurring today within all industrial societies. One is fundamental. It is probably the most distinctive feature of the time in which we live. Evidence of it appears in newspaper reports every day. You may read the signs within your own family, and you certainly encounter it in your sales work.

The dynamic is that, more and more, people want a "piece of the action." Generally people are no longer passive or tolerant of being told what is good for them. The classic "Simple Simon" is nearly extinct, having been replaced by new generations who are far better educated and more discriminating in their approach. All of us are exposed to much more information and wider ranges of choice. Young people, as customers, are sharp and sophisticated. Most of their purchasing lifetime is still before them. Simple, pat, rehearsed presentations, insincerity of any kind, or attempted manipulations by a salesperson turn them off. The authority of valid, factual information is acceptable. So are authentic and friendly personal relationships. But personal domination is not.

Newer generations—reared by the preceding—are on the way. It is unlikely that the present trend will be reversed, due to the fact that many educational, technological, and political indicators point in the same direction. We are in a new ball game, a situation that has rendered many textbooks about selling training methods and current sales practices irrelevant, and thus obsolete.

Let us take an instance of where customary selling precepts and practices have now gotten badly out of alignment with the customer approach of the "now" generation. And we're not using this term to refer to the younger customer exclusively. Many older customers are also more savvy than they used to be. They may not be so advanced or up-to-date in their general education, but they have access to a great deal of magazine information about product tests conducted on the customer's behalf by independent researchers. Other mass media are also increasing their sophistication.

The traditional "managed" sales interview dates from an era when customers were less well informed and more patient and formally polite. Typically, its sequence includes introductory and middle phases during which you concentrate mainly on outlining the product to your customer, which provides an understanding of its features and functions. This is where, it is hoped, the customer gains insights into the product's potential usefulness. Your presentation is factual and information-packed. You hope it provokes favorable feelings as the customer listens to what you say, but you have no certain way of knowing. Some salespersons recommend a brief question now and then to test the state of the customer's feelings and reactions. Many others prefer not to be interrupted at all. Details now, persuasion later. At this moment, and maybe for several more minutes, the salesperson is on stage; the customer has the role of audience and is expected to think about the product while listening and watching. In the final segment of the interview, the presentation proceeds to strengthen the customer's desire to purchase the product. This is the do-or-die stage; the sale will either be clinched or lost. It is here that the customer often turns cold, sensing the pressure of the sale. It is so obvious and artificial, it is an insult to intelligence.

There are many variations, of course. Some salespersons provide a lot of product information, followed by relatively little selling pressure. Others do the opposite. There are differences in subtlety and skill in appealing to the customer's emotions when trying to bring the purchase decision about. But all salespersons who consciously or unconsciously keep the information and selling aspects of the interview apart, and who build these into successive phases, share a common assumption—and it is a faulty one. The weakness is in separating thinking and emotions as though they were two distinct aspects of human experience.

Look at it in another way. Every thought can stimulate an emotion if the opportunity is provided. Every emotion can promote an insight too, often creating new awareness of logical links between different facts. Is there a key for bringing thought and emotion together? Can the advantages of understanding that logic provides, and the creativity and stimulus to action that emotion gives, be meshed all through the sales interview?

They can. The key to doing it is indicated by the meaning of two words, participation and involvement, taken together. "Participation" denotes engaging in an activity. "Involvement" means being drawn in and becoming invested and emotionally absorbed by what one is doing. Involvement does not necessarily follow from participation, but here is what happens when participation and involvement are linked and integrated.

Active participation in the interview helps the customer understand the product. It also stimulates a sense of involvement. The emotions growing along with absorption in the activity influence the customer to continue participating. No artificial stimulus such as prompting by the salesperson is needed. In turn, further participation strengthens emotional involvement; the customer feels more and more positively engaged and occupied in the joint consideration of the product and its relatedness to customer needs. This interplay between thought and emotions that is brought about by participation and involvement is what it takes to bring about a true commitment to buy. The dynamics of full participation and involvement, or the lack of it, underlie the selling process as it proceeds from opening to closing. Grid assumptions toward participation and involvement were presented in each of the basic chapters, and this review of a 9,9 orientation to participation and involvement tells us how basic this part of an interview is to effective selling.

COMMUNICATION

The salesperson and the customer arrive or fail to arrive at a successful closing through talking with each other. To the customer, your readiness to understand the situation is all-important. Objections and complaints, for example, are at the very heart of the customer's feelings. The same is true about participation and involvement—how willing you, the salesperson, are to have the customer take an active part in thinking along with you, analyzing what the product can do. Regardless of the customer's Grid style, he or she wants *you* to be thorough, open, and meaningful, catering to customer wants as though they were your own. Resistance, resentment, and antipathy are a customer's way of telling you you haven't been helpful. Customers *really* believe they are always right. It's their money to keep or spend, not yours.

We have reviewed how communication skills relate to effective selling. At the very heart of the communication process are four issues: (1) asking questions, (2) listening, (3) responding to the customer's point of view, and (4) handling your emotions. As you have seen, how you react in a give-and-take way with your customer is colored by your Grid style assumptions.

THE SALES ENCOUNTER FROM OPENING TO CLOSING

Let's move on. To sell something, you have to sell it to somebody. That means you have to get with a prospect. You have to conduct an interview, meet objections, and bring about a successful closing.

It is usually taken for granted that the person you contact is the one who will make the decision to buy. Yet "Who is my real customer?" is a vital issue in any salesperson's contact. If the person to whom you present your product is a message carrier to someone else, then the opportunity to influence the actual purchaser in a direct face-to-face way may be lost. Your message can be distorted when it is filtered through another person, or you may be stalled on a dead-end street with no hope of going farther. "I'll tell my boss" or "It's up to my wife" is a reaction that you need not hear if you have answered in advance the question "Who is my customer?"

Getting Prospects

Gaining access to another person's mind so that both of you can begin thinking, analyzing, and evaluating together is not a natural process that can be taken for granted. Skill in overcoming resistance—or if not resistance, inertia—is essential. This applies particularly in "cold canvassing." It also may be essential when you have been favorably introduced to the prospect by a third party or even when you have been directly invited by the prospect to come in and present your product. Opening up another person's mind is an initial step that is of crucial importance for effective selling.

This initial period in the personal selling process starts with eyeball contact and handshake. When successful, it ends with a positive level of interest. While the customer's attitude may have something to do with knowledge—or lack of it—about your product, the deeper issue is whether both of you can get together long enough for you to get into a sales interview, or whether you get turned off or out beforehand. You may meet three different initial attitudes on the part of the prospect. One is a positive and receptive attitude. A second is a neutral attitude or expression of disinterest. A third is negative, rejecting, or antagonistic. What is most important is how you deal with a person whose attitudes are less than positive to begin with.

The problem of "warm-up" is that of creating a favorable atmosphere—of refocusing the prospect's attention upon your reasons for being together. Without this attention, the prospect may remain inert. In dealing with a prospect whose attitude differs from yours, your efforts to sell may only promote a higher degree of resistance.

The Sales Interview

Unless already informed or prepared to act on faith, the customer needs to know about the product or service being offered before reaching a decision. The decision to purchase, except under the most unusual circumstances, is one over which you have no control. Even though you may influence the decision in various ways, you cannot force a person to take your product if the decision is not to buy. The function of a sales presentation is to build a customer's early opinion that personal needs may be met by the product into the conviction that they will be. This defines a major opportunity and also a major risk. If the customer is convinced your product will satisfy personal needs, the likelihood of making the sale is increased. If not, it is reduced. Much depends on how you conceive and conduct the sales interview.

Many studies by salespersons who have observed themselves and their sales colleagues through their careers speak as one voice concerning integrity. It is certainly a major contributor to continued success. From the outside, integrity is seen as an unfailing consistency between what a person says and what that person does. Customer confidence is founded on the premise that what the customer is being asked to buy is what the salesperson really is selling; that the needs the customer anticipates satisfying by the purchase will be satisfied. This means that the product does what it is described as having the capacity to do. It benefits the customer in the ways that the customer is led to expect.

A salesperson with integrity is one who helps the customer to develop a valid set of expectations regarding how well the product will solve the problem for which it has been bought. The distinction between what the customer is actually buying and what the customer thinks it is can be seen in the difference between the realistic properties of the product and expectations about it. The customer can be led to have a set of expectations that the product will do something, only to find out when using it that it doesn't. Then expectations are violated, and the purchaser is frustrated, dissatisfied, and unhappy, feeling "sold down the river." If expectations are satisfied or exceeded—that is, if the product does all or more than the customer believed it would— esteem for the product and for the salesperson is increased. The question of whether the customer's expectations are fulfilled by the product or are violated is related to how the product is presented and to the salesperson's carefulness in detailing what it actually can or cannot do. Unrealistic customer expectations can be corrected if you check to find out what the current understandings are before the purchase. Here is where you either maintain or lose your reputation for personal integrity, depending on whether your customer is satisfied or frustrated by the consequences of the purchase.

Working through Reservations, Doubts, and Objections

If customers were all passive and receptive to your desire to make a sale, or enthusiastic for what you have to offer, selling would be simple. But only under exceptional circumstances are these favorable conditions likely to be met. The job of selling is made harder because customers think and feel in a pros-and-cons way and often reach a state of uncertainty about moving to a closing. Even though the pros may far outweigh the cons, the cons may loom large and be brought into the interview in the form of reservations and doubts about the product being offered, its quality, its durability, the warranty it carries, the price terms, and so on. Selling is made infinitely harder because not only do customers think and feel, but their thoughts and emotions are unlikely to be identical with yours.

When two people are interacting and when each wants something from the other, neither is certain of the outcome, yet both want to achieve a result. The result each wants to achieve is not necessarily the result that each can achieve. The salesperson wants to make a sale; the customer may or may not be ready to purchase. Under these conditions, it is to be expected that a customer will raise questions that are not easily answered. Whenever a reservation, doubt, or objection is raised, you and the customer are in an area of possible disagreement. Just beneath the surface of any disagreement is potential or actual conflict.

It is a good working assumption that an objection is never limited to intellectual considerations. Rather, a feeling or an emotion tells the prospect that something is not right. Somehow, a number of factors are not in the right combination. They do not add up. They do not fit. These feelings arise when an objection to what you are saying, or to how you are saying it, or to what you are not saying is raised. The objection may emerge as antagonism toward you or reluctance about your product, or some mixture of the two. Every spoken objection, then, needs to be analyzed by the salesperson from two angles. Is the prospect's objection mainly rooted in insufficient understanding or in emotions? Either can block a sale. If the objection is rooted in emotions and you ignore them, pouring out technical answers, you are not tackling the real problem. If it is rooted in lack of understanding and you interpret it as an emotional reluctance, your attempts to provide encouragement will only increase doubts. More often objections are partly aroused by lack of understanding and supplemented by emotions of reluctance, doubt, antagonism, and resentment. When this is the situation, both aspects must be dealt with if uncertainty or lack of interest is to be converted into positive convictions.

Even more difficult are those reservations, doubts, and objections that are not voiced. You may interpret the absence of a positive reaction as disinterest when in fact the apparent disinterest only hides the interest a prospect is unprepared to reveal because of some privately held thought or feeling that the product is not right. The opposite is even true. The prospect may appear enthusiastic but for some unidentifiable reason may defer coming to a conclusion, and you cannot understand why.

The manner in which the salesperson deals with reservations and doubts may reduce or eliminate them entirely, may cause them to remain and become buried and lead the customer to become irritated or antagonistic, or may be so inadequate as to turn off the customer completely and result in a termination of the interview.

Meeting and resolving objections or disagreements makes the difference between a sale or the loss of one. Effective prospecting, even a sound sales presentation, may lead to nothing, depending on how objections are handled. This is so central to selling that it has been discussed deeply and thoroughly throughout the earlier chapters as the basis for increasing sales effectiveness.

Closing

The behavior of customers sometimes undergoes dramatic change as they near the point of decision. During the sales presentation, a customer may be free, open, and candid, positive toward the product and constructive toward the solution offered, creating the impression of intention to buy. But at the point of decision this customer may reverse field, asking for time to think it over, or procrastinate in some other way. Maybe this moment is chosen to introduce additional objections beyond those that had been resolved before. Alternatively, as the closing is approached, the customer may tell you of a negative decision. Or the customer may act as though it was never his or her intention to complete the transaction in the first place.

In other words, customer behavior during the closing—when the sales interview is just about completed but before a decision has been reached—is often difficult to explain or to account for in terms of what has occurred during your discussion with the customer. Why is this?

Rehearsing a possibility in one's mind is quite different from committing oneself in a positive act of decision. The first is "as if"; the second is for real. There tends to be less anxiety or uncertainty in a person's experience of emotions when rehearsing. But often new emotions may arise when acting for real. It is the difference between practicing a speech in private and standing before a live audience where actions have real consequences. Because the closing converts what was formerly an interest in buying into a positive or negative decision about doing so, it is a very important point in a salesperson's relationship with the customer. New tensions that can disturb the customer's constructive thinking may enter the picture as the customer feels confronted with committing the pocketbook.

An analogy may help here. It is one thing to make a matrimonial pitch when the wedding day seems far ahead in the future; it is quite a different feeling when one is facing the altar, about to get involved in a binding contract. This is like the problem of closing a sale. From the customer's point of view, is the pleasure of the product greater than the pocketbook pain? The customer inevitably arrives at a buy/no-buy decision, and your job in closing is to deal effectively with these subtle tensions to bring about a positive result.

The salesperson may have noticed a positive customer attitude toward the product and yet face insurmountable obstacles at the point of decision and find this difficult to explain. The explanation may involve two prior considerations. One is that the product, although appreciated, does not satisfy the need the customer is seeking to satisfy. In other words, the product is interesting but not pertinent. This reason for failing to bring about a positive closing will arise when the needs analysis has been inadequate.

Another barrier is related to expectations that cause the prospect to want something of higher quality, more versatile, or cheaper than anything that has been shown. Although what has been offered is interesting and the customer has expressed interest in the product, it does not measure up relative to expectations. This cause of failure to bring about a successful closing appears only when the salesperson has failed to be clear with the prospect as to expectations. The shock comes to the salesperson when the customer says, "No thanks, it's not what I've had in mind."

When the interview has been conducted in a 9,9 manner, the

closing often involves no more than the formalities. The reason is that the salesperson has selected the product based on the customer's needs and has met and successfully resolved reservations and doubts. Thus the closing becomes a mutually rewarding ending to a satisfying process and serves as a foundation for repeat business.

ESTABLISHED BUSINESS

Once the first sale is made, the question becomes "How do you turn your new customer into a steady one from whom you can enjoy increased sales volume?" Once a successful closing has been reached, any initial objections or resistances that you encountered have subsided. You are in accord, at least for a while. Even more important, if the customer remains satisfied with the product, the likelihood of shifting from your product to a competitor's is greatly reduced. This brings you to a point of maximum opportunity, and it also confronts you with a higher-risk situation.

What are the opportunities and the risks?

Maintaining Accounts

One opportunity is that you are in a favored position. The customer understands your product. If the customer is presently satisfied with your product and with the established relationship with you, you can build upon what you have already achieved. This produces a basis for increasing your sales results. It also affords you additional time that can be put into prospecting elsewhere, since much background effort has been invested that need not be repeated.

What are the risks? The major risk lies in any mental attitude that may cause you to drift into complacency. Since the natural tendency is to feel you "have the customer in the bag," your calls may be less frequent than would be desirable for sustaining the interest. Or, if there is competition for your time and some shortage of your product, the inclination might be to make this customer wait while you divert the product to a new customer. This same attitude can erode your servicing of already completed purchases and can lead to your giving less weight to complaints than they merit. What are the consequences for your relationship with an established account if you adopt these slovenly attitudes? The customer's initial satisfaction can slide away and turn into resentment. Before you know it the customer may be saying, "I'll show that bum!" The way to show you is to turn to your competitors on the assumption that they will do whatever it is that you are failing to do.

Complaints

The combination of a salesperson who has just the right product and the one-in-a-million customer who never has a complaint is hard to come by. This ideal set of circumstances would mean that the ultimate in customer satisfaction has been reached. Reaching it is as unlikely today as it will be tomorrow. In the realistic world, things go wrong. The product does not do everything it was expected to do; delivery is tardy; defects appear in the early phases of the product's use; a service call that was needed was not made on schedule. A host of problems such as these inevitably arise. If you are lucky, the customer will complain. If you are not, the customer just goes silent and business goes to your competitors.

Dealing with complaints is different in some significant ways from handling objections that arise during the sales interview itself. In handling objections successfully, you are raising the expectation that the customer will get what is wanted—or even more than was anticipated. But complaints arise because expectations have been violated. The source of almost every complaint is products or services that fail to yield the anticipated benefits. Violated expectations not successfully resolved can quickly turn good feelings toward you and your products into antipathy or wrath at your indolence or lack of integrity. Objections most frequently are based on thinking and reason, lack of information, or faulty logic. The reaction that accompanies almost every complaint is drawn from the reservoir of emotions, and these are not the emotions of warmth or enthusiasm. They are the emotions of disappointment or possibly antagonism, arising from the feeling of having been hoodwinked or sold a bill of goods or having been made a victim of unfulfilled promises.

How complaints and the emotions beneath them are dealt with may very well determine whether an established account can be retained and strengthened or whether it will be blown to smithereens. One basic human attitude can get in your way unless you recognize it and avoid letting it adversely influence your behavior. This is the basic tendency to turn away from the unpleasant, not allowing feelings to be stirred up. You are fearful of any risk of getting into a fight with the customer on whom you are dependent for your success. Negative emotions are catching, and when a customer complains, it is easy for you to catch the disease and become defensive. Not that you respond with complaints about the customer. Negativism on your part emerges as you procrastinate and try to wiggle your way around. The most positive approach is to face up to the complaint and take the actions essential for reducing frustration—by correcting the problem if the complaint is legitimate or by helping the customer see the objective situation if the complaint is without justification.

Rush Business

If it is possible to program the product requirements of established accounts without straining the company's production capacity, and if all current customer needs can be satisfied through optimal factory scheduling and production, one of the greatest problems of servicing established accounts will have been eliminated. As long as there are still openings in the upcoming production program, you will have little trouble coping with new business. But this happy state seldom lasts. It is inevitable that customer orders for products will not jibe perfectly with factory production or with service cycles. Under these circumstances you, the salesperson, are really in the middle. You come under pressure from the customer to get the order through in a hurry—and the customer sometimes seems to imply that you are superhuman and can respond instantaneously to every request. If you fail to meet a customer's request for rush deliveries, you risk losing future business.

Conversely, you sometimes come under pressure from your company. The factory manager might want you to get the customer either to defer or to speed up the previously agreed delivery schedule. The factory aims to keep its production-warehousing-distribution flows as steady as possible. Sometimes the customer agrees readily, if this poses no inconvenience, but at other times the customer balks and holds you to the previous commitment "or else. . . ."

So it is not unusual to find yourself between conflicting pressures from customer and company. The pressures increase in rush-business situations and when sudden special requests are made. All the important qualities of your personal behavior—the Grid elements—are called upon for dealing with these pressures, as are those of your company colleagues and the customer, to reach the desired outcome of sound problem solving.

SELF-MANAGEMENT

Salespersons are among the most freewheeling individualists in modern business society. They are usually under supervision from some central point, but when behind the counter or out in the field they are on their own.

How you manage yourself is up to you.

Scheduling and Time Management

Time is worth nothing in itself. It's what you do with it that counts. Some say, "Time is money." Others say, "Time on my hands," and still others, "No time to think." The real issue, of course, is that there are only so many hours in a day. How you think about those hours and what use you make of them are all-important. If you let time slip through your fingers so that it's gone before you know it, with nothing accomplished, you're not going to sell much. If you organize yourself to make good use of available time, getting an effective yield from every moment at your disposal, then time is money—in your pocket.

The effectiveness with which time is used is a very personal matter. Often explanations are given such as, "Jane is well organized, she knows how to use her time," or "Tom jumps from one thing to another in such an erratic way he has to be held together with bailing wire." A better explanation of how time is used points to the factor of your attitudes about how to use it rather than to any inherent quality of "organization" you might possess. Since the way you use time is influenced by your attitudes, when it becomes clear to you what these attitudes are, the next step is easier to take. This is to learn the skills of using your time more productively. Personal planning and scheduling are at the heart of it.

Prospecting

The professional approach to selling can result in unending interest, even excitement, as you explore new business opportunities. It is a self-evident truth that if you can't gain access to potential customers, you can't sell them. You may have an entire city or a regional territory to cover. Prospects are not as easily recognizable as features of the landscape; they have to be actively sought out. They have to be discovered before a sales approach can be made to them. If they are not sought out, they will go unnoticed, like buried treasure. Or you may operate within a small-space area, perhaps in a retail business area. Even so, you can locate new customers in the next block and gain access to them, if you maintain constant effort to study the kinds of customers with whom you have been successful and go about finding new ones like them.

In most sales organizations, people differ considerably in the degree of interest they have in searching out new prospects. They differ in how successful they are in finding them. Some are vigilant, eager, and quick to try out new approaches; others are not. One salesperson may have assumptions that restrict exploratory vision like a set of blinders. Another's assumptions work like radar, constantly scanning for new selling opportunities.

Servicing

The narrow view of selling is "Once sold, that's it." But there is a broader view too. It is this: The organization that sells has not completed the sale until the customer is on-stream with the purchase.

The period after the product has been delivered but before it has been brought into use is an integral part of the sale. Many problems can arise during this period. How you handle them can add to the customer's glow or cause a glower. You are the natural liaison that the customer turns to in the hope of dealing with unanticipated problems in making use of the product. Possibly you feel that you are not making the best use of your time if you go back to the customer you've already sold. And, conceivably, you may not be the best person to handle the situation; a technician may be far better equipped to handle the problem. But customer demands on your time are likely to be felt here too, and if you fail to respond to them in a sound way, you are putting a ceiling on your future sales.

Expenses

Another aspect of self-management relates to your attitudes toward expenses over which you have direct and personal control. Company policy may direct you to keep expenses to a minimum. In this way, maximum profit can be obtained from each selling activity. At the other extreme, expense control can be so loose that unjustifiable practices are tolerated. Sales managers know that the first-mentioned "rational" business approach above is often ignored, and for understandable reasons when viewed from the standpoint of the salesperson. Salespeople often bring up striking examples of how some expense incurred in the course of promoting sales has paid off handsomely. They tend to forget the frequency with which other expenses of equal magnitude did not. The salesperson's attitude may well be "In case of doubt it's better to load on a little in going after a sale than to risk losing it by not being willing to run up additional expense." These are matters of judgment, subtle but significant. Usually the salesperson's own freedom of judgment is narrowed by the company's expense policy and standard practices. It might be that these are so constricting that the flexibility of judgment is not available to the salesperson.

The last decade has seen an astounding breakdown in the ethics of use of money to make sales, in this country and abroad. There are literally thousands of examples of using "payments" to get contracts or import licenses, or to support political parties, and a whole new series of examples of gifts in exchange for sales and contracts is coming to the fore in government.

Sound expense guidelines are desirable from both the company's and the salesperson's viewpoint. But in the final analysis the bang per buck of expense—in terms of sales results—depends on your judgment.

Self-Steering

When you maintain sound attitudes toward steering yourself, you can look forward to continuously improving your effectiveness throughout your sales career. Since you need to think and plan before taking action —action that may need to be different from what you have been doing in the past—it is important for you to be aware of your own selling strategies and how to change them to be more effective.

CONCLUSIONS

Four conclusions from this brief survey of each of the major dimensions of a salesperson-customer relationship can be checked out further as you proceed. They are:

1. Your concept of what you are selling largely determines the characteristic strategy you adopt for dealing with customers. The 9,9 solution selling strategy produces the best results.

2. Your view of what is the customer's part in the interview influences the way you open, what information you provide and how you provide it, your response to objections that may be raised, and the way in which a closing is brought about or lost. Gaining the customer's active participation and involvement is basic to 9,9 solution selling.

3. Your personal integrity, which comes under review during and after every sale, relates to whether or not you are building up a long-term selling relationship with the customer based on mutual respect and confidence. Unfailing consistency in presenting your product in a valid way is the 9,9 approach.

4. Your attitudes toward self-management will be significant factors in determining the extent to which your selling is profitable to you and to your company. Enlightened personal management entails a 9,9 sense of self-respect.

Chapters 3 through 7 examined the salesperson-customer relationship for each of the major Grid styles, illustrating selling behavior based on 9,1; 1,9; 1,1; 5,5; and 9,9 assumptions. As you read these chapters, you probably found something of yourself in each of these styles. This is natural, because the descriptions presented are "pure" styles and everyone has dominant and backup styles for dealing with everyday situations. But one of the Grid styles was likely to be more characteristic and therefore a better description of you than the others. Another was probably the next most like you. Remember the difference between intentions and actual behavior in determining the results you get. You can avoid self-deception to the extent that you are able to separate what you *think* from what actually occurs—how you come through to the customer. The self-development chapter was intended to help you to heighten your awareness of what really happens while you are selling under your current Grid style assumptions, and to suggest ways for strengthening your sales effectiveness. The sales amateur continues to make the same mistakes, while the sales professional studies past actions and plots out how to change. With this book, you have a comprehensive approach to self-study and change.

APPENDIX

Grid Study of Behavioral Approaches

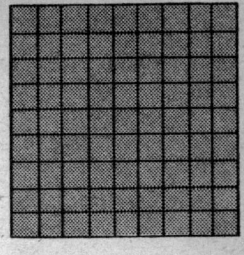

The original use of the Grid to analyze interactions between significant variables of management—production and people—occurred in our efforts as consultants to understand a basic conflict in a top management group. One faction maintained, "If we don't put the pressure on for higher production, we're going to sink." The other faction said, "We must ease up on the pressure and start treating people in a nicer way." Thus, a 9,1 orientation met a 1,9 orientation. This either-production-*or*-people way of conceiving the problem eliminated perception of other possibilities, such as getting people involved in the importance of being more productive.*

By treating these variables of production and people as independent yet interacting, we came to see many alternative ways of managing: not only 9,1 and 1,9 but also 1,1,

---

*From "Use of the Grid to Analyze Behavioral Science Approaches to Human Relationships," Blake, R.R., and Jane S. Mouton: *The New Managerial Grid*, Houston: Gulf, 1978.

5,5, 9,9, paternalism, counterbalancing, two-hat, statistical 5,5, and facades.

A way of thinking about human relationships that permitted such clear comprehension and comparison of alternatives led us to believe this formulation to be of general significance for understanding other human relationships. Thus we evaluated in greater detail how others had tried to deal with the subject of human relationships.

We found no systematic use of a two-dimensional geometric space as the foundation for conceptual analysis of assumptions about how to manage, but we were struck by the extent to which such a basis of analysis was being used, either implicitly or statistically. Theorists who used two variables *implicitly*, and without identification of the variables involved, included Horney and Fromm. Other theorists who approached the situation *statistically*, without explicit analysis of how assumptions and therefore behavior may change as a function of the character of the interaction of these variables, included Likert and Fleishman.

The following table, Catalog of Approaches to Human Relationships through a Grid Framework, shows the various implicit or statistical approaches that can be fitted into the Grid. Several explicit efforts to modify the Grid also are included and are commented on later.

As shown in the Catalog, regardless of their field of specialization, and with but a few exceptions, all investigators describe behavior as if relying on a two-dimensional framework. Factor analytic approaches reinforce conceptual analysis and lead to the conclusion that most meaningful variance in behavior can be accounted for by two factors.

There are exceptions, however. One is Bales, who described behavior in a three-variable geometric space, the third variable being related to an individual's acceptance or rejection of conventional authority. The added complexity did little by way of extending understanding of behavior. Another, by Schutz, added *inclusion* as a third dimension, but inclusion is the motivational scale for the 5,5-oriented theory only. Reddin and Hersey and Blanchard have added *effectiveness* as a third Grid dimension, but this is not a true third dimension since effectiveness is already determined by the first two and therefore is not independent of them.

There is an implicit third dimension within the Grid framework,

Catalog of Approaches to Human Relationships Through a Grid Framework*

Investigator	Source	Field	9,1	1,9	1,1	5,5	9,9	Statistical 5,5	Facades	Paternalism	Other
Argyris, C.	*Management and Organizational Development: The Path from XA to YB.* New York: McGraw-Hill, 1971.	Organization Behavior	xi, xii, 6-15,66-70, 73-74, 77-78, 85-88 105, 107, 134, 135, 138-140			13-14, 30-34, 56-57	xi, 15-20,21-22,24 42,57-61, 67-70, 85-89		19	3,62	
Argyris, C. & Schon, D.A.	*Theory in Practice: Increasing Professional Effectiveness.* San Francisco: Jossey-Bass, 1974.	Business Administration	66-84 101-102, 104, 105-106, 107-108, 149-155				85-95, 101, 102-104, 105, 106-107, 108-109				
Arkava, M.L.	*Behavior Modification: A Procedural Guide for Social Workers.* Missoula: U of Montana, 1974	Social Work	16-66					1-11		1-82	
Bach, G.R. & Wyden, P.	*The Intimate Enemy.* New York: William Morrow and Company, Inc., 1969.	Psychology	8-9, 45-46, 46-49, 71-73,75, 83,109-117,129, 141-150, 256-257, 311,312, 314	5,48,71-73,84-85, 97,102-108,311, 314,321-322	31-32, 312	5, 53-54 135-136	36,43 53,91 119-123, 137,161-165,257-258,343-348		7,10,13, 19,36, 103,120, 158,196-197,222-223,253-254	113	Sick 9,1 112-113, 151,158, 160,260 Distorted 1,9,75, 112,154, 156,160, 260,331 Change 173-174
Bales, R.F.	*Personality and Interpersonal Behavior.* New York: Holt, Rinehart & Winston, 1970.	Sociology	193-199, 213-219, 220-229, 230-237,	200-207, 252-257, 313-319, 320-326, 369-376	289-295, 332,339, 340-346, 347-353, 354-360, 361-368, 377-386	191, 258-264, 265-272, 327-331	208-212	190, 273-281,			Balance 5,5;191 Machiavellianism 238-241
Barber, J.D.	*The Presidential Character:* Englewood Cliffs, N.J.: Prentice-Hall, 1972.	Applied Politics Political Science	12-13,17-57,58-98, 99-142, 347-396, 413-442, 446-448	13,91, 173-206, 448-450	13,145-163,165, 166-167	170-173	12, 209-342, 452-454		79,86, 92-93	83	60,91	Two Hat: 86,87 Critique: 273-278, 331
Hall, G.D.	*The Achievers.* Chapel Hill, N.C.: Preston-Hill, 1973.	Business	23-38, 39-59, 132-152	73-83, 164-171	60-72, 153-163		104-124, 181-187		84-103, 172-180, 188-195		
Benne, K.D. & Sheats, P.	"Functional Roles of Group Members." *Journal of Social Issues* 4, no. 2 (1948): 41-49.	Clinical Psychology	45,46	44,45, 46	45	44	44		46		
Bennett, D.	*TA and the Manager.* New York: AMACON, 1976.	Business Consultant	14,19,26-27,30-32, 122,145 146-150, 161-162, 164-165, 230	14,26-27,32, 122,160-161,168-170,230-231	79,80, 145, 153,154, 160-161	18-19, 79-82, 129-137, 145,150-153	26-27, 81,82, 83,139-145, 154-157, 178,194-196,230		81,82, 91-116	231	Dom/Backup: 151-152, 181 Wide Arc: 230
Berne, E.	*Games People Play.* New York: Grove Press, 1964.	Psychiatry	21,111, 113	95,96			27, 178-179, 180-181, 182-183, 184		48-168		
Biestek, F.P.	*The Casework Relationship.* Chicago: Loyola U Press, 1957	Social Work	106-107	33-47	108	48-66	67-99, 100-119	23-32			
Bion, W.R.	*Experiences in Groups.* New York: Basic Books, 1959.	Psychoanalysis	152-153	147-150	152-153	150-152	156-158, 169				Dom/Backup: 160-165
Blake, R.R. & Mouton, J.S.	*The Grid for Sales Excellence: Benchmarks for Effective Salesmanship.* New York: McGraw-Hill, 1970.	Social Psychology	45-58	59-69	70-79	80-94	95-118	187	125-136	188	Dom/Backup: 13-15
Blake, R.R. & Mouton, J.S.	*The Grid for Supervisory Effectiveness.* Austin: Scientific Methods, Inc., 1975.	Social Psychology	11-28	29-43	44-58	59-78	79-107				Dom/Backup: 8-9

Catalog of Approaches to Human Relationships *(Cont.)*

Investigator	Source	Field	9,1	1,9	1,1	5,5	9,9	Statistical 5,5	Facades	Paternalism	Other
Branden, N.	*The Psychology of Self-Esteem.* New York: Bantam Books, 1969.	Psychiatry	188-190	150,151	194-195	185-188	109-139, 146				
Burns, T. & Stalker, G.M.	*The Management of Innovation.* New York: Barnes & Noble, Social Science Paperbacks, 1961.	Organization Behavior	96-125				96-125				
Buzzotta, V.R., Lefton, R.E., Sherberg, M.	*Effective Selling Through Psychology: Dimensional Sales and Sales Management Strategies.* New York: Wiley Interscience, 1972	Clinical Psychology	36-53 99-100a, 120-121, 127,264-270,285-286,301-318,319, 320-324, 338-339, 344-347, 357-358, 358-359	68-82, 99-100a, 122,124, 127,274-287, 287-288,301-318,319, 327-331, 340-341, 344-347, 357,359	54-67, 99-100a, 121,122, 127,270-274,286-287,301-318,319, 324,327, 339-340, 344-347, 358-359		83,98, 99-100a, 124,125, 127,199-224,277-283,288-289,301-318,319, 331-334, 341-343, 344-347, 356,359-360		113-117, 291-292		Dom/Back 101-112, 289-291
Durkheim, E.	"On Anomie." In C.W. Mills, ed., *Images of Man: The Classic Tradition in Sociological Thinking.* New York: George Braziller, Inc., 1960. pp. 449-485.	Sociology	455-461	460	460-461	449-461					
Etzioni, A.	*A Comparative Analysis of Complex Organizations.* (Rev. ed.) New York: Free Press, 1975.	Sociology	xxiv,5-6, 8,12,15 27-31,56-59,60-61, 66-67,75-82,84,106, 115,116-118,133, 287,455-460,471, 479,486-490,500-504		28,289	xxiv,5-6 6-8,12, 15,40-54, 56-59,61-72,78,81-82,89,92, 106,114-117,169, 305-311, 426-427, 455-460, 471,479 486-490 500-504	471	433-436, 437-438		xxiv,5, 6-8,12, 15,31-39, 62-67,72-75,78-82, 84-87,89, 106,112-113,116, 271,389-391,425-427,455-460,471, 479,486-490,500-504	Machiavellianism; 387
Fleishman, E.A.	"Twenty Years of Consideration and Structure." In E.A. Fleishman and J.G. Hunt, eds., *Current Developments in the Study of Leadership.* Carbondale: Southern Illinois University Press, 1973, pp. 1-40.	Industrial Psychology	25-26, 26-27, 29,32	23,25, 26-27, 29	26-27, 29,32, 36,37	29	23-24, 24-25, 26-27, 27-29, 32,35, 37	37			
Fromm, E.	*The Art of Loving.* London: Unwin Books, 1957.	Psychiatry	23,25, 31,43, -54-55	9,23,25, 42-43, 55-56	15-16, 23,83-84	10-11, 18-22, 25,74-76,80	24,26-28,29, 42,53-54,87, 104-109		82-63		
Gordon, T.	*Parent Effectiveness Training.* New York: Peter H. Wyden, 1970.	Counseling Psychology	10-11,41-44,83-86, 110,112-113,151, 152-153, 159,174-183,195, 207,248, 260-261, 263,280, 321-322, 323-324, 325,326-327	11,13-14, 43-44, 151,152, 154-155, 159-161, 164,190-193,246, 251-253, 324-325, 326	44,152, 183,185, 327	42-43, 110,113, 184,289, 322,323, 324,325-326,327,	12,30-31,33, 47-61, 194-264, 280-282, 305-306		261-263	22-25	11,166, 166-169, 177-178, 190-191	Wide Arc: 11,161-163

220

Investigator	Source	Field	9,1	1,9	1,1	5,5	9,9	Statistical 5,5	Facades	Paternalism	Other
Gordon, T.	T.E.T.: Teacher Effectiveness Training. New York: Peter H. Wyden, 1974.	Counseling Psychology	27-29,48-49,80-84, 84-85,86-87,184-185,186-189,191, 192-194, 198-206, 211-216	49,85-86, 184,186-188,189-190,191, 206-207	49,87, 206-207, 208-209	208		220-282		194-195, 213	Dom/Backup: 23-24 Wide Arc: 190-191
Hardman, D.G.	Authority Monograph. National Council on Crime & Delinquency	Social Work	219, 245, 246, 248	215-217, 219,249				249-255, 245-254	217,221, 247, 249-255		
Harrington, A	The Immortalist. Millbrae, Calif: Celestial Arts, 1977.	Philosophy	114,117, 118,119, 123-127, 137,139		117,118, 129-130	100-101, 114-115, 117,118, 127-129	136-139		144-145	120-121	
Harris, T.A.	I'm OK—You're OK. New York: Avon, 1969.	Psychiatry	72-73, 263	67-69	69-71, 142-143, 152	143-146, 153	74-77, 151-152, 153,302-304		75-76, 146-151, 152,262-263		
Heath, R.	The Reasonable Adventurer. Pittsburgh: The University of Pittsburgh Press, 1964.	Clinical Psychology	ix-x, xii 5-6,20-24,38,39 63-67	28-29		ix,xi,4-5,10-11, 14-20,37-38,39, 57-63	ix,x,7, 8-10, 30-36, 39	x,xii-xiii,5-7,24-28, 38,39, 67-69			
Hersey, P. & Blanchard, K.H.	Management and Organizational Behavior: Utilizing Human Resources. (2nd ed.). Englewood Cliffs, N.J.: Prentice-Hall, 1972.	Education	35-37,46-48,61,63, 70-76,92-93	61,63, 74-76	70-76	74-76	46-48, 61,63, 70-76	83-86, 121-123, 127-131		61,63, 133-143	Machiavellianism: 92-93 Wide Arc: 125 Change: 149-171
Horney, K.	Neurosis and Human Growth. New York: W.W. Norton & Co., 1950.	Psychoanalysis	17-39,76, 97,191-213,214-215,304-306,311-316	76-77,97-98,215-238,339-243,316-324	43-44,77-78,259-290,304, 324-328			312-315			Dom/Backup: 232-234 Sick 9,1: 247-256 Distorted 1,9:243-256
Horney, K.	The Neurotic Personality of Our Time. New York: W.W. Norton & Co., 1937.	Psychoanalysis	39,81-82, 98,162-187	36,85-87, 96-98, 102-161	99,191-192,212-97	28,96-97	104,107, 108,109, 113,163, 273-274	100-101			Distorted 1,9:259-280
Horney, K.	Self-Analysis. New York: W.W. Norton & Co., 1942.	Psychoanalysis	44,47-48, 56-57, 57-58, 58-59	54-55	48-52, 55-56, 57,58, 59-60, 62,108	58,108					Wide Arc: 44
James, M.	The OK Boss. Reading, Mass.: Addison-Wesley, 1975.	Adult Education	10-11,16-17,20-21, 25,35,39, 40,54,55, 56,57,59, 61,62,75, 76,77, 131,139,	13, 18-19,37, 39-40,75	14-15, 35,55, 56,57-58,59-61,62, 75-76, 135, 139-140	19,37, 77,132, 144	17,21, 54,55, 56,57, 59,61, 62,69, 76-77, 132-133, 139, 144-145, 161-163	27,38,64,	106-121, 124-127	12-13, 35,36, 39,73-75	Dom/Backup: 6-9
James, M. & Jongeward, D	Born To Win: Transactional Analysis with Gestalt Experiments. Reading, Mass.: Addison-Wesley, 1971.	Education	18,36,68-100,101-126,230	18,37, 127-159, 230-231	37,56, 56-57	18,57-58, 58-59, 224-226	18,36, 56-62, 235-238, 263-274	2-3, 127-229	29-35, 58	86, 229-230	
Jennings, E.E.	The Executive: Autocrat, Bureaucrat, Democrat. New York: Harper & Row, 1962.	Business Education	2,4,20-21,25,66-70,75-77, 83-86,86-90,114-163			2,4,90-91,91-97, 105-106, 164-195, 228-232	77-80, 254-256		85,250	25-26, 149, 157-160	Dom/Backup: 117
Jung, C.G.	Psychological Types. Princeton: Princeton University Press, 1971.	Psychiatry	346-354, 383-387		385-388, 388-391, 395-398, 401-403, 403-405	334-335, 354-355, 356-359, 363-366		365-370	384		Dom/Backup: 355-356, 362-363, 405-407

221

Catalog of Approaches to Human Relationships *(Cont.)*

Investigator	Source	Field	9,1	1,9	1,1	5,5	9,9	Statistical 5,5	Facades	Paternalism	Other
Ingass, J.A. & Solomon, G.H.	*The Psychology of Strength.* Englewood Cliffs, N.J.: Prentice-Hall, 1975.	Psychology	7-9,10-11, 14,15-17, 55-56, 56-57, 135-136	18-19,22, 24,78	20-21, 21-22, 23	11-12, 19, 57-58	3,9,12, 21,23-34,24-25,68-69,117, 130-135, 136-141, 142-145, 146-150, 151-168	26-27	13-14,17-18,19-20, 24-25,29-30,56,77		Wide Arc: 136
ovar, L.C.	*Faces of the Adolescent Girl.* Englewood Cliffs, N.J.: Prentice-Hall, 1968.	Adolescent Psychology	11-12, 73-83, 103-106	9-10, 53-68	79	10-11, 35-51, 63, 148-149	4-9, 107-125, 148-149				
Kunkel, F.M. & Dickerson, R.E.	*How Character Develops: A Psychological Interpretation.* New York: Charles Scribner & Sons, 1946.	Psychology	68-81	60-67	80-82		125-140, 157-159, 176-178				
Leary, T.	*Interpersonal Diagnosis of Personality.* New York: Ronald Press, 1957.	Clinical Psychology	19,64-65, 104,105, 135,137, 233,269-281,324, 331,332-340	64-65, 104,105, 135,233, 292-302, 303-314	19,23-24, 64-65,95-96,104, 105,135, 233,282-291	19,64-65, 135,233, 315-322	21,64-65, 135,233, 323-324		181-186, 188-191, 282-283, 284-285, 316,317, 318,324, 325,326	64-65, 93	Dom/Backup: 225-227 Distorted 1,9:284-286, 289,367 Sick 9,1: 341-350, 364,372
Likert, R.	*The Human Organization: Its Management and Value.* New York: McGraw-Hill, 1967.	Organization Behavior	3-12, 13-46			3-12, 13-46	3-12, 13-46, 47-100			3-12, 13-46	
Likert, R. & Likert, J.G.	*New Ways of Managing Conflict.* New York: McGraw-Hill, 1976.	Organization Behavior	19-40, 59-69			19-40	16-17, 19-40, 49-51, 51-56, 71-324			19-40	
McClelland, D.C.	*Power: The Inner Experience.* New York: Irvington Publishers, 1975.	Individual Psychology	7-8,8-12, 13-21,27, 49-51,52-76,77-78, 249,252-254,255-256,257, 258,260-261,264, 266,274-275,295-297,324, 326,328	27,104-122,255, 264,274, 289,322-323,325, 328		27,155, 157-158, 249	27,257, 258,260-261,263-266,269, 288,301-302,324, 325,329		301-302	35-36, 142-144, 260,289-290	Distorted 1,9:102, 104 Sick 9,1: 255 OD:254, 255
McGregor, D.	*The Human Side of Enterprise.* New York: McGraw-Hill, 1960.	Psychology	33-43				45-57, 61-246				
McGregor, D.	*The Professional Manager.* New York: McGraw-Hill, 1967.	Psychology	59-63, 79-80, 117-118, 118-125, 136-137, 138-140, 148-149	59-63	59-63	59-63, 144-145	29-30, 59-63, 79-80, 118,127-130,130-133,140, 162-182, 191-195			7-10, 142-144	Dom/Backup: 60
Maccoby, M.	*The Gamesman.* New York: Simon & Schuster, 1976.	Psychiatry	34,47-48, 76-85, 181-182, 183-184, 187-189, 212-213	183-187	94	34,35, 46-47, 48,50-75,86-97,189-209	179,212, 213-217	100,149	48-49, 91,92-93,98-120,121-171	240-241	

222

Investigator	Source	Field	9,1	1,9	1,1	5,5	9,9	Statistical 5,5	Facades	Paternalism	Other
May, R.	*Love and Will.* New York: W.W. Norton & Co., 1969.	Clinical Psychology	45-48, 57-59, 276-278	278-279	27-33	40-45, 279	55-56, 91-92, 146,283-286,303-304,306, 310-311				
Meininger, J.	*Success Through Transactional Analysis.* New York: New American Library, 1973.	Business Consultant	26-27, 28-29, 33,39-40,43-44,54-67,73-75,87-90,128-129	29-30, 34-36, 38,43-44,45-46,67-71,75-76,90-92,105-106,166-170,186-190	36,39-40,40-42,43-44,56-57,100-101,105-106,110-113,153,157	30-31, 57-60, 76-77	26-27, 36-37, 63-64, 101,113-114,129-130,158-166,175-177,178-185,186-206	66	7-10,60-63,78-99, 106-109, 173-175	153, 160-161	Wide Arc: 66 Change: 132-139, 194-204
Metcalf, H.C. & Urwick, L.	*Dynamic Administration: The Collected Papers of Mary Parker Follet:* New York: Harper & Bros., 1940.	Government and Administration	31,50-58, 96-101, 272-277			31-32,35, 210-213, 239	31, 33-49, 58-70, 111-116, 198-202		213-225, 240-246, 260-269, 279-281		
Missildine, W.H.	*Your Inner Child of the Past.* New York: Simon & Schuster, 1963.	Psychiatry	77,85-100,103, 106,108-109,125-126,130-133,138-139	77,133-136,157, 166,171-191,259-260,266-267,271-272	78-79, 101-103, 104-105, 107-108, 109-111, 121-124, 145-155, 156-159, 165-166, 166-167, 243-252, 254-259, 261						
Missildine, W.H. & Galton, L.	*Your Inner Conflicts—How to Solve Them.* New York: Simon & Schuster, 1974.	Psychiatry	35-36,37, 38-39,39-40,62,72-74,76,77, 81-82, 83-86, 131-133, 145-146, 154-155, 171-172, 172-180, 187-191, 196-201, 205-207	36,37-38,61, 76-77, 130	37,39, 53-59, 60,60-61,62, 62-63, 77, 120-127, 157-160, 162-163, 184-187		33-34, 262-263, 308-313				
Moment, D. & Zaleznik, A.	*Role Development and Interpersonal Competence.* Boston: Harvard University Press, 1963.	Business Administration	20,38,56, 62-63,67, 72,77,80, 85-86,87-88,89, 104-105, 122-123, 158-159, 160	20,39, 56,62-63,67, 72,77, 78-79, 80,83, 86-87, 89, 105-106, 123-124, 159-160	20,36-37,39, 56,62-63,67, 72,80, 83,87, 89-90, 106-107, 124-125		19-30, 36-37, 38,41, 53,56, 62-63, 68,72, 77,80, 85,89, 104, 120-122				
Mouton, J.S. & Blake, R.R.	*The Marriage Grid.* New York: McGraw-Hill, 1971	Social Psychology	41-67	97-113	123-137	151-169	181-201	80-85	76-80	69-74	Dom/Backup: 15-17
Reddin, W.J.	*Managerial Effectiveness 3-D.* New York: McGraw-Hill, 1970.	Business Administration	27,28-29, 31-32,42, 47,73-74, 94-95, 161,177, 192,194, 194-195, 194-196, 221-227, 262,263, 268-269	27,28-29, 31,42,68, 73,94, 194,215-219	43,48, 54,194, 209-213, 258-259, 263,264,	27,28-29, 30-31,41, 42-43,48, 72-73, 93-94, 194,205-209,213, 231-233	27,28-29, 29,32, 41,48, 74-75, 94,96, 192,194, 230-231, 233-234	52,53-54, 139-140, 149-150, 159-160, 169-178, 181-185, 256-257		42,47	Dom/Backup: 46-47,48, 49,152 Change: 163,307
Reid, W. & Epstein, L.	*Task-Centered Casework.* New York: Columbia U Press, 1972.	Social Work		155-156		136-138	1-260				

223

Catalog of Approaches to Human Relationships *(Cont.)*

Investigator	Source	Field	9,1	1,9	1,1	5,5	9,9	Statistical 5,5	Facades	Paternalism	Other
Riesman, D., Glazer, N., & Denney, R.	*The Lonely Crowd.* Garden City, N.Y.: Doubleday & Co., 1953.	Sociology Political Science Economic History	73,28-32, 41,57-63		278,281	23,24-28, 33,34-40, 41-42, 63-74, 278	33,278, 282,286, 296,328		302-305, 305-307	303	
Roberts, R.W. & Nee, R.H.	*Theories of Social Casework.* Chicago: U of Chicago Press, 1970	Social Work	181-218	33-75, 131-179			77-128, 313-351				
Schutz, W.C.	*The Interpersonal Underworld* (originally titled *FIRO: A Three Dimensional Theory of Interpersonal Behavior*). Palo Alto, Calif.: Science & Behavior Books, 1966.	Psychology	29,41,46, 47-48,89	31,36,41, 47,48,89	25-26, 28-29, 30-31, 41,42, 45-46, 47,48, 89	26-27	27,29-30,31, 37,41, 43,48, 87-89			43	Sick 9,1: 43 Distorted 1,9:42-43
Steiner, C.M.	*Scripts People Live: Transactional Analysis of Life Scripts.* New York: Bantam Books, 1974.	Therapy	53,54-46, 78-81, 115-119, 186-193, 197-196, 231-234, 236-237, 253-261	54,56, 76-78, 198-201, 211-213, 222-224	92-95, 115-119, 178-181, 218-220, 243-245		3,85-86, 352-361, 362-370, 382-383, 384		44-50, 121, 175-178, 304-305		Wide Arc: 39 Dom/Backup 37-38
Thomas, W.I. & Znaniecki, F.	"Three Types of Personality." In C.W. Mills, ed., *Images of Man: The Classic Tradition in Sociological Thinking.* New York: George Braziller, Inc., 1960, pp. 405-436.	Sociology	427			407-408, 409,411, 418-419, 421,423, 425,427, 428,434, 435-436	408,409, 411,416, 423,435, 436	408-409, 416,423, 433,435, 436		420	
Wheelis, A.	*The Quest for Identity.* New York: W.W. Norton & Co., 1968.	Psychiatry	18,85			16-19, 48-49, 85-89, 91-93, 126	19,20		85		
White, R. & Lippitt, R.	"Leader Behavior and Member Reaction in Three 'Social Climates'." In D. Cartwright and A. Zander, eds., *Group Dynamics: Research and Theory.* (2nd ed.) Evanston, Ill.: Row, Peterson, & Co., 1960, pp. 527-553.	Social Psychology	528-529, 529-532, 537,540-541,541, 546,549-553		528-529, 530,531, 532-534, 539-540, 549-552	528-529, 530,531, 532-536, 546-549, 549-553					

*Reproduced by permission from Robert R. Blake and Jane S. Mouton. "The Grid as a Comprehensive Framework for Analyzing Human Relationships." Austin, Texas: Scientific Methods, Inc., 1977.

however. It involves identification of motivation as a bipolar scale, ranging—in the 9,1 case, for example—from control, mastery, and domination on the plus end to dread of failure on the minus end of the scale. While adding a third dimension of motivation introduces further clarification as to what a 9,1 orientation is like, little in predictive utility is gained over that already available in a two-dimensional system.

Another concept of importance in understanding the Grid is that of *interaction*. Interaction between these variables can occur in either of two ways. The combination of any two quantities can occur in an arithmetic way. This needs to be distinguished from the fusion of two quantities in a "chemical" way. Hersey and Blanchard, for example, might see 9,9 as a combination of 9 units of task orientation, telling a subordinate in great detail "who, what, where, and how . . ." added to 9 units of relationships, involving extensive compliments and appreciation expressed in response to subordinate compliance. The "chemical" view, by comparison, produces a 9,9 character of interdependence in which shared participation, involvement, and commitment produce consensus-based teamwork. In the former case combination of variables is quantitative and arithmetic; in the latter, it is qualitative and organic, i.e., the *character* of the behavior itself changes, not just the amounts of the behavior.

For the reasons that (1) most investigations have found a two-dimensional basis sufficient and (2) three-dimensional formulations have added little to understanding beyond that already available from the use of two, we conclude that a framework for analyzing behavior that results from two variables is a sound and sufficient basis for comprehending managerial assumptions and practices.

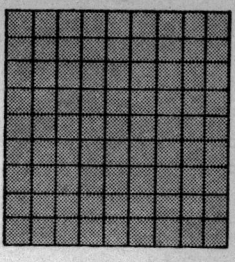

REFERENCES

Chapter 1

1. The technical literature of behavioral science research on which the Grid is based includes about 400 references. The source for these references is Blake, R. R., and Jane S. Mouton: *The New Managerial Grid*, Houston: Gulf, 1978. They are not repeated here. The literature noted in this book is limited to those sources of pertinence in understanding sales situations.

2. Miller, A.: *Death of a Salesman*, New York: Compass Books, Viking, 1958.

Chapter 2

3. Blake, R. R., and Jane S. Mouton: *The Managerial Grid: An Exploration of Key Managerial Orientations*, Austin, Texas: Scientific Methods, 1962.

4. Items taken from *The New Sales Grid Seminar*, Austin, Texas: Scientific Methods, 1980.

Chapter 3

5. Levitt, T.: *Innovation in Marketing: New Perspectives for Profit and Growth*, New York: McGraw-Hill, 1962; Mason, J. L.: "The Low Prestige of Personal Selling," *Journal of Marketing*, vol. 29, pp. 7–10, October, 1965; "Flimflam: The 10 Most Deceptive Sales Practices of 1968—So Far," *Sales Management*, vol. 101, pp. 33–36, Sept. 15, 1968.

6. Items taken from *A Grid Self-Analysis for*

Sales Excellence, Austin, Texas: Scientific Methods, 1969.

Chapter 4

7. Ibid.

Chapter 5

8. Ibid.

Chapter 6

9. Ibid.

Chapter 7

10. Ibid.

Chapter 8

11. Other approaches include counterbalancing; the 9,1–1,1 win-or-leave cycle; and the 9,1–1,9 wide-arc pendulum swing. Because these are not sufficiently common in everyday selling situations, they are not elaborated here. See Blake, R. R., and Jane S. Mouton: *The New Managerial Grid,* Houston: Gulf, 1978, chap. 8.

Chapter 9

12. The recognition and use of positive features of a good reputation are not always stimulated by facade tactics. See Husband, R. W.: *The Psychology of Successful Selling,* New York: Harper, 1953, p. 71.

13. Carnegie, D.: *How to Win Friends and Influence People,* New York: Pocket Books, 1958, p. 28.

INDEX

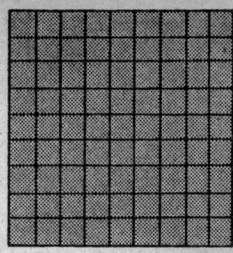

Acceptance:
   customer desire for, 11
   1,9 need for, 187
Accommodation in *5,5* orientation, 96, 111
Accounts, maintaining, 208–209
   9,9 approach to, 144
   9,1 approach to, 43
   5,5 approach to, 109–110
   1,9 approach to, 65–66
   1,1 approach to, 84–85
   (*See also* Established business)
Adjustment:
   of complaints, *5,5* approach to, 110
   to rush business, *5,5* approach to, 111
Affection for customer in mixed orientation, 155–156
Analysis, needs (*see* Needs analysis)
Antagonism, provoking, in statistical *5,5* approach, 158
   (*See also* Resentment)
Anxiety of *5,5*-oriented salesperson, 92
Apology in *5,5* complaint handling, 110
Approaches:
   behavioral, Grid study of, 217–225
   "cafeteria line," in needs analysis, 100
   contingency, 158–160
   9,9 manner of, 129
   9,9 problem-solving, 120, 142, 151
   sales, 194–195
   two-hat, 157–158
Approval:
   customer desire for, 12
   expression of, by facade builder, 167
   1,9 need for, 51–52, 187

Assumptions:
   actions and, 2
   defined, 8
   role of, in sales effectiveness, 8–9
Attitudes:
   as affecting sales, 1–2
   comparison of, with Grid, 183

Backup Grid strategy:
   and dominant style, 14, 175, 178
   1,1 orientation as, 73
Balancing of customer-salesperson needs, by *5,5*-oriented salesperson, 96
Bargaining in *5,5* orientation, 93, 96, 106, 111
Barriers:
   9,9 elimination of, 141
   9,9 identification of, 143
Behavioral approaches, Grid study of, 217–225
Behavioral change, 185
Behavioral science, 1
Bluffing in *5,5* orientation, 104–105
Burnout:
   low degree of concern and, 4
   9,9 avoidance of, 190
   in *1,1* orientation, 74
Business:
   established (*see* Established business)
   new (*see* Customers, new; Prospecting; Prospects, getting)
   rush (*see* Rush business)

INDEX

"Cafeteria line" approach in needs analysis, 100
Calls, 9,9 frequency of, 144
  (*See also* Accounts, maintaining)
Candor of 9,9-oriented salesperson, 125, 142
Caring in 9,9 orientation, 120
Change, behavioral, 185
Closing, 202, 206–208
  9,9 approach to, 142–144
  9,1 approach to, 41–43
  5,5 approach to, 107–109
  1,9 approach to, 64–65
  1,1 approach to, 83–84
Commitment, 1,1 lack of, 74
Communication, 201–202
  importance of, 2
  9,9 approach to, 128–130
  9,1 approach to, 29–32
  5,5 approach to, 96–97
  1,9 approach to, 56–57
  1,1 approach to, 77–78
Comparison:
  of attitudes of salesperson with Grid, 183
  of customers, 185–186
  of products, 9,9 objectivity in, 123
  (*See also* Knowledge, of product, customer, and competitor)
Comparison learning, development through, 181–186
  attitudes and Grid compared, 182–183
  customers compared, 185–186
  Grid positions compared, 182–183
  ideal Grid style, choice of, 183–184
  personal evaluation in, 185
  personal strategies and other salespersons' strategies compared, 184–185
Competitors:
  comparison of, 75
  criticism of, 104
  knowledge of, 196–197
  (*See also* Knowledge, of product, customer, and competitor)
Complaints, customer, 209–210
  9,9 handling of, 145, 180
  9,1 handling of, 43–44

Complaints (*Cont.*):
  5,5 handling of, 110–111
  1,9 handling of, 66
  1,1 handling of, 85
Compliments:
  facade builder use of, 168
  1,9 use of, 53–54
  (*See also* Flattery)
Compromise (*see* Bargaining in 5,5 orientation)
Concern:
  for customer, 4–5
  of 9,9-oriented salesperson, 122
  for quality of sales result by 9,9-oriented salesperson, 122
  for sales, 3–4
Confidence-building, 5,5 approach to, 97
Confidence of customer, 9,9 heightening of, 152
Conflict:
  5,5 avoidance of, 105–106
  as Grid element, 23
  9,9 confrontation of, 141–142
  (*See also* Complaints; Objections, customer)
Conformity, desire of 5,5-oriented customer for, 13
Consensus, customer-salesperson, 9,9 achievement of, 127, 141
Consequences:
  of actions, prediction of, 2
  of 9,1 approach, 45–46
Contingency approach, 158–160
Contribution to customer of 9,9-oriented salesperson, 127
Control of people, facade builder, 165, 167, 172
Controlling and motivating customers, 167–171
Convictions:
  as Grid element, 22
  of 9,1-oriented salesperson, 26, 40
Cover-up in facade building, 167
Criticism:
  avoidance of: by 5,5-oriented customer, 13, 92
  by 9,1-oriented salesperson, 51–52

Criticism (Cont.):
  disregard for, by 9,1-oriented salesperson, 25
  as a form of motivation, 168
Critique:
  as a form of learning, importance of, 146, 190
  of selling styles, 186–188
  (See also Comparison learning, development through)
Customer Grid, 9–14
  diagram, 10
Customer reactions:
  to 9,9 orientation, 148–151
  to 9,1 orientation, 45–49
  5,5 orientation, 112–116
  to 1,9 orientation, 68–69
  to 1,1 orientation, 86–88
Customers:
  complaints of (see Complaints, customer)
  concern for, 4–5
    of 9,9-oriented salesperson, 122
  controlling and motivating, 167–171
  emotions of (see Emotions)
  established (see Accounts, maintaining; Established business)
  evaluation of products by, 137
  expectations of (see Expectations, customer)
  feedback from, 186–188
  Grid styles (Customer Grid), 9–14
  identification of: 9,9 approach to, 133
    9,1 approach to, 33–34
    5,5 approach to, 99
    1,9 approach to, 59
    1,1 approach to, 79
  interruptions by (see Interruptions, customer)
  needs of, 96, 133
  new: 9,9 handling of, 131–133
    9,1 handling of, 32–33
    5,5 handling of, 98–99
    1,9 handling of, 58–59
    1,1 handling of, 78
  objections of (see Objections, customer)

Customers (Cont.):
  orientation of (see types of, below; Customer Grid)
  participation and involvement of (see Participation and involvement, customer)
  reactions of (see Customer reactions)
  reservations of (see Reservations, customer)
  respect of, for 9,9-oriented salesperson, 73
  salesperson knowledge of, 197–199
    (See also Knowledge, of product, customer, and competitor)
  trust of, for 9,9-oriented salesperson, 128, 148–149
  types of: 9,9-oriented, 14
    9,1-oriented, 9–11
    5,5-oriented, 13
    1,9-oriented, 11–12
    1,1-oriented, 12–13

Data (see Facts)
Death of a Salesman (Miller), 7
Deception (see Facades and facade building)
Defeat of 1,1-oriented salesperson, 88
Defensive listening (see Listening, defensive)
Dependency of 1,9-oriented salesperson, 7
Depolarization, 1,9 use of, 62
Development, salesperson (see Comparison learning, development through; Self-development)
Discounts, 1,9 use of, 60
Discouragement of 1,1-oriented salesperson, 73–74
Dominant style and backup Grid strategy, 14, 175, 178
  1,1 orientation as backup style, 73
Domination by reputation in facade building, 167

232 INDEX

Ego-building of customer in 5,5 orientation, 107
Elements, Grid, 19–24
 conflict, 23
 convictions, 22
 energetic enthusiasm, 23–24
 involvement, 21–22
 resilience, 24
 thoroughness, 20–21
Emotional adjustment of 5,5-oriented salesperson, 97
Emotions:
 buy decision and, 124
 criticism and, 170
 failure and, 188–190
 9,9 handling of, 119–121, 139–140
  understanding of, 129–130, 137
 9,1 handling of, 51–52, 149
  sensitivity to, 56
 5,5 handling of, 97
 1,1 handling of, 72, 77–78
 and two-hat approach, 157–158
Enthusiasm:
 energetic, as Grid element, 23–24
 9,9 orientation and, 136
 5,5 orientation and, 116
 1,1 lack of, 71–72, 76–78
 to overcome apathy, 150
 resiliency and, 188, 190
Established business:
 9,9 approach to, 144–146
 9,1 approach to, 43–44
 5,5 approach to, 109–111
 1,9 approach to, 65–67
 1,1 approach to, 84–86
 (*See also* Accounts, maintaining)
Ethics of 9,9-oriented salesperson, 191
Evaluation:
 customer, of products, 137
 salesperson, 183, 185
 of styles, 177
 (*See also* Criticism; Critique)
Exaggeration by 5,5-oriented salesperson, 104
Excellence, 9,9 standards of, 120
Expectations, customer, 48
 establishing: by 9,9-oriented salesperson, 134–135

Expectations (*Cont.*):
 by 9,1-oriented salesperson, 35–36
 by 5,5-oriented salesperson, 101
 by 1,9-oriented salesperson, 60–61
 by 1,1-oriented salesperson, 79–80
Expenses:
 control of, 181, 213
 9,9 management of, 147
 9,1 management of, 45
 5,5 management of, 112
 1,9 management of, 67
 1,1 management of, 86
Expert, sales, thoroughness of, 20–21

Facades and facade building, 163–174
 boomerang effects of, 174
 consistency in, 165
 criticism and, 170
 customer motivation and, 167–171
 defined, 163–164
 vs. Grid styles, 164, 165, 169
 helpfulness and, 172
 honesty vs. subterfuge, 164–167
 initiative and, 171
 integrity and, 174
 mastery and, 165, 167, 172
 personal, 163–164
 praise and, 168
 purpose of, 164, 172–173
 reputation building and, 166–167
 social ethics disregard and, 172
Facts:
 emotions as, 122
 human relationships and, 191
 integrity and, 180–181
 in 9,9 buy decision, 136
 sales interview and, 151
 use by 9,9-oriented salesperson, 123–125
 (*See also* Logic)
Fads, 135
 (*See also* Gimmicks)
Failure:
 and emotions, 189–190
 9,1 fear of, 25–26, 42–43
Feedback, 146
 from customer, 186–188

Feedback (Cont.):
   negative impact of, 187
   personal, in Grid Seminar, 175–177
Feelings, customer, 9,9 respect for, 130
   (*See also* Emotions)
Flattery:
   1,9-oriented customer and, 11–12
   1,9-oriented salesperson use of, 58
   (*See also* Compliments)
Flexibility, 5,5-oriented salesperson and, 103, 112, 113, 160
Follow-up, complaint, by 9,9-oriented salesperson, 145
Friend as evaluator, 185
Friendliness:
   in 9,9 approach, 149
   in 1,9 approach, 6, 7

Gimmicks in sales presentation, 102, 164
Gossip, 1,9 use of, 53
Grid, Customer, 9–14
   diagram, 10
Grid elements (*see* Elements, Grid)
Grid Seminars, 177, 178
Grid study of behavioral approaches, 217–225
Grid styles:
   vs. facade, 164, 165, 169
   Grid positions, comparison of, 182–183
   Grid sales strategies, 5–8, 184–185
   diagram, 6
   evaluation of, 176–181
   (*See also* Strategies, sales)
   ideal, 183–184
   of 9,9-oriented salesperson, 7–8
   of 9,1-oriented salesperson, 5, 25
   of 5,5-oriented salesperson, 7
   of 1,9-oriented salesperson, 6–7
   of 1,1-oriented salesperson, 7
   ranking of, 175
Guilt, avoidance by 1,9-oriented salesperson, 157–158

Half-truths in cloaking true intentions, 166

Helpfulness of 1,9-oriented salesperson, 55, 65
Hiding in cloaking true intentions, 165–166
Hopelessness of 1,1-oriented salesperson, 74
Humor:
   9,9 use of, 121
   9,1 use of, 32
   5,5 use of, 93
   good humor, 107
   1,9 use of, 52
   1,1 lack of, 72

Ideal Grid style, 183–184
Identification of customers (*see* Customers, identification of)
Implications of selling, 193–194
Indifference of 1,1-oriented salesperson, 73–74
Inflexibility of 9,1-oriented salesperson, 44–45
Information (*see* Facts)
Initiative, 171
   avoidance of, by 1,1-oriented salesperson, 79
   of 1,9-oriented salesperson, 52
Integrity:
   customer perception of, 39
   lack of, in facade, 174
   of 9,9-oriented salesperson, 120, 142, 180
   of 5,5-oriented salesperson, 104, 108
   passive, of 1,1-oriented salesperson, 81
Intentions, facade and:
   cloaking true, 165–166
   concealment of true, 164
Interaction, spontaneous, between prospective customer and 9,9-oriented salesperson, 133–134
Interrogation of customer:
   by 9,1-oriented salesperson, 30
   by 5,5-oriented salesperson, 96–97
Interruptions, customer:
   9,9 response to, 130
   9,1 response to, 31
   5,5 response to, 97

INDEX

Interruptions (*Cont.*):
  1,9 response to, 57
  1,1 response to, 77
  (*See also* Objections, customer)
Interview, sales, 203–204
Intrigue, facade as cover for, 164
Involvement as Grid element, 21–22
  (*See also* Participation and involvement)

Jokes (*see* Humor)

Knowledge:
  of competitor, 196–197
  of customer, 197–199
  of product, 195–196
  of product, customer, and competitor, 195–199
    by *9,9*-oriented salesperson, 121–125, 150–151, 179–181
      integrated knowledge, and team selling skills, 147
    by *9,1*-oriented salesperson, 27–28
    by *5,5*-oriented salesperson, 93–95
    by *1,9*-oriented salesperson, 53–54
    by *1,1*-oriented salesperson, 75–77
  of team of specialist purchasing agents, 147

Learning, comparison (*see* Comparison learning, development through)
Limits, acknowledgment of, by customer and *9,9*-oriented salesperson, 126
Listening, defensive:
  by *9,1*-oriented salesperson, 30
  by *1,9*-oriented salesperson, 54, 56
  by *1,1*-oriented salesperson, 76
  (*See also* Communication)
Logic:
  and *9,9*-oriented salesperson, 181, 191
    human relationships, knowledge of, 129
  and *9,9*-oriented customer, 151
  and *1,9*-oriented customer, 150
  during opening, 132

Logic (*Cont.*):
  during purchase decision, 119
  during sales presentation, 135
  and *5,5*-oriented salesperson, 160
  (*See also* Facts)
Love, feeling of, in *1,9* orientation, 155

Machiavelli, Niccolò, 167
Management:
  self- (*see* Self-management; Self-steering)
  time (*see* Scheduling and time management)
Maneuvers, deceitful, in facade building, 173
Manipulation, extensive, and *1,9*-oriented facade, 169
Mastery and facade building, 165, 167, 172
Maternalism as combination of *9,1* and *1,9* Grid styles, 155–157
Membership, need for, of *5,5*-oriented salesperson, 91–92
Miller, Arthur, 7
Mixed theories, 155–160
  two-hat, 157–158
Motivating and controlling customers, 167–171
Motives, personal, and facade-type behavior, 173

Name-dropping:
  effect on *5,5*-oriented customer, 13
  in facade building, 167
  by *9,9*-oriented salesperson, 139
  by *5,5*-oriented salesperson, 103
Needs, felt, of customer:
  and *9,9*-oriented salesperson, 133
  and *5,5*-oriented salesperson, 96
Needs analysis:
  by *9,9*-oriented salesperson, 133, 143
  by *9,1*-oriented salesperson, 34
  by *5,5*-oriented salesperson, 99
  by *1,9*-oriented salesperson, 59
  by *1,1*-oriented salesperson, 78–79
New customers (*see* Customers, new)

Objections, customer, 204–206
  9,9 handling of, 139–142, 184
  9,1 handling of, 28, 40–41, 46
  5,5 handling of, 105
  1,9 handling of, 56, 62–63
  1,1 handling of, 81–83
Objectivity, in product comparison, of 9,9-oriented salesperson, 123
Obligation, creation of, by 9,1-oriented salesperson, 29
Opening, 202–203
  9,9 approach to, 131–133
  9,1 approach to, 32–33
  5,5 approach to, 98–99
  1,9 approach to, 58–59
  1,1 approach to, 78
Openness of 9,9-oriented salesperson, 125, 142
Opinion molders, use by facade builder, 167
Optimism of 1,9-oriented salesperson, 63
Orientation:
  customer (*see* Customer Grid; Customers, types of)
  salesperson (*see* Grid styles; Strategies, sales)
Ostracism, 1,1 avoidance of, 72

Participation and involvement, customer, 199–201
  9,9 approach to, 125–128, 136–139, 150
  9,1 approach to, 28
  5,5 approach to, 95–96
  1,9 approach to, 54–56
  1,1 approach to, 76–77
Past practices, 5,5 reliance on, 93
Paternalism as combination of 9,1 and 1,9 Grid styles, 155–157
Perseverance of facade strategist, 171
Persistence, 1,1 lack of, 83
Perspective of 9,9-oriented salesperson, 130, 153
Persuasion, 5,5 art of, 97
Pessimism of 1,1-oriented salesperson, 74
Popularity, 5,5 concern for, 91

Positions, Grid, comparison of, 182–183
Positive reinforcement, 5,5 use of, 108
Praise, facade builder use of, 167, 168
Precedents, 5,5 reliance on, 93
Preciseness, lack of, in 1,1 presentation, 80
Presentation, sales:
  9,9 approach to, 135–136
    and 1,9-oriented customer, 149
  9,1 approach to, 36–40
  5,5 approach to, 102, 108
  1,9 approach to, 61–62
  1,1 approach to, 80–81
Prestige:
  customer need for: effect on purchasing decision, 124
    and 5,5 approach, 101
  5,5-oriented salesperson need for, 92, 116
  product: 5,5 customer and 9,1 approach, 48
    and 9,9 approach, 139
Pricing in sales presentation, 108
Principles, behavioral science, 1
Problem solving (solution seeking) of 9,9-oriented salesperson, 120, 142, 151
Product comparison, 9,9 objectivity in, 123
Product knowledge, 195–196
  (*See also* Knowledge, of product, customer, and competitor)
Properties of a 9,9 orientation, 179–181
Prophecy, self-fulfilling, 1,1 giving up as, 77
Prospecting, 212
  9,9 approach to, 147
  9,1 approach to, 45
  5,5 approach to, 112
  1,9 approach to, 67
  1,1 approach to, 86
Prospects, getting, 202–203

Questioning of customer:
  by 9,1-oriented salesperson, 30
  by 5,5-oriented salesperson, 96–97

236 INDEX

Rankings, Grid style, 175
Rapport, customer-salesperson, 94, 143
Rationalization in facade building, 173
Reactions, customer (*see* Customer reactions)
Reinforcement, positive, 5,5 use of, 108
Rejection, 1,9 fear of, 51
Relationships, salesperson-customer, 2
Repetitiveness, 9,9 avoidance of, 131
Reputation in facade building, 166–167
Resentment:
   customer, of paternalistic salesperson, 156
   as customer reaction to 9,1 orientation, 31, 46
   9,9 approach to, 149
   1,1 avoidance of, 72
Reservations, customer, 204–206
   9,9 approach to, 135, 142
   1,9 approach to, 63
Resilience:
   as Grid element, 24
   of 9,9-oriented salesperson, 146
   strengthening of, 188–190
Resistance, customer, to 1,1-oriented salesperson, 87
   (*See also* Objections, customer; Reservations, customer)
Respect, customer, for 9,9-oriented salesperson, 149
Retreat of 1,1-oriented salesperson, 73
Rumor, 1,9 use of, 53
Rush business, 210–211
   9,9 approach to, 145–146
   9,1 approach to, 44
   5,5 approach to, 111
   1,9 approach to, 66–67
   1,1 approach to, 85–86

Sales approach, 194–195
   (*See also* Approaches)
Sales expert, thoroughness of, 20–21
Sales Grid (*see* Grid styles)
Sales Grid strategies, 5–8, 184–185
   diagram, 6

Sales Grid (*Cont.*):
   evaluation of, 176–181
   (*See also* Strategies, sales)
Sales interview, 203–204
Sales presentation (*see* Presentation, sales)
Sales prospects (*see* Prospecting; Prospects, getting)
Sales strategies (*see* Strategies, sales)
Sales techniques (*see* Techniques, sales, of 5,5-oriented salesperson)
Sales volume in 9,1 approach, 25
Salespersons:
   approaches of (*see* Approaches; Theories)
   closing by (*see* Closing)
   communication of (*see* Communication)
   complaints handling (*see* Complaints, customer)
   concern of (*see* Concern)
   conflict handling (*see* Conflict)
   and customer expectations (*see* Expectations, customer, establishing)
   customer involvement and (*see* Participation and involvement, customer)
   emotions handling (*see* Emotions)
   established business handling (*see* Accounts, maintaining; Established business)
   evaluation of, 183, 185
   (*See also* Criticism; Critique)
   expenses handling (*see* Expenses)
   facade building and (*see* Facades and facade building)
   feedback to (*see* Feedback)
   5,5 bargaining, 93, 96, 106, 111
   Grid Seminars for, 177, 178
   identification of customers (*see* Customers, identification of; Customers, types of)
   interruptions handling (*see* Interruptions, customer)
   knowledge: of competitor, 196–197
     of customer, 197–199
     of product, 195–196

INDEX 237

Salespersons (*Cont.*):
  (*See also* Knowledge, of product, customer, and competitor)
  listening by (*see* Listening, defensive)
  management by (*see* Scheduling and time management; Self-management; Self-steering)
  name-dropping by (*see* Name-dropping)
  needs analysis by (*see* Needs analysis)
  new business (*see* Customers, new)
  objections handling (*see* Objections, customer; Reservations, customer)
  opening by (*see* Opening)
  orientation of (*see* Grid styles; Strategies, sales)
    customer reactions to (*see* Customer reactions)
  presentation by (*see* Presentation, sales)
  prestige and (*see* Prestige)
  prospecting by (*see* Prospecting; Prospects, getting)
  rapport, customer-salesperson, 94, 143
  relationships, salesperson-customer, 2
  rush business handling (*see* Rush business)
  sales interview by, 203–204
  and selling, implications of, 193–194
  servicing customers (*see* Servicing)
  styles of (*see* Grid styles; Styles)
  thinking process of (*see* Elements, Grid; Facts; Logic)
  training of (*see* Comparison learning, development through; Grid Seminars)
  (*See also specific traits, attributes, or emotions, for example:* Acceptance; Accommodation; Affection; Antagonism)
Scheduling and time management, 211–212
  9,9 approach to, 147
  9,1 approach to, 45
  5,5 approach to, 112

Scheduling (*Cont.*):
  1,9 approach to, 67
  1,1 approach to, 86
Science, behavioral, 1
Security:
  expectation of, in 1,1 orientation, 72
  sense of, in 5,5 orientation, 91
Self-alienation of 1,1-oriented salesperson, 74
Self-confidence of 5,5-oriented salesperson, 105
Self-correction, 186–187
Self-deception, 24
  in facade building, 173
  overcoming, 177–178
Self-development, 175–191
Self-diagnosis, 183
Self-esteem, reduction of, by facade strategist, 168
Self-fulfillment as 9,9 motivation, 120
Self-management, 211–214
  by 9,9-oriented salesperson, 146–148
  by 9,1-oriented salesperson, 44–45
  by 5,5-oriented salesperson, 111–112
  by 1,9-oriented salesperson, 67
  by 1,1-oriented salesperson, 86
Self-reliance of 9,9-oriented salesperson, 121
Self-steering, 214
  by 9,9-oriented salesperson, 147
  by 9,1-oriented salesperson, 45
  by 5,5-oriented salesperson, 112
  by 1,9-oriented salesperson, 67
  by 1,1-oriented salesperson, 86
Self-worth, 1,1 erosion of, 74
Selfishness, 9,9 avoidance of, 120
Selling:
  fundamentals of, 2
  implications of, 193–194
Selling strategies (*see* Grid styles; Strategies, sales)
Seminars, Grid, 177, 178
Sensitivity and facade building, 169
Servicing, 212–213
  by 9,9-oriented salesperson, 147
  by 9,1-oriented salesperson, 45
  by 5,5-oriented salesperson, 112

INDEX

Servicing (*Cont.*):
  by *1,9*-oriented salesperson, 67
  by *1,1*-oriented salesperson, 86
Silence of *1,1*-oriented salesperson, 76
Situational selling, 158–160
Solution seeking (problem solving) of *9,9*-oriented salesperson, 120, 142, 151
Solution selling of *9,9*-oriented salesperson, 119, 151
Spouse as evaluator, 185
Statistical *5,5* approach, 158–160
Status:
  customer need for, 101
  in purchasing decisions, 124
  status consciousness of *5,5*-oriented customer, 88
Status quo, *5,5* support of, 116
Steering (*see* Self-steering)
Strategies:
  Grid (*see* Grid styles)
  sales: combinations of, 16
    comparison of, 5–8, 184–185
    critique of, 186–188
    evaluation of, 176–181
    9,9, review of, 178–181
    salesperson's personal, 5
Strategist, facade (*see* Facades and facade building)
Styles:
  dominant, and backup Grid strategy, 14, 175, 178
    1,1 orientation as backup style, 73
  evaluation of, 177
  experimenting with, 186
  (*See also* Grid styles)
Superficiality of *5,5* product knowledge, 93
Sympathy, appearance of, in facade building, 169

Tactics in facade building, 169
Teamwork by *9,9*-oriented salesperson, 147

Techniques, sales, of *5,5*-oriented salesperson:
  closing, 107–108
  and customer differences, 114
  for customer pseudo participation, 95
  customer reactions to, 112–113
  high-pressure, 108
  reliance on, 92, 164
  sales presentation, 102
Tentativeness of *5,5*-oriented customer, 13, 48
Theories:
  mixed, 155–160
  two-hat, 157–158
  Sales Grid as set of, 2
  (*See also* Approaches)
Thoroughness, 160
  5,5 lack of, 103
  as Grid element, 20–21
Time management (*see* Scheduling and time management)
Trade-off in *5,5* orientation, 106
Trade-out in *5,5* orientation, 96
Trial-and-error selling methods, *5,5* use of, 92
Trickery, facade as cover for, 164
Trust, customer, of *9,9*-oriented salesperson, 128, 148–149

Versatility of *9,9*-oriented salesperson, 151, 184
Visiting, *9,9* frequency of, 144
  (*See also* Accounts, maintaining)
Volume-selling, *9,1* drive toward, 25

Wife as evaluator, 185
Win, *9,1* desire to, 26
Win-lose as *9,1* orientation, 40
Withdrawal of *1,1*-oriented salesperson, 72
Work, undercover, in facade building, 167

Yielding by *1,9*-oriented salesperson, 62

How to get what you want from everyone...and make them love you in the process!

WINNING BY NEGOTIATION

Tessa Albert Warschaw

At last—a revolutionary new strategy for success that makes winning a way of life! Learn how to take a positive, constructive approach to getting what you want from your spouse, parents, friends, landlord, or employer with the least amount of conflict—*Winning By Negotiation!*

___ **WINNING BY NEGOTIATION**   06748-3/$3.50
Tessa Albert Warschaw

Price may be slightly higher in Canada.

Available at your local bookstore or return this form to:

BERKLEY
Book Mailing Service
P.O. Box 690, Rockville Centre, NY 11571

Please send me the titles checked above. I enclose _____ Include 75¢ for postage and handling if one book is ordered; 25¢ per book for two or more not to exceed $1.75. California, Illinois, New York and Tennessee residents please add sales tax.

NAME_____

ADDRESS_____

CITY_____ STATE/ZIP_____

(Allow six weeks for delivery.)

WOMEN'S BUSINESS BOOKS

___872-16806-9	**THE LANDAU STRATEGY** Suzanne Landau & Geoffrey Bailey	$2.50
___872-16816-6	**MONEY MANAGEMENT FOR WOMEN** Rosalie Minkow	$2.50
___872-16909-X	**RE-ENTERING** Eleanor Berman	$2.25
___872-16899-9	**SUCCESSFUL NEGOTIATING SKILLS FOR WOMEN** John Ilich & Barbara S. Jones	$2.25
___872-16835-2	**WHAT EVERY WOMAN NEEDS TO KNOW ABOUT THE LAW** Martha Pomroy	$3.95
___867-21064-8	**WOMAN TIME** Personal Time Management for Women Only! Diana Silcox with Mary Ellen Moore	$2.95
___515-07358-X	**SALES THE FAST TRACK FOR WOMEN** Gonnie McClung Siegel	$3.50

Available at your local bookstore or return this form to:

JOVE
Book Mailing Service
P.O. Box 690, Rockville Centre, NY 11571

Please send me the titles checked above. I enclose _____ Include 75¢ for postage and handling if one book is ordered; 25¢ per book for two or more not to exceed $1.75. California, Illinois, New York and Tennessee residents please add sales tax.

NAME_____

ADDRESS_____

CITY_____ STATE/ZIP_____

(allow six weeks for delivery.)

65

THE BEST BUSINESS GUIDES AVAILABLE TODAY FROM JOVE PAPERBACKS

_____ 867-21053-2	**CHANGE YOUR JOB, CHANGE YOUR LIFE** Arbie Dale	$2.50
_____ 867-21130-X	**GETTING RICH YOUR OWN WAY** Srully Blotnick, Ph.D.	$2.95
_____ 867-21054-0	**HOW TO BE A SUCCESSFUL EXECUTIVE** J.P. Getty	$2.50
_____ 515-07397-0	**HOW TO BE RICH** J.P. Getty	$2.95
_____ 08100-0	**HOW TO MAKE MEETINGS WORK** Doyle & Straus	$3.50
_____ 867-21198-9	**INCOME FROM YOUR OWN HOME BUSINESS: CATER FROM YOUR KITCHEN** Majorie P. Blanchard	$2.95
_____ 872-16616-3	**MASTERY OF MANAGEMENT** Auren Uris	$2.25
_____ 867-21009-5	**MONEYSMARTS** Michael Assael	$3.25
_____ 867-21086-9	**PLAYBOY'S INVESTMENT GUIDE** Michael Laurence	$2.95

THE BEST BUSINESS GUIDES AVAILABLE TODAY FROM JOVE PAPERBACKS

_____ 867-21125-3	**POWER NEGOTIATING** John Illich	$2.50
_____ 07897-2	**SECRETS OF A CORPORATE HEADHUNTER** John Wareham	$3.50
_____ 515-07140-4	**SIMPLIFIED ACCOUNTING FOR NON-ACCOUNTANTS** Rick Stephan Hayes and C. Richard Baker	$3.50
_____ 867-21112-1	**STREET GAMES** Alan Lechner	$2.95
_____ 867-21035-4	**SUCCESSFUL REAL ESTATE INVESTING FOR THE SINGLE PERSON** Jack Cummings	$3.95
_____ 872-16646-5	**20 MINUTES A DAY TO A MORE POWERFUL INTELLIGENCE** Arbie M. Dale & Leida Snow	$2.25
_____ 867-21088-5	**THE VERY, VERY RICH AND HOW THEY GOT THAT WAY** Max Gunther	$2.95
_____ 867-21083-4	**ZEN AND CREATIVE MANAGEMENT** Albert Low	$3.50

Price may be slightly higher in Canada.
Available at your local bookstore or return this form to:

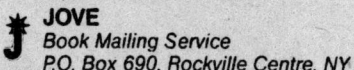
JOVE
Book Mailing Service
P.O. Box 690, Rockville Centre, NY 11571

Please send me the titles checked above. I enclose _____. Include 75¢ for postage and handling if one book is ordered; 25¢ per book for two or more not to exceed $1.75. California, Illinois, New York and Tennessee residents please add sales tax.

NAME_____
ADDRESS_____
CITY_____STATE/ZIP_____
(allow six weeks for delivery)   66B

Bestsellers you've been hearing about—and want to read

__	**GOD EMPEROR OF DUNE** Frank Herbert	07272-X-$3.95
__	**19 PURCHASE STREET** Gerald A. Browne	07171-5-$3.95
__	**PHANTOMS** Dean R. Koontz	05777-1-$3.95
__	**DINNER AT THE HOMESICK RESTAURANT** Anne Tyler	07173-1-$3.95
__	**THE KEEP** F. Paul Wilson	06440-9-$3.95
__	**HERS THE KINGDOM** Shirley Streshinsky	06147-7-$3.95
__	**NAM** Mark Baker	07168-5-$3.50
__	**FOR SPECIAL SERVICES** John Gardner	05860-3-$3.50
__	**THE CASE OF LUCY BENDING** Lawrence Sanders	06077-2-$3.95
__	**SCARFACE** Paul Monette	06424-7-$3.50
__	**THE NEW ROGET'S THESAURUS IN DICTIONARY FORM** ed. by Norman Lewis	07269-X-$2.95
__	**WAR BRIDES** Lois Battle	06155-8-$3.95
__	**THE FLOATING DRAGON** Peter Straub	06285-6-$3.95
__	**CHRISTMAS AT FONTAINES** William Kotzwinkle	06317-8-$2.95
__	**STEPHEN KING'S DANSE MACABRE** Stephen King	06462-X-$3.95

Prices may be slightly higher in Canada.

Available at your local bookstore or return this form to:

BERKLEY
Book Mailing Service
P.O. Box 690, Rockville Centre, NY 11571

Please send me the titles checked above. I enclose _____. Include 75¢ for postage and handling if one book is ordered; 25¢ per book for two or more not to exceed $1.75. California, Illinois, New York and Tennessee residents please add sales tax.

NAME _____

ADDRESS _____

CITY _____ STATE/ZIP _____

(allow six weeks for delivery)